AN INTERREGIONAL MODEL OF ECONOMIC FLUCTUATIONS

To my parents
To Leny

An Interregional Model of Economic Fluctuations

JACOB J. VAN DUIJN

*Interfaculty for Graduate Studies
in Management, Rotterdam*

SAXON HOUSE | LEXINGTON BOOKS

© Jacob Johan van Duijn 1972

Published by

SAXON HOUSE, D. C. Heath Ltd.
Westmead, Farnborough, Hants, England.

Jointly with

LEXINGTON BOOKS, D. C. Heath & Co.
Lexington, Mass. U.S.A.

ISBN 0 34701009 1
LC 72 10679

Printed in Great Britain by Redwood Press Limited, Trowbridge, Wiltshire

Contents

List of Symbols

Upper-case letters indicate variables. All variables are expressed in constant prices, except for variables that are ratios and those that measure population or labour. The latter are in thousands of men per period. A variable becomes a parametric constant through addition of a subscript 'o' to the variable.

Lower-case letters indicate parameters.

Variables dated '(t)' refer to period t. If the variable is a stock variable, '(t)' refers to the stock as measured at the beginning of period t.

Superscripts are used to specify the general definition of a variable, except for the numerals and the time coordinate '(t)', which are exponents when written as superscripts.

Variables

A	government investment; also autonomous investment in general
B	balance of trade
C	consumption
D	disbursements (J. S. Chipman's model of Section 1.4.3)
E	excess demand
F	production realization rate
G	government consumption; also autonomous consumption in general
H	unemployment benefits
I	(total) investment
J	private investment
K	capital stock
L	labour force
M	rate of immigration
N	population
Q	capital utilization rate
R	raw materials
S	savings
U	unemployment rate
V	inventory
W	wage income
X	output
Y	income
Z	demand

Parameters

a^1
a_2 propensities to consume

b adjustment coefficient private-investment function
c interregional trade coefficient private-consumption function
e $(=1+g)$ coefficient of expectations
f desired inventory–sales ratio
g growth rate autonomous expenditures
h unemployment benefits as fraction of wage income
k interregional trade coefficient private-investment function
l labour force participation rate
m rate of technical progress
p population growth rate
q coefficient weighting present and past desired investment in private-investment function
r rate of replacement; also rate of depreciation
s adjustment coefficient inventory-investment function
u labour–output ratio
v capital–output ratio
w target employment rate
y reaction coefficient migration function
z coefficient weighting trend level of private investment

Superscripts
a   anticipated
d   demanded
eu measured in efficiency units
FC full capacity
FE full employment
M   maximum possible
p   planned
r   realized (demand)
s   supplied; sold
*   desired or optimal; also denoting Golden Age values
‾   trend level
′   corrected for extra production because of existing excess supply

Subscripts

i, j regional subscripts; when two subscripts are used, the first refers to the producing region, the second to the receiving region
o   level in initial period $(t=0)$

Acknowledgement

I wish to express my gratitude to the members of my dissertation committee, especially to Professors Hans Brems and Harold F. Williamson, Jr., whose valuable comments and advice have been of great value to me during the course of this study.

I am most grateful to the Department of Economics and the Graduate College of the University of Illinois, which awarded me two University Fellowships and one University Dissertation Fellowship during my three years at the University.

1 Introduction

1.1 A Short Outline of the Present Study

This text is concerned with the study of regional economic fluctuations in a closed national economy. Its main purpose is to answer the following questions. How are regional and national fluctuations of output and unemployment affected by the economic characteristics of regions and by the trade relationships that exist among them? Through what forms of regional intervention can the central government attain its goals of interregional equity and economic stability at the lowest possible level of unemployment?

Within the framework of a closed economy the regional and national economic fluctuations are studied by simulating a non-linear interregional growth model capable of generating business cycles as well as steady-state growth. The two principal components of this model are: (a) Mechanisms to generate fluctuations, and (b) Mechanisms to transmit these fluctuations.

Fluctuations are transmitted through matrices that give propensities of one region to import from another region. Such matrices can be specified for each demand component. In the interregional model of this study this is done for both private consumption and private investment.

In order to concentrate on the cyclical properties of the interregional model, I shall first construct a national model of economic fluctuations that is identical to the interregional model in its economic contents. This model is called the prototype model. It incorporates contributions of different business cycle theorists, the most important being the essential feature of J. R. Hicks' cycle theory: the presence of full capacity and full employment ceilings which keep the movement of output in check over a period of time. It is the belief of the author that capacity constraints are indispensable in interregional models of economic fluctuations. Capacity bottle-necks can limit the expansion of a particular region, even if the country as a whole is characterized by excess productive capacity. Limited mobility of resources, however, can prevent production factors, whether labour or capital goods, from being available where they are needed.

Capacity constraints cause an economic model to become non-linear. This means that no analytical solution of the model can be obtained. In such a situation, I use the simulation technique as an alternative model to gain insight into the behaviour of the endogenous variables over a time period, to determine the stability of the economic system described by the model, and to see how sensitive the model is to changes in initial conditions, parameter values, and in a further stage, to alternative policy actions.

Following the presentation and simulation of the prototype model in Chapter 2, Chapter 3 introduces the interregional model. This model is the basis for all our subsequent investigations, although on several occasions I shall refer back to the prototype model, interpreting it as an interregional model in which all productive resources are perfectly mobile. The simulations in Chapter 3 and all following chapters are made for a hypothetical three-region economy.

Chapter 4 is a short chapter that gives national averages of the simulations of Chapter 3, which are then compared with prototype model simulations for the same sets of parameter values.

As an introduction to Chapter 6, the first of four chapters in which forms of intervention by the central government are discussed, Chapter 5 develops a method to determine long-term trends in an economy characterized by fluctuating growth.

Chapters 6, 7, 8 and 9 are attempts to answer the second of our two questions. Through what forms of regional intervention can the central government attain its goals of economic policy? Regional policy is seen here as an interregional problem. Chapter 6 deals with the reallocation of government expenditure as a means to pursue these goals. In Chapter 7 the trade between regions, and therefore the location of industry is the subject of discussion, and Chapter 8 looks at migration as a mechanism to equalize regional unemployment. Chapter 9, in addition to introducing a single government expenditure as a tool of short-term economic policy, examines a special aspect of economic policy, namely its timing in a cyclical economy.

1.2 Basic Assumptions

The following assumptions pertain to the prototype model as well as the interregional model.

First, time in our models is divided into discrete homogeneous periods. From an operational standpoint, period analysis is more useful than continuous analysis because empirical data are always discrete. From a theoretical standpoint, period analysis can be defended on the grounds that economic decision makers think in period terms, even though empirically obtained values of economic variables are admittedly the outcome of a large number of decisions that are not all taken at the same time. In our model I shall assume that decisions are made at the beginning of each period and based on the most recent information available, usually the outcomes of the previous period. I have attempted to specify the models

2

such that the length of the time period will be one year, and the values of the parameters that have the dimension time have been selected with this in mind.[1] If one can choose between a quarterly and an annual model, it is obviously more desirable to operate on a quarterly model. In time, aggregation obscures certain important developments,[2] and accurate timing of contracyclical policy measures requires more information than annual models can provide. On the other hand, quarterly data are available for only a few countries, and in general quarterly models are much more difficult to construct. For these reasons I chose one year rather than one quarter as the length of the time period.

Secondly, the models do not contain a monetary sector. At first sight, this seems to be a serious short-coming since empirical estimates of the fixed-investment function indicate that at least the long-term rate of interest has a significant effect on investment,[3] and this effect alone would justify the inclusion of a monetary sector. In empirically tested models, however, the discount rate, as set by the monetary authority, and the money supply are exogenous variables, instruments of national monetary policy. The ultimate goal of deriving the interregional model from our prototype model is to apply *regional* economic policy, and on the regional level monetary policy through manipulations of the discount rate (such that interest rates would differ interregionally) would be very difficult to administer.[4] Thus, it is readily acknowledged that money has an important influence on the economy, but the inclusion of a monetary sector would add the possibility of applying monetary policy to the models, something I do not consider feasible on the regional level.

Thirdly, the levying of taxes by the government is not made visible in this model. Tax policies, although important instruments for a government on the national level, are difficult to administer regionally, and could even be unacceptable on constitutional grounds.[5] For these reasons taxes are left out of the model. The addition of equations determining taxation would again provide instruments that would be of no use on the level on which I want to apply economic policy, that is on the regional level.

In the fourth place, all variables in our models are measured in constant prices except for those that are ratios and those that measure population or labour. This does not imply that prices are not allowed to vary. It does imply the assumption that price movements do not affect the course of the real variables such as to necessitate price equations for all outputs and production factors in the models. In short, our models have no money illusion in them. This rather important assumption asks for a justification, since there are a number of reasons why price variables could be included in a model that serves to describe economic fluctuations. Six of these reasons are given below. They are followed by six counter-arguments which led

3

to the decision not to complicate and enlarge the prototype and the inter-regional model, as the additional benefits of price equations were thought to be very small.

(a) Prices as a market clearing mechanism reduce excess demand to the point at which demand can be met by production plus existing inventory. However, in our models I assume that planned production in excess of productive capacity will affect demand components in a proportionate way.

(b) Factor prices determine the income distribution. Empirically, the wage share of personal disposable income falls during booms and rises during recessions. This may affect the cyclical movements of the real variables. Nevertheless, it is rather doubtful whether the cyclical redistribution of disposable income affects aggregate consumption significantly enough (at least for the degree of income inequality found in the post-war United States economy).[6] Fluctuations in investment are affected by profits, but not nearly as much as by sales.

(c) The cyclical movements of the prices of capital goods and labour may lead to factor substitutions. But I am using a Leontief production function, where no such substitution of one factor for another is possible.

(d) In an interregional model, prices may provide a mechanism to allocate the production of capital and consumption goods among regions. But within a national economy of moderate geographical size the price level of consumption and capital goods is not likely to vary greatly interregion-ally. To the extent that, because of location and different production tech-niques, regions have a comparative advantage in the production of certain goods, this is reflected in the matrices of the interregional model, that give the trade patterns, and in the regional capital–output and labour–output ratios. I assume that these coefficients do not change during the short time which our models describe, unless through government interference.

(e) The inclusion of price equations in the model makes it possible to follow the course of prices over an interval. However, price stability is not con-sidered a goal of economic policy in the economy discussed here.

(f) Tax functions in economic models are always in money terms. Thus, during persistent inflation the percentage of real gross national product (GNP) going to the government sector will increase. But to prevent such an increase, it is more and more felt appropriate to build in clauses in tax systems to correct for this effect.

An assumption which only applies to the interregional model is that transport costs and other distance factors are considered as having only a negligible influence on the interrelationships between regions. This means that the system of regions is seen as a set of spatially separated points. Within each region perfect mobility of resources and output exists, but between regions the resources are immobile (unless mobility is explicitly introduced, as in Chapter 8); the mobility of outputs is thus regulated by the trade matrices of the interregional model.

It should be clearly stated that the prototype model does not reflect an attempt to build a sophisticated model that accurately describes the movements during a time interval, of economic variables as recorded after World War I. For such a model the reader should consult econometric models such as the Brookings or the Wharton-EFU model. The prototype and the interregional model are relatively crude models of economic fluctuations, built around the idea that it is rather unrealistic to look at an interregional system without recognizing the fact that economies do not grow at constant rates, but that fluctuations occur with time. The crudeness of the models is reflected in the length of the time period, which is one year rather than one quarter. The choice of one year as the length of the time period makes it impossible for this model to produce short subcycles, such as the inventory cycle. Furthermore, it leads to a pattern of heavier fluctuations than will be observed in reality, since only annual figures can be considered, instead of distributed lags of quarterly figures, which would certainly tend to smooth some of the heavy fluctuations.

It should be realized throughout the study that the emphasis in this text is on regional economics, rather than business cycle theory. This does not imply that I shall not try to come as close as possible to observed patterns of fluctuations with the specification of our models. It does imply that only a certain level of accuracy can be accomplished, given that I do not wish to replace the prototype model with a much more complicated quarterly model. A major reason for keeping the model simple is that only this will enable us to come to grips with the impact of regional diversity on a national economy.

The prototype model, therefore, is what it says it is: a standard-type model exhibiting features of more precise models that might grow out of it, but omitting features considered inessential for the purpose of this study.

1.3 Models of Economic Fluctuations

Fluctuations in demand are generally held to be the cause of fluctuations in output. Of all demand components, investment is likely to be the most variable. Historical evidence shows that investment has fluctuated proportionally more than consumption and it is not surprising that the explanation of investment behaviour lies at the heart of every theory of economic fluctuations.[7]

The acceleration principle as an explanation of investment and consequently of economic fluctuations has played a major role in business-cycle

5

theories. In Section 1.3.1 one very prominent theory built around this acceleration principle is described: J. R. Hicks' theory of the cycle, which not only used the multiplier accelerator but introduced ceilings and floors in the economy to keep economic fluctuations in check.

A looser formulation of the acceleration principle has been used in the economic literature during the last two decades and is known as the capital stock adjustment principle (see Section 1.3.2). The essence of both Hicks' theory and the capital stock adjustment principle will be found in the national and interregional model in this study.

1.3.1 *Hicks' Constrained Multiplier-Accelerator Model*

Hicks was the first economist to advance a complete, non-linear theory of the business cycle (J. R. Hicks [1950]). Hicks built his theory on the following assumptions.

(*A*1) investment consists of autonomous investment, *A*, and induced investment, *J*. The induced-investment function is the familiar acceleration principle, lagged one period:

$$J(t)=v[X(t-1)-X(t-2)],\qquad(1.1)$$

where X is the output, income, and v the acceleration coefficient.

Autonomous investment, defined by Hicks as 'public investment, investment which occurs in direct response to inventions, much of the "long-range" investment which is only to pay for itself over a long period',[8] grows at a constant rate, g:

$$A(t)=A_o(1+g)^t.\qquad(1.2)$$

The level of autonomous investment and the fact that gross induced investment can only fall to zero determine the floor of the system. Hicks assumes that autonomous investment will be reduced a little below its normal level in a slump, although he does not indicate this downward adjustment in his graphical presentation.

(*A*2) consumption depends on output of the previous period:

$$C(t)=aX(t-1).\qquad(1.3)$$

(*A*3), a full-employment ceiling, checks the upward movement of income. The ceiling itself has an upward trend. In his verbal analysis, Hicks distinguishes an investment ceiling and a consumption ceiling; in his graphical analysis there is only one ceiling, which is growing at the same rate as autonomous investment, and therefore also at the same rate as equilibrium output.

6

If the equilibrium condition is added,

$$X(t) = C(t) + J(t) + A(t) \qquad (1.4)$$

from (1.1) to (1.3), these equations together form a multiplier-accelerator model with a lagged investment function and two parameters, a and v. The resulting linear non-homogeneous second-order difference equation

$$X(t) = (a+v)\,X(t-1) - vX(t-2) + A_o(1+g)^t \qquad (1.5)$$

may yield four different types of time paths, depending on the values of the two parameters. Assuming that the coefficients are such that a divergent movement will set in, whether cyclic or simply explosive, Hicks introduces his non-linearities to meet this difficulty:

Assumption ($A3$), the existence of a full employment ceiling, precludes the upward movement of income from proceeding beyond the ceiling level.

The working of the accelerator on the downswing being different from that on the upswing will provide a floor of the system: net induced disinvestment can only take place through the wearing out of existing capital goods. But net induced disinvestment means that gross induced investment has fallen to zero. It cannot fall any further, and neither can output. Autonomous investment, growing at the constant rate g, will make this lower buffer a regularly increasing one.

Unfortunately, Hicks did not formalize his complete model of the cycle. His mathematical treatment of it was restricted to equations (1.1) to (1.5), which represent only the unconstrained system. In other words, Hicks built a model for what he called 'the elementary case'[9] in which he takes a one-period delay for both the investment and consumption function. It is easy, however, to build a model which also accounts for the other assumptions of Hicks' theory. The more complete Hicksian model could look like this:

$$X^{FE}(t) = X_o^{FE}(1+g)^t \qquad (1.6)$$

$$J(t) = \max\left[0,\ \{v[X(t-1) - X(t-2)] + rK(t)\}\right] \qquad (1.7)$$

$$A(t) = A_o(1+g)^t \qquad (1.2)$$

$$C(t) = aX(t-1) \qquad (1.3)$$

$$X^p(t) = C(t) + J(t) + A(t) \qquad (1.8)$$

$$X(t) = \min\left[X^p(t),\ X^{FE}(t)\right] \qquad (1.9)$$

$$F(t) = X(t)/X^p(t) \tag{1.10}$$

$$K(t+1) = (1-r)K(t) + F(t)[J(t) + A(t)]. \tag{1.11}$$

In this model, X^p is the planned production,

$\quad\quad\quad\quad X^{FE}$ is the full employment output,

$\quad\quad\quad\quad K$ is the capital stock (measured at the beginning of period t),

$\quad\quad\quad\quad F$ is the production realization rate, and

$\quad\quad\quad\quad r$ is the rate of replacement, also rate of depreciation.

The buffers of this system are given by (1.6), (1.7), (1.2) and (1.9); (1.6) and (1.9) represent the full employment ceiling and the confrontation of supply and demand; (1.7) and (1.2) show that autonomous plus gross induced investment together cannot fall below the level given by autonomous investment, growing at the rate g.

Since its publication in 1950 several critics have pointed out deficiencies in Hicks' model. In this paragraph I shall summarize some of the weak points in Hicks' analysis that are of importance to us.

(a) The supply side of the economy is only represented by the full employment ceiling. No reference is made to the state of technology of the economy.

(b) The full employment ceiling is not the only ceiling. Limitations on the availability of capital may restrain the growth of income as well. On a disaggregated level sectoral ceilings may exist.

(c) In the formal analysis, investment is only seen as demand creating. The capacity generating character of investment is ignored.

(d) Inventory investment is left out. Hicks distinguishes working capital and liquid capital, the latter understood to be inventory. In the formal analysis, however, only fixed capital is considered.

(e) In the non-linear model the growth of autonomous investment is crucial for output to get off the floor in a depression.[10]

(f) On empirical grounds, the acceleration principle has been rejected by some economists in favour of profits as the major explanatory variable in the investment function. Others do not dismiss the principle altogether, but reject it in its naïve version in favour of the capital stock adjustment principle.[11]

(g) The theory lacks a mechanism which allocates the available resources among producers of capital and consumption goods if demand hits the ceiling.

The prototype model will meet the deficiencies of Hicks' model mentioned in points (a) to (g).

Criticism of a different nature has come from J. S. Duesenberry[12], who argues that no major depression in the past has been caused by shortages of capital goods or labour. That is, capacity constraints have not caused the downturn in the later stages of an upswing. A response to his comments can be found in Section 4.3.

1.3.2   The Capital Stock Adjustment Principle

One deficiency of the Hicks model noted in the preceding section was its use of the naïve accelerator as the induced-investment function. For some critics this was the major weakness of the model,[13] even though Hicks used the acceleration principle in its non-linear form, with zero being the minimum level of gross induced investment.

Shortly after the publication of Hicks' cycle theory, an alternative approach was suggested by R. M. Goodwin [1951] and H. B. Chenery [1952], independent of each other; this came to be known as the flexible accelerator. The flexible accelerator belongs to a class of investment functions in which investment decisions vary directly with income and inversely with capital stock. This class of investment function is based on what is generally referred to as the capital stock adjustment principle.[14] In an equation the capital stock adjustment principle can be expressed as

$$J(t) = \alpha X(t-1) - \beta K(t). \tag{1.12}$$

The flexible accelerator as introduced by Goodwin and Chenery can be described in the following way. Let the desired or optimal capital stock at the beginning of period t, $K^*(t)$, be related to the last known output, $X(t-1)$. Let the coefficient which relates the two variables be v, where v is the optimal capital–output ratio, so that

$$K^*(t) = vX(t-1). \tag{1.13}$$

According to the capital stock adjustment principle, businessmen try to adjust their actual capital stock as measured at the beginning of period t, $K(t)$, to the desired or optimal stock $K^*(t)$:

$$J(t) = b[K^*(t) - K(t)]. \tag{1.14}$$

In this equation, b is the adjustment coefficient $(0 \le b \le 1)$, indicating to what extent businessmen adjust their capital stock to its desired level in one period. Inserting (1.13) into (1.14) gives

$$J(t) = bvX(t-1) - bK(t). \tag{1.15}$$

If $b=1$ (capital stock completely adjusted to its optimal level) holds for every period, net induced investment is proportional to the change in output, and the flexible accelerator is reduced to its naïve version. Algebraically, $b=1$ implies $K(t)=K^*(t-1)=vX(t-2)$. Equation (1.15) then becomes

$$J(t)=v[X(t-1)-X(t-2)],\qquad(1.16)$$

which is equation (1.1) of Hicks' 'elementary case'. As can be readily seen, the flexible accelerator is obtained as a particular case of the capital stock adjustment principle with $\alpha=bv$ and $\beta=b$.

The somewhat looser general formulation of the capital stock adjustment principle of Equation (1.12) had already been used before Hicks' cycle theory and the two articles by Goodwin and Chenery were published. This broader version is associated with the names of M. Kalecki [1939] and N. Kaldor [1940]. They built their business cycle models around this type of investment function more than a decade before Goodwin and Chenery introduced the flexible accelerator.

In subsequent chapters the Goodwin-Chenery capital stock adjustment version—the flexible accelerator—will be applied. It retains the basic idea of the acceleration principle that investment will be directed towards bringing capital stock into the desired relationship with the level of output recently prevailing. However, it rejects the mechanical and rigid relationship postulated by the naïve accelerator.

1.4 Interregional Models: Earlier Contributions

In this section, I shall discuss three articles and one book that clearly stand out as pioneering contributions to the field of interregional model building. A fourth article discussed has the merit of bringing together a number of business cycle theories with the intention to translate them into interregional models.

Of the first three papers, Vining's article is definitely closest to an interregional business cycle model. Vining's main interest lay in business cycles and he emphasized the region as a concept which helped him to explain the cause of cycles. The value of the next two studies is more mathematical: Metzler's article and Chipman's article and book contain simple multisector demand models, for which the authors derived the stability conditions. Although these conditions have only value for models in which no inequalities restrict the behaviour of the variables, these studies nevertheless represent original and highly important contributions from a more general point of view, and both are recognized as such. The fourth article, written by Airov, is a comprehensive study on interregional business cycle models and to the knowledge of the present author the only of its kind. Unfortunately, the article contains a number of errors. The discussion in this chapter is first a correction and restatement of the models Airov presented and second a comparison of these corrected models.

1.4.1 Vining's 1949 Model

Every study on interregional business cycle models should mention R. Vining as the first economist to write on the interregional variations in economic fluctuations. The article discussed here is one of a sequence of papers which Vining wrote between 1945 and 1949, all on the regional aspects of business cycles.

Vining delineates his regions according to their sensitivity for generating business cycles. Even though this might seem a rather narrow concept for defining regions, it gives a good insight into the cause of business cycles. Vining's thesis with respect to these causes follows naturally from his delineations: national business cycles are weighted averages of regional cycles. To demonstrate this in the article under discussion Vining describes a model he built for four regions: two are relatively stable, while the other two are given characteristics of relative instability. Arguing that his model is too bulky and awkward, Vining does not present it mathematically. My rendition of it can, therefore, only be seen as a tentative approach based on Vining's non-mathematical description in his paper. The (simplified) model might have been as follows:

$$Y_i(t) = C_i(t-1) + I_i(t-1) \tag{1.17}$$

$$C_{ij}(t) = c_{ij}[a_j Y_j(t) + G_j] \tag{1.18}$$

$$C_i(t) = \sum_j C_{ij}(t) \tag{1.19}$$

$$I_i(t) = \sum_j k_{ij}\{\bar{A}_j + v_j[Y_j(t) - Y_j(t-1) + \text{random change}_j\} \tag{1.20}$$

$$i = 1, 2, 3, 4).$$

Here, Y is the income, output,
   G is the autonomous consumption,
   $\bar{A}$ is the equilibrium level autonomous investment, and
   c and k are interregional trade coefficients. Where two subscripts are used, the first refers to the producing region, the second to the receiving region.

Equation (1.17) indicates that consumption and investment outlays in this period are the next period's income. The constant term in the con-

11

sumption function is added, so I can distinguish between the marginal propensity to consume and the average propensity. Investment expenditures per region are composed of three parts: (a) A basic level of investment, $\bar{A}$; (b) Induced investment, depending on the change in income. Vining calls this a 'systematic component', which in his verbal specification is induced by changes in consumption. Besides that, investment good exports will lead to changes in investment expenditure in the unstable regions. Both effects are brought together here in the second part of (1.20); (c) Random alterations in investment, determined by random draws which are cumulated from period to period to give the alteration for a particular period. What will make the four regions different in this simple model is the specification of the parameters c_{ij} and k_{ij}, in addition to possible differences in marginal propensities to consume and capital productivity.

Vining's goal was the same as that of the present study: to construct economic models—I shall build more complicated models than Vining did—with which interregional variations in economic fluctuations can be generated. Vining's interest focussed on the phenomenon of the business cycle. His regions as concepts in business cycle analysis [15] were the product of his search for the root of this phenomenon. In that respect, Vining distinguishes himself from Metzler and Chipman who were principally interested in the stability conditions of multiple region systems.

One point of criticism should not be omitted, as its importance extends to the models I shall present in the ensuing chapters. It regards the elements of space in these interregional models. Vining states: 'It is my thesis that we should explicitly introduce a spatial dimension into our conception of the economic structure of the nation.'[16] W. Isard, however, in his comments on Vining's paper correctly remarks that this model 'contrary to his intentions is independent of the space factor'.[17] This is all very true. Vining's model, and my models too, describe one-point economies that are divided into as many parts as one wishes, to indicate the number of regions one desires.

Finally, as with so many other models, this model is purely demand oriented so that supply does not enter the picture. This may be the most essential difference between this and the interregional models I shall present in the following chapters. Indeed, for a one-region economy Vining's model would, in the initial equilibrium situation, be the most simple macro-demand model: $Y = C + I$; $C = aY$; I exogenous. Of course, Vining added to this a disturbance mechanism in the form of random investment shocks. Thus this model is an early contribution to the business cycle theories of the 'erratic shock' type, as Allen calls the theories in which random disturbances prevent cycles from dying away.[18]

1.4.2 Metzler's 1950 Model

Metzler's paper (Metzler [1950]) on interregional/international trade was written well before it was published. The author felt, however, that there was no widespread interest in the subject in 1945 when he wrote his article, and therefore he did not submit it.

Metzler's model is simple; it contains the basic ingredients that are necessary to set up an *n*-region system. This simplicity is understandable in the light of the author's main goal: to establish stability conditions for an *n*-region system just as these conditions had already been established for 1- and 2-regions systems.

Metzler starts out with the well-known identity:

Income = Consumption + Net investment + Exports − Imports,

where, in our notation,

$$\text{Income} \qquad = Y_i$$

$$\text{Consumption} \quad = C_i^r = \sum_j C_{ji} \text{(consumption goods received)}$$

$$\text{Net investment} = I_i^r = \sum_j I_{ji} \text{(capital goods received)}$$

$$\text{Exports} \qquad = \sum_j (C_{ij} + I_{ij} + R_{ij}) \; (i \neq j)$$

$$\text{Imports} \qquad = \sum_j (C_{ji} + I_{ji}) \; (i \neq j).$$

Here, R stands for raw materials. From these specifications, indicated by Metzler, I can conclude that

$$Y_i = \sum_j (C_{ij} + I_{ij}) + \sum_j (R_{ij} - R_{ji})$$

or

$$Y_i = C_i + I_i + \sum_j (R_{ij} - R_{ji}). \tag{1.21}$$

To express the relationship of imports/exports and 'expenditures' (consumption + net investment) to income, Metzler introduces an 'import function' and an 'expenditure function', where the import function is the imports equation above and the expenditure function the sum of consumption received and capital goods received, with all variables written

13

as implicit functions of Y_i. Metzler's next step is to set up a system of equations for n regions; after several rearrangements this system can again be written as (1.21).

As indicated above, Metzler did much more than just presenting his model. He also stated the stability conditions and derived the interregional multiplier. In addition, Metzler looked at the effects of an income change in region i on the balance of trade of the other regions in the system.

The approach of analysing an interregional model that Metzler followed has not changed over the years. When dealing with linear models I am principally interested in the stability of the system, the effects of an exogenous change on the regions' incomes through multiplier effects, and the balance of trade effects of changes in the system. In that respect Metzler's article stands as a classic in regional economics.

1.4.3   Chipman's 1950 Model

Chipman's book and article (Chipman [1950-1 and 1950-2]) should first be seen as elaborations of the theory of the multiplier. This is where his main interest was. Chipman set himself the task of extending the 2-country multiplier for which the basic formulae and stability conditions were derived by Metzler [1942], to formulate a model for an n-sector economy. Chipman's model is similar to Metzler's. There are non-specified expenditures, called 'disbursements' by Chipman, that depend on income, or 'receipts', Y. As in Metzler's model, the derivatives of the disbursement functions with respect to Y give the marginal propensity to spend matrix. Writing the change in disbursements as dD, the change in 'receipts' for sector i in period t can be written:

$$d Y_i(t) = d D_i + \sum_j c_{ij} a_j d Y_j(t-1).$$ (1.22)

In this notation 'spending' refers only to consumption. $[c]$ is a distributive matrix, whose column entries add up to one. The next step for Chipman is to evaluate the multiplier. For the receipts vector he finds (using matrix notation):

$$d Y(t) = ([1] - \{[c]\, a\}^t) \cdot ([1] - [c]\, a)^{-1} \cdot dD.$$ (1.23)

With the matrix $[c]$ such that $[c]^t$ approaches the zero matrix as t becomes large, the receipts vector will converge to

$$\lim_{t \to \infty} d Y(t) = ([1] - [c]\, a)^{-1}\, dD.$$

A 'multiplier vector' can be easily derived from the receipts vector. Chipman now goes on to give the necessary and sufficient conditions for stability of systems of difference equations, known as the Schur conditions. Finally, as an example of possible further development a multiplier-accelerator model is presented. This model is identical to the first of Airov's four models discussed below.

Comparing Chipman's work with Metzler's 1950 article it is not hard to find a number of similarities. Both authors built simple n-sector models, concentrating their attention on the properties of these models. Chipman had the advantage of having a number of articles to refer to at the time he wrote his study. Metzler's article, written in 1945, deserves credit for being the more pioneering of the two. Both works, however, stand out as fundamental building blocks for the construction of linear interregional business cycle models.

1.4.4 Airov's 1963 Summary

Airov's summary article (Airov [1963]) can be considered the first comprehensive study in regional business cycle theory. Taking four different business cycle models (the multiplier-accelerator model, one of Metzler's inventory cycle models, Goodwin's flexible accelerator, and the capital stock adjustment model), Airov restated these models in matrix notation for an n-region economy to allow for the effects of interregional trade. Solving his models he obtained difference equations that described how the cyclical movements were propagated through the regions, following an outside shock. Airov's analysis, however, contains a number of errors resulting from the application of ordinary algebraic operations where matrix operations should have been used.

In this section I shall examine the regionalization of the four business cycle models Airov dealt with, to see what results can be obtained when the necessary corrections are made.

The most essential error in Airov's article results from the fact that he does not distinguish between capital goods produced by region i and outlays for capital goods by region i. This confusion is carried through all four models. It is only in the first model that it does not affect the final result. To clear up this matter:

$I_i(t)$ is the net investment produced by region i in period t (this includes, of course, all exports of investment goods to other regions within the economy),

$I_i^d(t)$ is the net demand for investment goods to be produced by region i in period t, and

$I_i^r(t)$ is the net outlays for investment by region i in period t (this includes all imports of capital goods from other regions in the economy).

A similar notation can be used for consumption goods, C, and autonomous expenditure, A. In the simpler models, where no supply restrictions exist (such as in the case with the following models): $I_i(t)=I_i^d(t)$, and also $C_i(t)=C_i^d(t)$ and $A_i(t)=A_i^d(t)$. On the other hand, $I_i(t)$ will always be different from $I_i^r(t)$. The following two definitional equations, employed in all four business cycle models by Airov, will make this clear. In vector notation:

$$X(t)=C(t)+I(t)+A(t) \tag{1.24}$$

$$K(t+1)=K(t)+I^r(t), \tag{1.25}$$

where the capital stock, $K(t)$, is measured at the beginning of period t.[19] Obviously, capital goods produced add to a region's output, capital goods obtained (outlays for investment) will be added to its capital stock, and the two are not the same as one is led to believe by Airov. Let us now state the four business cycle models in our own version, in vector notation, and solve them. For all models I shall assume that all regions have the same marginal propensity to consume, a, the same adjustment coefficient, b, and the same capital–output ratio, v.

(a) *Interregional Multiplier-Accelerator Model*

$$X(t)=C(t)+I(t)+A(t) \tag{1.24}$$

$$C(t)=[c]\,aX(t-1) \tag{1.26}$$

$$I(t)=[k]\,v[X(t-1)-X(t-2)] \tag{1.27}$$

$$A(t)=\bar{A} \tag{1.28}$$

According to the model as given by Airov, the entries of the vector A indicate that A_i is produced by region i's industries. Autonomous expenditures in region i are therefore goods originating in region i. The solution of the model is:

$$X(t)=(a[c]+v[k])\,X(t-1)-v[k]\,X(t-2)+\bar{A}. \tag{1.29}$$

(b) *The Interregional Inventory Accelerator*

This model is an interregional version of one of Metzler's inventory cycle models (Metzler [1941, pp. 125–6]), in which the following variables are introduced:

C^a, the anticipated sales of consumption goods,
C^d, the demand for consumption goods,
V^*, the desired or optimal level of inventories,
V^p, the planned inventory investment, and
V, the actual level of inventories (at beginning of period).

Furthermore, in this model, f stands for the ratio between desired inventory and anticipated sales.[20] Adjusted to our notation Metzler's model reads:

$$X(t)=C^a(t)+V^p(t)+A(t) \tag{1.30}$$

$$C^a(t)=C^d(t-1) \tag{1.31}$$

$$C^d(t)=[c]\,aX(t) \tag{1.32}$$

$$V^*(t+1)=[f]\,C^a(t)\ \text{(where $[f]$ is a diagonal matrix)} \tag{1.33}$$

$$V^p(t)=V^*(t+1)-V(t) \tag{1.34}$$

$$V(t)=V^*(t)-[C^d(t-1)-C^a(t-1)] \tag{1.35}$$

$$A(t)=\bar{A}\,. \tag{1.28}$$

The possibility that production plus existing stock might fall short of demand for a particular period was not discussed by Metzler in his original article. Let us assume that $V^*(t)>[C^d(t-1)-C^a(t-1)]$ for all t. Furthermore in this version the producers of consumer goods are the ones who hold an inventory.[21]

From (1.31) to (1.35) an equation can be derived for $V^p(t)$ expressed in $X(t)$ and $X(t-1)$:

$$V^p(t)=a[1+f]\,[c]\,[X(t-1)-X(t-2)].^{22} \tag{1.36}$$

The solution of the model is:

$$X(t)=a[2+f]\,[c]\,X(t-1)-a[1+f]\,[c]\,X(t-2)+\bar{A}, \tag{1.37}$$

where $[2+f]$ and $[1+f]$ are again diagonal matrices.[23]

(c) *The Interregional Flexible Accelerator*

Goodwin's model (Goodwin [1948] and [1953, p. 69]) in its interregional version is reproduced as follows by Airov. In his notation:

$$Z(t)=C(t)+I(t)+A(t) \tag{1.38}$$

$$Y(t)=[\mu]\,[Z(t)-Y(t)] \tag{1.39}$$

$$C(t)=MY(t) \tag{1.40}$$

$$I(t)=B[\lambda]\,Y(t)-P[\lambda]\,K(t) \tag{1.41}$$

17

$$K(t)=K(t-1)+I(t-1) \quad \text{or} \quad \Delta K(t)=I(t) \tag{1.42}$$

$$A(t)=\bar{A}. \tag{1.28}$$

Here, $Z(t)$ is aggregate demand and $Y(t)$ is aggregate supply. M is the matrix of consumption coefficients, B and P are matrices of capital coefficients, and $[\mu]$ and $[\lambda]$ are diagonal matrices which contain time constants of a distributed lag.

As it stands the model is incomplete. In general, $Z(t) \neq Y(t)$, which means that demand for productive capacity will not be fully realized or will be over-realized depending on the sign of $[Z(t)-Y(t)]$. The model lacks an outlet in the form of inventories and even with these stocks included one will have to assume that they will never be depleted. This all makes it hard to derive any meaningful difference equation from this model. For instance $I(t)$ in (1.38) [our $I^d(t)$], will be different from the $I(t)$ that eventually will be produced if $Z(t)>Y(t)$. Therefore the $I(t)$ of (1.42) cannot be substituted back in (1.38). For a different reason, outlined above, $I(t)$ in (1.41) is different from $I(t)$ in equation (1.42).[24]

A solvable interregional flexible-accelerator model would be the following. Assuming $I^d(t)=I(t)$, in our notation:

$$X(t)=C(t)+I(t)+A(t) \tag{1.24}$$

$$C(t)=[c]\,aX(t-1) \tag{1.26}$$

$$I(t)=[k]\,[bvX(t-1)-bK(t)] \tag{1.43}$$

$$A(t)=\bar{A} \tag{1.28}$$

$$I^r(t)=bvX(t-1)-bK(t) \tag{1.44}$$

$$K(t+1)=K(t)+I^r(t). \tag{1.25}$$

Here, (1.44) is derived from:

$$I_i^r(t)=b_i[K_i^*(t)-K_i(t)]$$

and

$$K_i^*(t)=v_iX_i(t-1).$$

Because of the assumed interregional equality of a_i, b_i and v_i, the difference equation in X is fairly simple:

$$X(t)=\{(1-b)\,[1]+a[c]+bv[k]\}\,X(t-1)$$
$$-\{1-b)\,a[c]+bv[k]\}\,X(t-2)+b\bar{A}. \tag{1.45}$$

18

(d) *The Interregional Capital Stock Adjustment Principle*

Airov's interregional version of the capital stock adjustment principle is correct, again with the exception of the equation which defines the change in capital stock. The model is identical to the flexible-accelerator model, with the exception of the consumption function, which is unlagged:

$$C(t)=[c]\,aX(t) \tag{1.46}$$

and the equations for investment demand and realized investment, which are replaced by:

$$I(t)=[k]\,[\alpha X(t-1)-\beta K(t)] \tag{1.47}$$

and

$$I^r(t)=\alpha X(t-1)-\beta K(t). \tag{1.48}$$

Here α and β are scalars, that is we assume that these parameters are the same for all regions.

The solution of the capital stock adjustment model not unexpectedly resembles the one given as (1.45):[25]

$$X(t)=([1]-a[c])^{-1}\,[\{(1-\beta)\,([1]-a[c])+\alpha[k]\}\,X(t-1)$$
$$-\alpha[k]\,X(t-2)+\beta\bar{A}]. \tag{1.49}$$

The crucial equations in all four models presented here are the investment equations, whether they are equations for fixed business investment (models 1, 3 and 4) or inventory investment (model 2). The reader will have recognized the naïve accelerator (model 1), Goodwin's flexible accelerator (model 3) and the capital stock adjustment principle (model 4) from Section 1.3. From that section we know how these models are related to each other. The difference equation solutions of the three fixed-investment models reflect these relationships. For instance, the solutions of the naïve- and flexible-accelerator models are identical for $b=1$, and—except for the lag in the consumption function—the capital stock adjustment model becomes the flexible-accelerator model if $\alpha=bv$ and $\beta=b$. Metzler's inventory-accelerator model is not so easily derived from any of the other three. The main features of this model will be adapted for the prototype model (see Section 2.2.3).

It should again be noted that the solutions of all four models were derived under the assumption that all a_i, b_i and v_i are identical among regions. This greatly simplified the solutions since it permitted the use of

19

scalars instead of diagonal matrices everywhere these parameters appeared in the difference equations.

1.5 Terminology and Notation

The prototype model and the interregional model are capable of generating growth with fluctuations, or cyclical growth, as well as steady-state growth. Where output paths are cyclical I use the following terminology to describe the phases of these cycles.

A complete cycle can be divided into an *expansionary* or *upswing phase* and a *contractionary* or *downswing phase*. The *peak* period, or *upper turning point* marks the end of the expansionary phase, the *trough* or *lower turning point* the end of the contractionary phase. Both turning points are relative extremes, measured in rates of unemployment. Occasionally the periods immediately following the trough period are labelled the *recovery phase*. More specifically, these are the periods during which output (not the un-employment rate) is lower in absolute terms than the preceding peak out-put. Also, depending on the amplitude of the downswing part of the cycle, the contractionary phase is alternatively called *recession* or *depression*. The phases of the cycle are schematically shown in Figure 1.1.

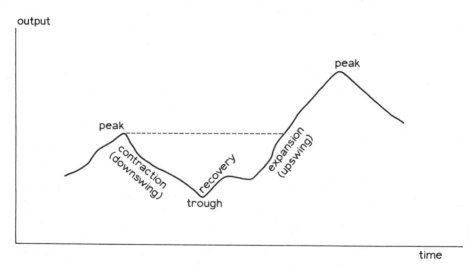

Figure 1.1　The Phases of the Business Cycle

The alternative of cyclical growth is *steady-state growth*. By this I mean growth at proportionate rates which are constant over a period of time.[26] Since I employ only one rate of growth for the output variables in our models, steady-state growth is also at the same time *balanced growth*, defined by Samuelson and Solow [1953] as identical proportionate rates of growth of output for all goods.

The prototype model and the interregional model, which are both constrained models, have two upper boundaries or ceilings: the *full capacity* ceiling, determined by the existing capital stock, and the *full employment* ceiling, determined by the existing labour force. Occasionally the word *capacity* is used to indicate productive capacity in general (capital stock and labour force), instead of just the capital stock.

In the second part of this study, two goals of regional economic policy are distinguished: *interregional equity* and *stability*. *Interregional equity* is defined as the interregional equality of trend rates of unemployment at the lowest possible level. In the context of economic policy, *stability* is measured in terms of the fluctuations of the (regional) unemployment rates over a period of time, with steady-state growth representing the case of perfect stability. When used as a concept of dynamic equilibrium analysis (such as in Sections 1.4, 7.2 and 7.3), stability is defined as a property of dynamic processes, which are said to be stable when the time paths of economic variables converge to some equilibrium position.

A word on notation: the *List of Symbols* (page viii) lists all the symbols used in the economic models of the following chapters. The equations of the models are identified by the number of the chapter in which they first appear, followed by a serial number, all in parentheses. To refer to sections of chapters (which are also numbered serially within a chapter), the chapter and serial number are used without parentheses.

In addition a number of abbreviations is used throughout this text. These abbreviations are:

P.M.   Prototype model
I.M.   Interregional model
c-u.r. Capital utilization rate (the variable Q)
u.r.   Unemployment rate (the variable U in percentage points)

Notes

[1] Very often in dynamic analysis the gestation lag of investment is chosen as the length of the time period. Although analytically convenient this division of time is not a very operational one, since all parameters that have a time dimension have to be made consistent with it.

[2] For example, U.S. real GNP was higher in 1960 than in 1959. Yet quarterly figures show that a recession started in mid-1960, and continued into 1961. See M. K. Evans [1969, p. 502].

[3] See Evans [1969, Chapter 5].

[4] Regionally differentiated control of bank credit other than through differentiated interest rates might be more feasible.

[5] See Engerman [1965, p. 314].

[6] See Evans [1969, p. 45].

[7] A distinction should be made here between national, regional and interregional models. Where in a closed national economy investment will be the most variable component, in a regional economy exports (exogenous for the regional economy) could be the cause of most fluctuations. In the interregional context, however, exports and imports are no longer seen as exogenous variables, but as the sum of consumption goods, capital goods and possibly raw materials traded by regions to each other. Fluctuations in investment demand will then cause fluctuations in exports more often than fluctuations in other demand components.

[8] J. R. Hicks [1950, p. 59].

[9] J. R. Hicks [1950, p. 67].

[10] See A. M. Martirena-Mantel [1968, p. 89].

[11] Still another theory is Jorgenson's, which combines the neo-classical production function (with labour-capital substitution) and the capital stock adjustment principle (see below). See D. W. Jorgenson and J. A. Stephenson [1967].

[12] See J. S. Duesenberry [1958, p. 280].

[13] See, for example, Kaldor [1951, p. 198] who refers to the acceleration principle as a 'crude and highly unstable tool for analysis—and also an obsolete one, that an economist of Mr. Hicks' subtlety should have long ago discarded'.

[14] Allen [1967, pp. 69 and 73] refers to the capital stock adjustment principle as 'Matthews' capital stock adjustment principle', using R. C. O. Matthews [1959] as his reference. This seems somewhat misleading. Matthews wrote an early article on capital stock adjustment theories (see Matthews [1954]) and may have labelled this type of investment function in this way, but he certainly was not its originator.

[15] See Vining [1946-2].

[16] Vining [1949, p. 90].

[17] See discussion in the *American Economic Review*, following Vining [1949].

[18] See R. G. D. Allen [1967, p. 367].

[19] Airov uses $K(t)$ in two different ways without mentioning it; in the first two models K is measured at the end of the period, in the last two at the beginning.

[20] Not for the ratio between desired inventory and actual sales, as Airov puts it.

[21] The alternative assumption is that the receiving region wishes to have

a buffer between the demand of its households and the available goods (own production plus imported goods). The assumption I have made is the more elegant one when it comes to writing this model in matrix notation.

[22] This equation is the equivalent of Airov's equation (4.2.3). However, in Airov's (4.2.3) the equivalents of the matrices $[1+f]$ and $[c]$ are interchanged, which means that in his reduced-form equation for planned-inventory investment the optimal inventory of region i depends upon all f_j's $(j=1, ..., n)$ which clearly by the definition of f_j cannot be the case.

[23] In Airov's solution (4.2.10) the matrices $[c]$ and $[2+f]$, $[1+f]$ respectively are again interchanged.

[24] Airov, however, solves the model, thereby multiplying matrices and vectors with each other as if they were ordinary algebraic numbers. The final difference equation therefore has no meaning, unless interpreted as the solution for the uninteresting case of a single-region model.

[25] Airov's solution of this model—his (4.4.12)—is not correct, even apart from his failure to distinguish between I^r and I.

[26] See Hahn and Matthews [1964]; also Allen [1967, p. 77].

2 The Prototype Model

2.1 Introduction

In this chapter the national version of our interregional model of economic fluctuations is introduced. The main advantage of presenting a national rather than an interregional model at this stage is that omission of the interrelationships among regions allows us to concentrate more on the properties of the model *per se*. The interrelationships in an inter-regional model can be complicated, even in a system with only three regions, the number of regions I shall consider. The discussion of the national version will show what impact the different behavioural assumptions, made in this model, have on the fluctuations with time of the variables I am interested in, such as planned production, actual output, investment, capital utilization and, most of all, unemployment. Following Klein's (in Klein *et al.* [1961, p. 9]) terminology for such an aggregated model—as opposed to a disaggregated (interregional) model—I have called this national model the prototype model (P.M.) of this study.

This chapter gives a full description of the P.M. (Section 2.2), followed by a summary in equation form (2.3). In Section 2.4 simulations of the P.M. are discussed. An alternative version of the investment function of the P.M. is presented in Section 2.5.

2.2 Description of the Model

2.2.1 Economic Environment

The P.M. describes a closed national economy with three sectors: the household sector, the production sector and the central government. For a discussion of the assumptions that underlie this model the reader is referred to Section 1.2.

2.2.2 Supply

Supply functions are indispensable in describing economies which operate close to the full employment or full capacity level, as some western European economies have been doing since World War II. The simplest function to describe the potential output of an economy is the Leontief or fixed-proportion function, where v, the capital–output ratio, and u, the labour–output ratio are the fixed coefficients. The yearly value of the capital–output ratio on the aggregate level has been found to be

25

fairly constant. On the other hand, the value of u will depend on the way in which labour is measured. In this model I shall measure labour in efficiency units, that is I shall assume that the disembodied technical progress in the economy can best be described to be of the labour-augmenting, Harrod-neutral type. The parameter u is then defined as the ratio between efficiency units of labour (expressed as number of men) and full employment output, and will depend in value on the unit of measurement of output. In equation form the production function will be:

$$X^M(t) = \min\left[K(t)/v, L^{eu}(t)/u\right],$$

where X^M is the maximum or potential output, K the capital stock (measured at the beginning of period t), and L^{eu} the labour measured in efficiency units.

In this and in following equations u and v represent the average as well as the marginal labour– and capital–output ratio.

Most empirical estimates of potential output have related X^M only to the labour factor, the best known being Okun's, which takes the unemployment rate 'as a proxy variable for all the ways in which output is affected by idle resources'.[1] Here, I deal with both full employment and full capacity output. Since the amount an economy can produce depends in part on the demand pressure, our measure of potential output should be thought of as the upper level to which an economy can go at a certain point in time.

As far as disembodied technical progress is concerned, the standard choice is between Hicks-neutral, Harrod-neutral and Solow-neutral technical progress, although this does not exhaust the list of possible forms of neutrality.[2] Harrod- and Solow-neutrality provided a somewhat better fit than Hicks-neutrality in a test done by Beckmann and Sato for the United States, Japan and Germany, in which the implied production function was of the CES-type.[3] The choice of Harrod-neutrality enables us to express technical progress as the annual growth rate of full employment output per man, a parameter which might be more easily approximated than other measures of technical progress.[4] The equation for $L^{eu}(t)$ then reads as follows:

$$L^{eu}(t) = lN_o(1 + p + m)^t, \tag{2.1}$$

where l is the labour force participation rate,

        N_o is the population in initial period,

        p is the rate of population growth, and

        m is the rate of technical progress.

In equation (2.1) the product of the two rates of change, p and m, is neglected. This can only be done when these rates are small numbers. The sum of the two rates gives Harrod's natural or ceiling growth rate: $g = p + m$.[5] The assumed constancy of the labour force participation rate is a rough approximation, since this rate clearly responds to employment opportunities, as has been shown for instance by Strand and Dernberg [1964] and Bowen and Finegan [1965]. The labour force has a tendency to rise during an economic expansion and to fall during the contraction phase. This empirical observation can be accommodated by assuming that L^{eu} represents the upper bound to which the actual labour force can expand during periods of high pressure on the labour market. Thus, the unemployment rate as given in this model will be measured relative to this 'upper bound labour force', and will be on average an over-estimation of the true unemployment rate. On the other hand, the labour force participation rate has shown a tendency to fall during the past decade in most western countries. To cope with this effect, a time trend could be included in (2.1) such that l would become a function of time.

Full capacity and full employment output follow from our production function:

$$X^{FC}(t) = K(t)/v \qquad (2.2)$$

$$X^{FE}(t) = L^{eu}(t)/u \qquad (2.3)$$

and potential output is the minimum of these two for any period:

$$X^{M}(t) = \min\left[X^{FC}(t),\, X^{FE}(t)\right]. \qquad (2.4)$$

2.2.3 Planned Production

Planned production for a particular period in a closed economy consists of three parts:
Planned production of private consumption goods,
Planned outlays for public consumption,
Planned production of capital goods (private plus public).
I shall deal with each of these three components in turn.

When discussing planned production a clear distinction should be made between production to stock and production to order. Production to stock is undertaken in anticipation of demand, while production to order is undertaken to fulfil demand already exerted. The stock in the latter case is the stock of unfilled orders. In the United States most manufacturers produce both to order and to stock, according to G. L. Childs [1967, p. 4]. The industries without unfilled orders are examples of almost pure production to stock, but all other industries produce both to order and to stock. Since the P.M. distinguishes only between the production of consumption and capital goods, I assume as a rough approximation that the production of consumption goods can be characterized as production to stock, and the production of capital goods as production to order.[6]

Planned production of private consumption goods then comprises two parts, namely production to satisfy anticipated demand and production to bring the inventory to the desired level. Anticipated demand will be determined by demand for consumption goods in the past. At the beginning of period t the most recent information on past demand is that of period t-1. The expectations of the producing firms then determine how past demand will be used to arrive at a value for anticipated demand for period t.[7] The most neutral assumption with respect to the firms' expectations is an expected rate of growth of demand equal to the long-term growth rate of the economy. This assumption implies that the effects on present expectations of extremely high or low actual rates of growth in the past are neglected, that is, firms do not expect booms or depressions to continue at the same rate. If they did, their expectations would aggravate the cyclical fluctuations. The above assumption can be expressed in the following simple equation:[8]

$$C^a(t) = eC^d(t\text{-}1),\qquad(2.5)$$

where C^a is the anticipated sales of consumption goods,
  C^d is the demand for consumption goods, and
  e = one plus the expected rate of growth, or $1+g=1+p+m$.

The inventory investment equation for consumption goods in our model is the flexible accelerator of Metzler's stock adjustment equation (Metzler [1941]), in which the optimal level of inventories, V^*, depends on the level of anticipated sales for the period, as follows:

$$V^*(t) = fC^a(t)\qquad(2.6)$$

$$V^p(t) = s[V^*(t) - V(t)].\qquad(2.7)$$

Here, V^* is the desired or optimal level of inventories,
  V^p the planned inventory investment,
  V the actual level of inventories (at the beginning of the period),
  f the desired inventory–sales ratio, and
  s the adjustment coefficient, representing the fraction of desired minus actual inventories adjusted each period.

The equation for planned production of consumption goods now follows:

$$C^p(t) = C^a(t) + V^p(t).\qquad(2.8)$$

The next component of total planned production to consider is planned public consumption. By this I mean that government expenditures that are of a consumptive nature, such as wages and salaries paid to government personnel, education, social care and public health. It is appropriate to assume that these expenditures grow at the same rate as full employment output. Or:

$$G^p(t) = G_o(1+g)^t, \qquad (2.9)$$

where G^p is the planned outlays for public consumption, and G_o the public consumption in the initial period.

The third component, planned investment, equals the sum of private investment demand and public investment demand. A discussion of these two demand categories will be postponed until Section 2.2.5.

$$I^p(d) = J^d(t) + A^d(t), \qquad (2.10)$$

where I^p is the planned total investment, J^d the private investment demand, and A^d the public investment demand.

The equation for planned production now follows:

$$X^p(t) = C^p(t) + G^p(t) + I^p(t). \qquad (2.11)$$

2.2.4 Actual Production

Whether or not all planned production can be realized depends on the productive capacity of the economy. The smaller of the two variables X^p and X^M will determine actual production, X:

$$X(t) = \min[X^p(t), X^M(t)]. \qquad (2.12)$$

Once the actual level of production has been determined for the period, the unemployment and capital utilization rates (abbreviated u.r. and c-u.r. in the text, U and Q in the equations respectively) can be derived from X, the u.r. being one minus the fraction of labour efficiency units used:

$$U(t) = 1 - [uX(t)/L^{eu}(t)], \qquad (2.13)$$

and the c-u.r. expressing the ratio between capital stock used and total capital stock:

$$Q(t) = vX(t)/K(t). \qquad (2.14)$$

Furthermore, the relation between planned production and actual production can be expressed as a ratio, F, where

$$F(t) = X(t)/X^p(t). \qquad (2.15)$$

In this real model, the variable F should be indicative of the price increases that would take place in a nominal model if the economy operates close to its productive capacity ceilings. If $F=1$, all plans can be carried out; if $F<1$, production plans exceed the existing productive capacity. In the latter case, the variable F also indicates what fraction of each producer's plans can be realized. I assume that in their bidding for productive capacity, all producers can realize the same fraction F of their original plans. For our national model, this implies that capital stock and labour are perfectly mobile within the space considered (in this case the nation). The unreality of this implication is one reason for subdividing the economy into regions for which we may or may not assume that capital stock and labour, or labour alone, can cross the regional borders.

The assumption of actual production proportionally to production plans is laid down in the following equations:

$$C(t)=F(t)\ C^p(t) \tag{2.16}$$

$$G(t)=F(t)\ G^p(t) \tag{2.17}$$

$$I(t)=F(t)\ I^p(t), \tag{2.18}$$

in which the variables without the superscript indicate actual production.

Of the three components of planned production, C^p and G^p are the most stable with time. Because of the accelerator in the investment function (see Section 2.2.5), planned investment will show a more fluctuating pattern. The variable F is most likely to drop below 1 when investment is at or close to its peak level during a cycle. For private and public consumption this means that their shares in national output will drop somewhat during these expansion periods, even though the absolute value of consumption may rise because of reduced unemployment. For public consumption in particular the implication is that the level of these government expenditures is not completely exogenous, as is often assumed in economic models. Indeed, the level of public consumption will follow a contracyclical pattern, being relatively higher during the recession phase than during the expansion phase of the cycle. For total government expenditure this pattern might be reinforced, depending on the assumptions made with respect to public investment (again see 2.2.5).

2.2.5 Demand

In this section I deal with private demand and public investment demand. (Public consumption was introduced in Section 2.2.3, as part of planned production.)

In most empirical work the consumption function has as determining

30

variables disposable income and lagged realized consumption.[9] In this model I shall use national income instead of disposable income, and unemployment benefits as a third explaining variable. National income is preferred to disposable income since the latter variable can be determined only if equations are used to explain the income distribution, the size of retained profits and taxed income. This I want to avoid in order to keep the P.M. as simple as possible.

An indication of how the income distribution looks will be given by the propensity to consume out of national income, another by the way unemployment benefits are determined. In this model I shall assume that the unemployment benefits are a fraction h of real wage income per 1000 men. This real wage income is W_o in the initial period. It grows at the rate of technical progress, m, and for period t is therefore equal to $W_o(1+m)^t$. The number of unemployed in thousands in period t is $[L^{eu}(t)-uX(t)]/(1+m)^t$. A fraction h of this number times real wage income $W_o(1+m)^t$ will be equal to [10]

$$H(t)=h\cdot W_o\cdot u\cdot[X^{FE}(t)-X(t)],\tag{2.19}$$

where H is unemployment benefits.

Knowing the three determinants of the demand for consumption goods, I can write

$$C^d(t)=a_1X(t)+a_2C^s(t-1)+H(t).\tag{2.20}$$

Here, C^s is the actual sales of consumption goods. In this specification of the consumption function the long-term marginal propensity to consume equals $a_1/(1-a_2)$; $H(t)$ could be seen as representing subsistence consumption. No savings will be made out of the transfer incomes. The presence of lagged realized consumption establishes the influence which past patterns of consumer behaviour will have on present consumption demand.

Private investment demand in this model is determined by the flexible accelerator (see Section 1.3.2). Net investment depends on the gap between the existing capital stock, K, and the desired or optimal capital stock, K^*. This process of adjusting the capital stock to its desired level will as a rule take a number of years, not only because it takes time before a change in investment determinants can be materialized in actual expenditures, but also because of uncertainty with respect to the future level of demand.

First, the determinants of desired capital stock must be specified. At the beginning of period t the most recent information to base the desired level of the capital stock on is last period's planned production, $X^p(t-1)$. This variable gives the best indication available of what the future demand for productive capacity might be.[11] As with the planned production of con-

31

sumption goods, the most neutral assumption regarding the expectations of firms is growth of planned production at the long-term growth rate, $g = p + m$. Since the construction of capital goods will on average take at least a year (the time that elapses between the first expenditure and the addition of the goods to the stock), firms extrapolate past planned production to arrive at an estimation of next year's planned production, and from there at the capital stock they desire to have at the beginning of next year.

One condition associated with use of $X^p(t-1)$ as an explanatory variable must be made. Last period's planned production may have been exceptionally high, so high that the realization of a capital stock matching the extrapolated planned production would lead to a full capacity output exceeding full employment output. Even if actual production next period would take place at the full employment level, this would then go along with excess capacity, and firms certainly will want to avoid this. An upper limit to extrapolated planned production is therefore given by next period's full employment output, and the equation for desired capital stock will be as follows:[12]

$$K^*(t) = \min \left[v \cdot e^2 \cdot X^p(t-1), \, v \cdot e^2 \cdot X^{FE}(t-1) \right]. \tag{2.21}$$

Squaring the parameter $e \, (= 1 + g)$ means that the expectations parameter is applied twice, that is, I extrapolate from $t-1$ to $t+1$. The expression $e^2 \cdot X^{FE}(t-1)$ is equal to $X^{FE}(t+1)$ since full employment output grows at the rate g. K^* has the time index t with it, since it stands for the optimal capital stock as conceptualized at the beginning of period t.

It is unlikely that the whole gap between actual and desired capital stock will be eliminated in one period. As stated above, there are two types of reasons for this: uncertainty regarding the correctness of the expectations, and the existence of technical lags. Apart from these lags, with which I deal in equation (2.23), firms will define as desired investment that fraction of the gap they want to eliminate in one period. The more cautious they are, the lower the adjustment coefficient b will be. Desired investment, J^*, includes replacement investment, which is assumed to equal depreciation. The asymmetry of equation (2.22) accounts for the obvious fact that negative gross investment is an impossibility:

$$J^*(t) = \max \left\{ 0, \, b \left[K^*(t) - (1-r) \, K(t) \right] \right\}. \tag{2.22}$$

Here, r is the rate of depreciation, equalling the rate of replacement.

The equation which expresses actual demand for capital goods in period t, $J^d(t)$, will have to specify the lag structure of the investment function. It takes time to work out investment plans, to have them approved, to appropriate funds, etc. Evidence has been accumulated (see for instance Evans [1969, pp. 95–105]) that investment expenditure, following a change in its determinants, rises for a time, reaches a peak, then falls such that expenditures during the second year of adjustment are usually larger than the first year. To account for this I shall assume that actual demand for investment is a weighted average of this period's and last period's desired investment, such that the latter variable has a larger weight:

$$J^d(t) = (1-q) J^*(t-1) + q J^*(t). \qquad (2.23)$$

The parameter q $(0 \leq q \leq 1)$ is a measure of the speed with which the most recent information enters investment demand (see F. Modigliani and H. M. Weingartner [1958, p. 40]). By selecting appropriate values for the parameters b and q I can ensure that the total lag between change in determinants (X^p in our case) and actual investment is in accordance with what has been found empirically.[13]

The third component of demand that remains to be discussed is public investment demand, comprising the construction of new roads, waterways, buildings and so on. In this model, government investment demand will be determined partly by the long-term growth rate of the economy, partly by the cycle phase in which the economy finds itself. Equation (2.24) below shows that the size of government contracyclical expenditure is determined by the difference between the target output level and actual output, both of the last period. From the standpoint of reducing the periodicity of fluctuations in the economy this is not necessarily the optimal policy (see A. W. Phillips [1954]). The only goal the government has in mind, however, is to reduce unemployment, and every time output drops below the target output, it will act. In period t the most recent information available to the government is that of period $t-1$:

$$A^d(t) = A_o(1+g)^t + \max [0, w X^{FE}(t-1) - X(t-1)]. \qquad (2.24)$$

In this equation, w is the target employment rate, set by the government. With public investment carried out in period t, the government attempts to eliminate the gap between the target level of production and actual production. The asymmetry of this equation is necessary to avoid negative investment which would have to take place if actual output is to exceed the target level.

2.2.6 Actual Sales

The remaining four equations in the model are all definitional. Actual sales of consumption goods equal to the demand for consumption goods or to actual production plus inventories at the beginning of the period, whichever is smaller:

$$C^s(t) = \min[C(t) + V(t),\ C^d(t)].\qquad(2.25)$$

Total sales will be equal to actual production plus or minus inventory changes. The simplest way to write total sales, X^s, is as follows:

$$X^s(t) = C^s(t) + G(t) + I(t).\qquad(2.26)$$

2.2.7 Capital Stock and Inventory Next Period

Finally, to complete the model, two equations are needed to determine the level of capital stock and inventories at the beginning of next period:

$$K(t+1) = (1-r)\,K(t) + I(t)\qquad(2.27)$$

$$V(t+1) = V(t) + C(t) - C^s(t).\qquad(2.28)$$

2.3 Summary of the Model

Supply

$$L^{eu}(t) = l \cdot N_o(1 + p + m)^t\qquad(2.1)$$

$$X^{FC}(t) = K(t)/v\qquad(2.2)$$

$$X^{FE}(t) = L^{eu}(t)/u\qquad(2.3)$$

$$X^M(t) = \min[X^{FC}(t),\ X^{FE}(t)]\qquad(2.4)$$

Planned production

$$C^a(t) = eC^d(t-1)\qquad(2.5)$$

$$V^*(t) = fC^a(t)\qquad(2.6)$$

$$V^p(t) = s[V^*(t) - V(t)]\qquad(2.7)$$

$$C^p(t) = C^a(t) + V^p(t)\qquad(2.8)$$

$$G^p(t) = G_o(1+g)^t\qquad(2.9)$$

$$I^p(t) = J^d(t) + A^d(t)\qquad(2.10)$$

$$X^p(t) = C^p(t) + G^p(t) + I^p(t)\qquad(2.11)$$

Actual production

$$X(t) = \min[X^p(t),\ X^M(t)]\qquad(2.12)$$

$$U(t) = 1 - [uX(t)/L^{eu}(t)] \qquad (2.13)$$

$$Q(t) = vX(t)/K(t) \qquad (2.14)$$

$$F(t) = X(t)/X^p(t) \qquad (2.15)$$

$$C(t) = F(t) \, C^p(t) \qquad (2.16)$$

$$G(t) = F(t) \, G^p(t) \qquad (2.17)$$

$$I(t) = F(t) \, I^p(t) \qquad (2.18)$$

Demand

$$H(t) = h \cdot W_o \cdot u[X^{FE}(t) - X(t)] \qquad (2.19)$$

$$C^d(t) = a_1 X(t) + a_2 C^s(t-1) + H(t) \qquad (2.20)$$

$$K^*(t) = \min[v \cdot e^2 \cdot X^p(t-1), \, v \cdot e^2 \cdot X^{FE}(t-1)] \qquad (2.21)$$

$$J^*(t) = \max\{0, \, b[K^*(t) - (1-r) \, K(t)]\} \qquad (2.22)$$

$$J^d(t) = (1-q) \, J^*(t-1) + qJ^*(t) \qquad (2.23)$$

$$A^d(t) = A_o(1+g)^t + \max[0, \, wX^{FE}(t-1) - X(t-1)] \qquad (2.24)$$

Actual sales

$$C^s(t) = \min[C(t) + V(t), \, C^d(t)] \qquad (2.25)$$

$$X^s(t) = C^s(t) + G(t) + I(t) \qquad (2.26)$$

Capital stock and inventory next period

$$K(t+1) = (1-r) \, K(t) + I(t) \qquad (2.27)$$

$$V(t+1) = V(t) + C(t) - C^s(t) \qquad (2.28)$$

2.4 Simulations of the Model

This part of Chapter 2 describes some of the simulations made with the P.M. In Section 2.4.1 the values assigned to the parameters, parametric constants and lagged endogenous variables are discussed. The next section describes a representative model run, called the 'base run', to illustrate how the model works. Then additional simulations with slightly different parameter values are presented in order to see how sensitive the P.M. is to these variations (Section 2.4.3).

2.4.1 Values Assigned to Parameters, Parametric Constants and Lagged Endogenous Variables

To start a simulation, values will have to be assigned to sixteen parameters, four parametric constants and seven lagged endogenous variables. The values I assign to the lagged endogenous variables are usually not crucial for the movement of the system over a period of time. Of course, they determine the level of activity—just as the parametric constants do—but other than with the latter data their effect on the course of the system gradually diminishes, either through a multiplier-type process (if the initial conditions implied a departure from the long-term trend in a non-explosive model) or, more slowly, through the working of the upper boundaries of the system (if the system shows oscillatory movements, whether explosive or damped).

The long-term behaviour of the simulated economy is not affected by the values of the lagged endogenous variables, that is cycle length, peak and trough u.r.s are the same for a large range of reasonable values assigned to the lagged endogenous variables. The exact course of un-employment over a cycle may differ slightly for different initial values, but these differences will usually cancel each other out.[14] These observations imply some freedom in choosing the values of the lagged en-dogenous variables, the main condition being that they are consistent with each other and with the values of the parametric constants. The values of the parameters, on the other hand, are crucial to the operation of the system, though some are less sensitive than others; to make our model realistic values must be chosen in accord with empirical results.

The first values to determine are those of the supply side of the model: the growth rates p and m, the labour force participation rate l, the technical coefficients v and u, and the parametric constant N_o, giving population in the initial period. Three of these values can be assigned arbitrarily. For l I have selected a realistic value in the neighbourhood of .40. The product of l and N_o determines the potential labour force in the initial period, and the size of this labour force is entirely up to us, as we are not trying to approach levels of supply factors for a particular country. Convenient numbers are therefore required. In all computer runs we used $l = .40$ and $N_o = 2500$. N_o is measured in efficiency units, where 1000 men give one efficiency unit. Thus, I start the simulations with 2500 efficiency units, equalling a population of 2.5 million. Since $l = .40$, the labour force is one million. The parameter u measures the number of efficiency units required for a unit of output. This number is arbitrarily taken to be 10, so that full employment output equals 100 in the initial period. The number of efficiency units grows at a rate $p + m$, the combined rate of population growth and technical progress.

The population growth rate for most OECD countries during the 1960s has been around 1% annually, but the labour force participation rate has shown a tendency to fall somewhat. I shall treat the latter as a parameter and select for the base run a population growth rate of 1%. The growth of output per man (which is the way in which I measure technical progress) has been over 3% for the OECD countries during the 1960s; taking a conservative value, I will assume a potential growth of output per man of 3%.[15] The final parameter on the supply side to be estimated is v, the capital–output ratio. Kuznets [1961] gives 2.0–2.5 as the approximate value of v for the United States economy on an annual basis (output is then gross output). I shall take 2.5 as the aggregate value for the base run, and not discriminate between marginal and average capital–output ratio, assuming that the v remains constant over the periods of observation.

I shall move on to the planned-production parameters now. Four values must be selected: the expectations coefficient, e, which I shall set equal to one plus the long-term growth rate of the economy ($e=1.04$); the optimal inventory–consumption output ratio, f; the inventory–investment adjustment coefficient, s, and G_o, giving the level of public consumption in the initial period. The inventory–investment part of the model has been tested by L. R. Klein [1950] for the United States; Klein found that 62% of the gap between desired and actual inventory was adjusted in one year. That gives .6 as a reasonable value for the parameter s. The inventory–sales ratio in the United States for the post-war period has been around .125 on an annual basis (see Evans [1969, p. 377]). This is the actual, not the desired ratio, and sales here include non-consumption goods. As an approximation, however, I shall use the value .125 for our f.

It is clear that G_o, the last parameter of the planned-production section of the model, is a crucial parameter because of its policy impact. This will be particularly evident when I come to the interregional model. Right now I shall have to determine a range within which G_o will vary. An indication of the extent to which government contributes to GNP in two mature western European economies is given by public expenditure figures for the Netherlands and Belgium in A. P. Barten [1970, pp. 85–6]. These data show that in two small countries, geographically so close together, relatively large differences can exist in public expenditure as part of GNP: in the Netherlands this percentage went up from roughly 18% in 1953 to a little more than 20% in 1966; in Belgium it rose from roughly 14% to 16% in the same period. Public expenditure in these figures is public expenditure on goods and services. It includes, besides public consumption, gross investment in transport and education. Simulations with our model showed that, given the other parameters, G_o has to be around 18 (which means around 18% of GNP in the initial period) for unemployment to be at tolerable levels. Thus, 18 is the value I selected for the base run. The effect of alternative initial values is discussed in Section 2.4.3.

The 'actual-production' segment of the P.M. involves no new parameters. I continue, therefore, with a discussion of the demand parameters: h, a_1, a_2, b, r, q, w and the parametric constant W_o. The parameter h gives the fraction of real wage income that is paid to the unemployed. This fraction will be fairly low for most countries; a value of .3 seems reasonable. By increasing this value the impact on the economy of this kind of stabilizer can be examined. The second parameter associated with unemployment benefits is the initial real wage, W_o. In the initial period income will be approximately 100. Assume that 75% of this income is labour income (an assumption which will not be contradicted by the actual facts for most western economies), and recall that in the base period a fully employed labour force consists of 1000 efficiency units; then real wage per efficiency unit under full employment conditions is 75% of .1, or $W_o = .075$.

The consumption function in our model has output, lagged sales of consumption goods and unemployment payments as explanatory variables instead of the more usual disposable income and lagged sales. This means that I shall have to adjust the empirically tested marginal propensity to consume out of disposable income to a marginal propensity to consume out of GNP, thereby keeping in mind that unemployment-benefits recipients are assumed to have a marginal propensity to consume of one. Evans [1969, p. 57] discusses several empirical estimates of the United States consumption function. One that measures variables in constant dollars, and uses the correct deflator is[16]

$$C_t = 5.04 + 0.66 \ Y_t^d + 0.28 \ C_{t-1}.$$

With this equation as our guide, $a_1 = .45-.50$ and $a_2 = .25-.30$ seem to indicate a fair range for the two propensities to consume of equation (2.19). For the base run, $a_1 = .45$ and $a_2 = .30$ were selected. An a_1 of .45 for the United States economy would imply that personal disposable income is approximately 68% of GNP; together the two marginal propensities would imply a long-term marginal propensity to consume out of GNP of .63. Neither of these two results is far off the mark.[17] The unemployment benefits act as a variable intercept in our consumption function, most likely to grow over time as the u.r. varies around some average value.

The first of the three investment-function parameters I shall discuss is r, the rate of replacement. Jorgenson and Stephenson [1967] tested this parameter for United States manufacturing industries, and estimated the over-all rate (durables plus non-durables) at .0273. For the base run and for other runs I took .027 as the best available estimate.

The next two parameters of the investment function are very important. Desired investment depends on the value of b, the adjustment coefficient, while actual investment demand is determined by the lag structure, with q giving the weights of present and past desired investment. Empirical estimates of any of these two parameters are hard to obtain. At most, simulations with the model made certain values for b improbable, while empirical findings suggest that q should have a value below .5. As it turns out, values of b slightly over and of q slightly under .5, together with the rest of the lag structure of the model, give rise to moderately fluctuating cycles; this is an acceptable result in the light of post-war experience. For the base run I chose the values of the investment parameters to be .6 (b) and .4 (q). Variations of these parameters will show their sensitivity.

Our last demand component is public investment. Let part of government demand for investment grow at the long-term growth rate of the economy, with the initial level, A_o, equalling 3 in the base run. That is, roughly 3% of national product will be contributed by public investment programmes which are independent of the cyclical situation. However, the government in our model actively pursues a full employment policy, just as the governments of some western countries have done this since World War II. Recall that our full employment concept is an absolute upper ceiling independent of which phase of the cycle the economy is in. The government may aim at this input level or at some lower level, depending on the intensity of its desire to reduce unemployment. In the base run I assumed the former. In Section 2.4.3 runs with lower values of w will be discussed, including the value zero (no government interference at all).

Since the remaining equations of the P.M. are definitional and do not contain new parameters, I can summarize the values assigned to the parameters and parametric constants for the base run:

Values assigned to parameters

$a_1 = .45$	$f = .125$	$m = .03$	$s = .60$
$a_2 = .30$	$g = .04$	$p = .01$	$u = 10$
$b = .60$	$h = .30$	$q = .40$	$v = 2.5$
$e = 1.04$	$l = .40$	$r = .027$	$w = 1.00$

Values assigned to parametric constants

$G_o = 18$	$A_o = 3$	$N_o = 2500$	$W_o = .075$

Finally, we have to assign values to the lagged endogenous variables in order to start the computer runs. We have chosen the value of the parametric constant N_o such that $X^{FE}(0) = 100$. A matching capital stock is $K(0) = 250$. Assume a rate of growth of .04, then at the beginning of period 1, K will have to be 260 to allow for a full capacity output, which equals full employment output. The initial values of X^p and X are both set equal to 100, those of C^d and C^s to 72, and the value of J^* in period 0 is assumed to be 18 (which is a little high to assure that the system starts off with positive excess demand). The remaining endogenous variable, V, is given a value of 8 at the beginning of period 1 (which will lead to positive investment demand). Again, there is considerable freedom in selecting these values. I have chosen them such that excess demand results in the initial period. Summarizing:

Values assigned to lagged endogenous variables

$C^d(0) = 72$	$J^*(0) = 18$	$V(1) = 8$	$X^p(0) = 100$
$C^s = 72$	$K(1) = 260$	$X(0) = 100$	

2.4.2 The Base Run

All simulations of the P.M. were carried out for 60 periods. The key figures of the computer runs are recorded, however, over periods 24 to 60: the first periods were omitted from the computer print-out, since the initial conditions would have too great an influence on the time series of these first periods to make them comparable with other runs. Key figures of the base run and all other runs (to be discussed in the next section) are brought together in Table 2.1. Figure 2.1 presents time paths of the main endogenous variables, recorded during the periods 24 to 60 of the base run.

The print-out for the periods 24 to 60 of the base run shows two complete cycles, approximately identical to each other, each 14 periods long. During these two cycles, the variations in the unemployment rate (which variable I take as the indicator of the general level of activity) are moderate. At the

Explanation

1. *U low-high*: lowest and highest unemployment rates recorded between periods 24 and 60, or steady-state u.r. if simulation generated steady-state or heavily damped growth.
2. *Q low*: lowest capital utilization rate recorded between periods 24 and 60, or steady-state c-u.r. if simulation generated steady-state or heavily damped growth.

40

Table 2.1

Prototype Model Simulations (Base Run and Variations)

Run	Variation	U low-high	Q low	F low	CL
1604	base run	1.0–5.5	.97	.94	$9+ 5=14$
1613	$b = .5$	2.1–5.4	.99	.93	$6+ 9=15$
1612	$b = .7$	0.2–6.1	.96	.94	$9+ 5=14$
1633	$b = 1.0$	0.0–6.8	.94	.89	$7+ 6=13$
1619	$q = .3$	1.0–5.7	.97	.94	$10+ 5=15$
1620	$q = .5$	1.1–5.5	.97	.95	$9+ 5=14$
1631	$b = .7; q=.3$	0.2–5.8	.97	.94	$9+ 5=14$
1632	$b = .8; q=.2$	0.0–7.9	.94	.93	$6+ 8=14$
1634	$b = 1.0; q=.2$	0.0–10.9	.91	.90	$6+ 8=14$
1618	$a_1 = .45; a_2=.28$	1.3–10.2	.93	.95	$9+ 5=14$
1617	$a_1 = .48; a_2=.30$	2.1	1.00	.91	—
1635	$a_1 = .48; a_2=.32$	2.3	1.00	.90	—
1621	$G_o = 15$	8.2	.97	1.00	—
1622	$G_o = 21$	2.1	1.00	.93	—
1627	$v = 2$	8.1	.95	1.00	—
1628	$v = 3$	2.5	1.00	.92	—
1601	$A_o = 0$	1.9–6.8	.98	.90	$6+ 7=13$
1605	$A_o = 6$	2.9	.99	1.00	D
1614	$w = .95$	2.2–9.0	.96	.86	$5+ 9=14$
1608	$w = 0$	2.0–19.2	.93	.74	$6+11=17$
1609	$A_o = 6; w=0$	0.1–7.6	.91	.75	$6+11=17$
1610	$A_o = 9; w=0$	0.0–14.0	.91	.80	$10+ 8=18$
1611	$A_o = 15; w=0$	0.0–5.3	.92	.95	$11+ 7=18$
1602	$A_o = 0; w=.95$	3.0–11.2	.96	.83	$5+ 7=12$
1625	$A_o = 0; w=.90$	3.8–15.9	.96	.77	$6+ 7=13$
1603	$A_o = 0; w=0$	4.0–23.5	.94	.70	$6+ 9=15$
1615	$h = .5$	1.1–4.0	.99	.94	$5+ 8=13$
1616	$h = 0$	1.2–12.2	.92	.95	$13+ 7=20$
1629	$A_o = 0; w=0; h=0$	6.8–55.1	.65	.58	$8+14=22$

3. *F low*: lowest production realization rate recorded between periods 24 and 60, or steady-state F if simulation generated steady-state or heavily damped growth.

4. *CL*: cycle length (expansionary + contractionary stage). Steady-state growth is indicated with a dash, heavily damped growth with a D. If no clear cyclical pattern is discernible this is indicated by a question

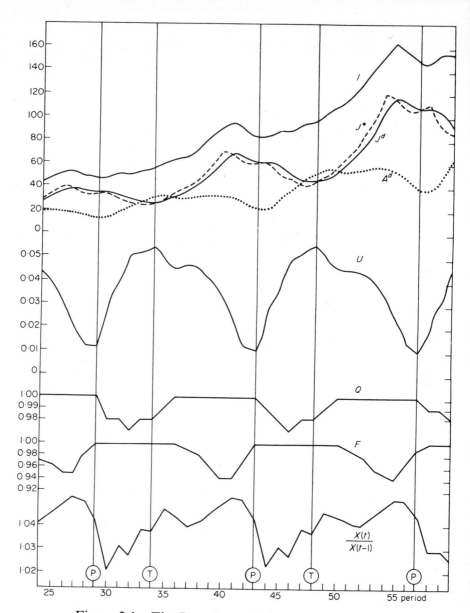

Figure 2.1   The Base Run of the Prototype Model

mark. If a subcycle exists, its length is given in the upper right-hand
side of the *CL*-column, preceded by a + sign.
5. The *base-run parameters* are listed on page 63.

height of the recession the rate of unemployment is 5.5% (periods 34 and 48),
during the peak periods, 1.0 and 1.1% (periods 29, 43 and 57). Output
never falls in absolute terms during any phase of the cycle, neither does
consumption, whether measured as consumption plans, demand or sales.
It is investment that causes the variations in the rate of growth of output
and in the rate of unemployment.

Figure 2.1 shows how J^*, J^d and I behave during a cycle. Since $J^d(t)$
is a weighted average of $J^*(t)$ and $J^*(t-1)$, with a heavier weight on the
latter, I expect that during the upswing or expansionary phase $J^*(t) > J^d(t)$,
and *vice versa*. This is true, with the exception that both J^* and J^d are already in the downswing when the economy still has to reach its peak.
Hence the model generates a phenomenon that has also been observed in
reality, and that has made new orders for durable producers' goods (J^d in
our model) one of the most important early indicators of revivals and
recessions. During the recession, only J^* indicates that a recovery is forth-
coming before the actual trough occurs, while J^d reaches its low when
general economic activity does.

The story of actual total investment, I, is again a different one. This
variable includes public investment, which is partly independent of the
cyclical situation and partly related to unemployment. Thus, at all times
I will be greater than J^d (which stands for private demand for capital goods,
not actual private investment), but the gap will be wider during a recession
than during a boom. The result is that actual investment expenditure falls
in absolute terms only a few periods before the upper turning point,
when unemployment is at its lowest level and the decline of private
investment demand is announcing the coming recession. This is also a
result that has been typical for actual post-war cycles in the United
States.

The rise and fall of investment demand can only be explained in terms
of the gap between desired and actual capital stock. During the expansionary stage the gap has been narrowed and the economy has come closer to
its full employment level. At that point, firms become more hesitant to expand their capital stock further, as they are aware of the tightness of the
labour market. No substitution between labour and capital is possible
in the model. It is the reduced desire to expand the capital stock that will
result in a turning point. A comparison of the time series of planned output,
X^p, and full employment output, X^{FE} (made from a computer print-out)

43

will clearly show that the latter variable becomes a constraint only during the final three periods before the peak. In all other periods $X^P < X^{FE}$. The computer print-out will also show the effectiveness of the full employment constraint on private investment. Desired investment drops immediately after X^P exceeds X^{FE} for the first time.

Inventory investment in this model reinforces the instability caused by the fluctuations of investment. During the recession the inventory reaches its desired level, to fall below it when the economy starts expanding again. The movement of this stock is closely related to that of the variable F. This variable measures the degree to which production plans can be realized. When $F = 1$ for a number of periods, one expects the inventory to grow to its optimal level; when $F < 1$, the stock will be reduced in size to meet consumption demand that cannot be realized through production. In general the F-ratio is the best indication in this model of price increases that will result from a discrepancy between supply and demand. In a policy context, government could set a tolerable minimum level for F. An $F = 1$, will, however, not be in general reconcilable with low u.r.s and a full usage of capacity $(Q = 1)$. From Figure 2.1 I conclude that recessions go together with $F = 1$ and $Q < 1$, while the expansionary stage is characterized by falling U, $Q = 1$ and $F < 1$. On the whole, the base run produces tolerable minimum values for Q and F: .97 and .94 respectively. It is inevitable that firms will have excess capital goods during the contractionary stage. During eight of the 14 periods which together form a complete cycle, however, the economy operates at full capacity; the full capacity ceiling is therefore an effective boundary. The full employment ceiling is effective too, but indirectly: it prevents firms from aiming at a capital stock for which no matching labour force would exist.

2.4.3 Some Parameter Variations

In this section I shall look at the sensitivity of the P.M. economy to parameter variations. On the basis of additional simulations I shall discuss those sets of parameter values for which cycles will be generated and those for which the output path will be a steady-state path. Furthermore, I shall consider what determines the amplitude and length of the cycles generated. The simulations with which the impact of different parameter values was tested are summarized in Table 2.1. See also Figure 2.2 for an illustration of two of the variational runs.

The P.M. economy operates within an upper and a lower boundary. The upper boundary, or ceiling, comes into operation when output reaches the full capacity or the full employment level. The lower boundary, or floor, consists of government autonomous and contracyclical investment, of government consumption and unemployment benefits. With our

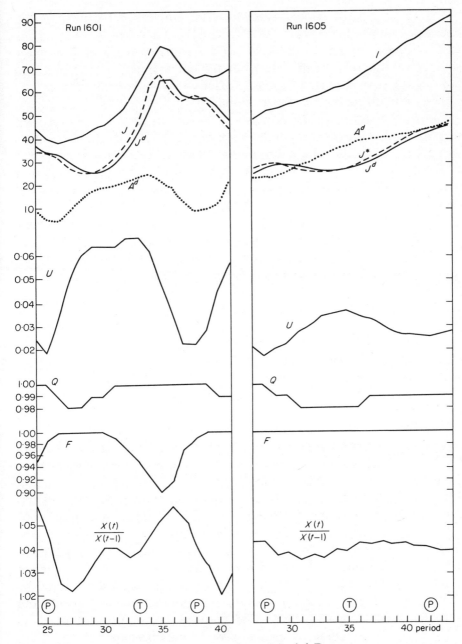

Figure 2.2   Prototype Model Runs

45

definition of desired capital stock the full employment ceiling mostly operates in an indirect way, by restraining businessmen from investing up to a level where the capital stock cannot be matched any more with the necessary amount of labour. So while full employment is not reached in most cases, it is the fear of excess capacity that makes the full capacity ceiling an indirectly active upper boundary.

Our model is a model of economic fluctuations, that is, it is specified such that for a range of acceptable parameter values it will generate cyclical output paths. Whether or not time paths will be cyclical depends on the level of planned production over a period of time relative to the upper and lower boundaries of the system. In two cases steady-state growth instead of growth with fluctuations will be the rule:

(a) When the demand structure is such that an excess demand of stable demand components (e.g. private and public consumption) causes planned production to exceed maximum possible production continually. This I will call 'upper' steady-state growth: output moves along the ceiling. Examples are runs 1617, 1635 and 1622 (excess consumption demand), and run 1628 (excess investment demand).

(b) When government autonomous investment and contracyclical investment (which responds to the unemployment level) cause an excess supply of capital goods, relative to the total demand level, such that the accelerator mechanism of private investment demand ceases to operate. This I will call 'lower' steady-state growth: output moves along the floor. Examples are runs 1621, 1627 and 1605.

When neither (a) nor (b) holds, the time path of output is cyclical.

Simulations of the model show that if cycles are generated these are either constant in amplitude or slightly damped. Explosive time paths (whether oscillatory or non-oscillatory) are excluded by the presence of the upper and lower boundaries; time paths that would be explosive in an un-constrained economy become constant amplitude cycles in our model.

With private investment being the most volatile output component, the amplitude of the cycles will be determined by the volatility of investment behaviour (indicated by the adjustment coefficient b), and by the degree to which the government will attempt to mitigate the instability caused by investment through contracyclical and/or autonomous investment, and through unemployment benefits. Fluctuations will be heaviest when all fiscal policy is eliminated (run 1629)[18] and become milder when successively the various contracyclical measures are introduced (see run 1603, which has $h = .3$; run 1601, with $h = .3$ plus $w = 1$; and finally, the base run which has both contracyclical and autonomous government expenditures).

Investment behaviour and the intensity of government stabilization measures also determine the length of the cycle:

The larger that b is, the faster the gap between desired and actual capital stock will be closed, and the shorter therefore the expansionary stage and the whole cycle will be (see sequences 1613, 1604, 1612 and 1633).[19]

The less the government uses its contracyclical measures to interfere with the outcomes of the market process, the longer the cycles will be. See, for instance, runs 1608 ($w=0$) and 1616 ($h=0$), which have cycle lengths of 17 and 20 periods respectively, as compared with the 14 periods of the base-run cycle. Typically, the cycle is longest when w and h are both zero in addition to $A_o=0$, namely 22 periods (run 1629). Autonomous government investment, on the other hand, affects the cycle length in a different way than contracyclical expenditures do: the higher autonomous investment, the longer the cycles will be (runs 1601, 1604, 1603, 1609, 1610 and 1611). The explanation for this is that higher autonomous investment causes more excess supply of capital goods in a depression. Under these circumstances it takes more time before the accelerator starts pushing the economy out of the depression to the ceiling, and the cycle as a whole will therefore be longer.

2.5 Alternative Specifications of the Investment Function

Our specification of the investment function, as adopted for the P.M. [equations (2.10), (2.21) to (2.24)], is obviously not the only possible one. Indeed, our equation for desired capital stock, (2.21), is not likely to be found in empirical work, since X^p is not a variable that can be readily measured. Yet in this analytical model, the specification of (2.21) gives better results than simpler investment functions would. I shall illustrate this by discussing the implications for our model of two desired-capital stock functions, which were tested as alternatives for (2.21):

$$K^*(t)=v\cdot e^2\cdot X^s(t-1) \tag{2.21a}$$

$$K^*(t)=v\cdot e^2\cdot X^p(t-1). \tag{2.21b}$$

The first of these two equations uses actual sales as the explanatory variable. In empirical models actual sales are often used as the output variable, and this desirable feature would make (2.21a) an acceptable equation in the P.M. In our model, however, X^s is not used as an exogenous variable (as it would be in empirical models), but generated within the model as an endogenous variable whose magnitude is determined by demand or actual production, whichever is smaller.

Once actual production is less than demand the link between desired

47

capital stock and demand is broken, and basically the model ceases to be a demand model: X^s does not reflect unsatisfied demand, and entrepreneurs lack an incentive to bring their capital stocks to a level high enough to satisfy demand. Computer runs with (2.21a) instead of (2.21), and with the adjustment coefficient b equal to unity give continually increasing u.r.s with time, output moving along the full capacity ceiling. Actual investment in these simulations is too low to realize all production plans. The rate of growth of output is positive, but decreasing as time proceeds.

The simplest way to bring in demand in investment considerations is by substituting $X^p(t-1)$ for $X^s(t-1)$ in the desired-capital stock function. X^p reflects both consumer and producer demand, and with (2.21b) the causality between demand and production is certainly restored in the model. Simulations of the P.M. with (2.21b) instead of (2.21), and without autonomous investment behaviour, produce time series that are even more unrealistic, however, than those with $X^s(t-1)$: zero u.r.s and no production of consumption goods in the long run, since all productive capacity is eventually applied to the production of capital goods. The explanation for this outcome is that planned production leads a life of its own in the new specification, a life in which the productive capacity barrier does not play a role any more. The causal chain which leads to only investment as output is the following: a high planned-production level leads to a high level of desired investment in the next period. This high level of J^* by itself is likely to give rise to an X^p that is even higher than last period's, whereupon J^* goes up again, and so on. The consideration that labour is increasingly unable to produce planned production is absent in (2.21b). Finally, desired investment becomes so high that consumption goods are no longer produced.

The inclusion of autonomous investment will considerably mitigate the explosive character of the (2.21b) model. Positive autonomous investment will take away some of the pressure on private investment to close the gap between desired and actual capital stock, as it adds capital goods to the stock regardless of the size of X^p. Still J^* reaches unrealistic highs during the upswing phase, when in addition the production of consumption goods is cut in half, enough to make the combination of positive autonomous investment plus equation (2.21b) an undesirable investment function. Table 2.2 gives a comparison between some runs of the P.M. and comparable runs made with the alternative (2.21b) model. The table shows that all parameter combinations tested produce zero u.r.s at least once between periods 24 and 60, except for run 1408 (with $G_o = 15$ instead of 18) which gives exactly the same steady-state growth, converging time path as its counterpart run, 1621. If X^p never exceeds X^{FE}, the modified model and the P.M. become identical, and that is the case

Table 2.2

Prototype Model Simulations with Simplified Investment Function

Run	P.M. Run	Variation	(2.21b) Model Run				P.M. Run			
			U low-high	Q low	F low	CL	U low-high	Q low	F low	CL
1401	1601	$A_o = 0$	0.0–12.3	.79	.82	17	1.9– 6.8	.98	.90	13
1402	1603	$A_o = 0; w = 0$	0.0–31.1	.57	.58	21	4.0–23.5	.94	.70	15
1403	1604	base run	0.0–10.2	.82	.86	18	1.0– 5.5	.97	.94	14
1404	1605	$A_o = 6$	0.0– 8.1	.85	.90	19	1.7– 4.8	.97	1.00	—
1406	1612	$b = .7$	0.0–11.8	.74	.80	21	0.2– 6.1	.96	.94	13
1407	1613	$b = .5$	0.0–10.2	.89	.88	16	2.1– 5.4	.99	.93	15
1408	1621	$G_o = 15$	8.2	.97	1.00	—	8.2	.97	1.00	—
1409	1622	$G_o = 21$	0.0–10.5	.75	.77	18	2.1	1.00	.93	—
1410	1633	$b = 1.0$	0.0–21.6	.27	.30	?	0.0– 6.8	.94	.89	13

with runs 1408 and 1621. In all other cases, however, the modification of the desired-capital stock function makes the simulated economy much more explosive, to which lower minimum values of Q and F testify. The cycles generated by the modified model are longer, as is to be expected when the full employment ceiling is no longer keeping investment plans in check.

Notes

[1] See A. M. Okun [1962, p. 99]. Other methods of estimating potential GNP have been summarized by M. E. Levy [1963]. A more recent article on potential output is E. Kuh [1966].

[2] See M. J. Beckmann and R. Sato [1969].

[3] Beckmann and Sato [1969].

[4] For example, in many OECD publications one will find the actual growth of real GNP divided up in growth of employment and growth of output per employed person. See, for example, OECD Economic Studies [1966, p. 28].

[5] See R. F. Harrod [1939, pp. 30–1]; also D. Hamberg [1971, p. 16].

[6] D. A. Belsley [1969, p. 74] divided the 19 U.S. 2-digit industries into 13 with unfilled orders and six without. The six 'pure' production to stock industries were food and kindred products, tobacco manufactures, apparel and related products, chemicals and allied products, petroleum and coal products, and rubber and plastic products.

[7] Here, I ignore the influence of actual demand before period $t-1$ on anticipated demand. In empirical work one would, of course, choose for a specification including a geometrically declining weighted average of past demand.

[8] Recalling Metzler's equation for anticipated sales in Metzler [1941]: $C^a(t) = C^s(t-1) + \varepsilon(C^s(t-1) - C^s(t-2))$, where C^a is the anticipated sales, C^s the actual sales and ε is Metzler's coefficient of expectations, our (2.5) is in fact Metzler's equation for a growing economy $(e > 1)$ with $\varepsilon = 0$, assuming all demand is realized.

[9] See, for instance, Evans [1967].

[10] h times real wage income times number of unemployed $= h \cdot W_o(1+m)^t$ $\times [L^{eu}(t) - uX(t)]/(1+m)^t = h \cdot W_o \cdot u \cdot [X^{FE}(t) - X(t)]$.

[11] In the derivation of most empirical investment models based on the flexible accelerator, actual sales, $X^s(t-1)$ or past actual output, $X(t-1)$, is taken as the variable that determines desired capital stock. In this model, however, $X^p(t-1)$ is the only variable that properly reflects the demand for capital stock. Both $X^s(t-1)$ and $X(t-1)$ only tell us what was actually sold or produced, without indicating to what extent, if at all, demand for

capital stock could not be satisfied. An empirically measured $X^s(t-1)$ or $X(t-1)$ of course also reflects existing demand, but in this analytical model demand–supply adjustments take place only once every period, namely at the beginning of each period.

[12] Hickman [1965, p. 8] remarks that 'rates of capacity utilization can differ, and have differed, substantially from labor force utilization over the postwar years, and it is the former rather than the latter that are relevant for investment demand'. The specification of (2.21) seemingly contradicts this statement, but actually it is in total agreement with it. By comparing expected planned production with full employment output next period, firms are able to prevent less than full capacity utilization in the near future (if their expectations are correct). The simulations we made with the lagged capital utilization rate as explanatory variable in the equation for $K^*(t)$, led occasionally to very low c-u.r.s, and the explanation for this is that $Q(t-1)$ does not give any information about the future labour force that will have to match the capital stock.

[13] D. W. Jorgenson and J. A. Stephenson [1967, p. 17] found that 'investment expenditure lags behind its determinants by six to twelve quarters or from a year-and-a-half to three years on the average. For each industry, investment expenditure is unaffected by changes in its underlying determinants for at least two quarters'.

[14] See Chapter 9 in which dynamic multipliers are given for the base run of the P.M.

[15] What actually is measured is the growth of output per employed person. In an economy operating below full employment but with decreasing unemployment this figure will be higher than the potential growth of output per man. See OECD Economic Studies [1966, pp. 21–6]. There it is reported that the Council of Economic Advisers for the United States gave $3\frac{1}{2}$ to $3\frac{3}{4}\%$ per year as the underlying rate of growth for the first half of the 1960s.

[16] C here includes purchases of durable goods (as our C does); Y^D stands for personal disposable income. The sample period is 1929–1962; $R^2 = .999$.

[17] Evans [1969, p. 288] presents a table showing personal disposable income divided into wage income and rentier income as a share of GNP at different stages of four post-war U.S. cycles. This share has varied between 66% and 72% over the period 1949–1960. Blyth [1969] gives .64 as the most probable value of the long-term marginal propensity to consume out of GNP for the United States, however without showing how he obtained this number (see Blyth [1969, pp. 47 and 50]).

[18] Note that I assumed the level of government consumption to be independent of fiscal policy.

[19] The expansionary stage of run 1613 seems to contradict this rule. The explanation for the short expansionary stage, if $b = .5$, is that in that case the second of the two troughs (generated by the P.M. for almost all parameter combinations) is the relatively lower one and therefore taken as the starting point of the recovery. As it turns out, all runs in which the contractionary stage is longer than the expansionary stage have a second trough which is deeper than the first one.

3 The Interregional Model

3.1 Introduction

The interregional model (I.M.) presented in this chapter is the basis for all further investigations in this study. It combines the business cycle theory of the P.M. with interregional trade to make it an interregional model of economic fluctuations. Having explained the economic contents of this model in the previous chapter, here I shall stress the roles of inter-regional relationships and regional characteristics in determining the be-haviour of the regional and national economies over an interval of time.

The organization of this chapter is as follows. Section 3.2 describes the model, and is followed by a summary in equation form (3.3). Simulations with selected sets of parameter values are discussed in Section 3.4.

3.2 Description of the Model

3.2.1 Economic Environment

The interregional version of the P.M. describes the economies of n re-gions which are interrelated through the trade of consumption and capital goods, and which together form a closed economy. Each region contains a household sector and a production sector. The central government serves all regions. All assumptions made with respect to the P.M. also pertain to its interregional version.

3.2.2 Supply

The supply equations are identical to those of the P.M. with the regional subscripts added:

$$L_i^{eu}(t) = l_i N_{oi}(1 + p_i + m_i)^t \tag{3.1}$$

$$X_i^{FC}(t) = K_i(t)/v_i \tag{3.2}$$

$$X_i^{FE}(t) = L_i^{eu}(t)/u_i \tag{3.3}$$

$$X_i^M(t) = \min\left[X_i^{FC}(t), X_i^{FE}(t)\right]. \tag{3.4}$$

3.2.3 Planned Production

It is only necessary to add subscripts to the planned-production equa-tions of the P.M. to get the equivalent equations for the interregional version:

$$C_i^a(t) = eC_i^d(t-1) \tag{3.5}$$

$$V_i^*(t) = f_i C_i^a(t) \tag{3.6}$$

$$V_i^p(t) = s_i [V_i^*(t) - V_i(t)] \tag{3.7}$$

$$C_i^p(t) = C_i^a(t) + V_i^p(t) \tag{3.8}$$

$$G_i^p(t) = G_{oi}(1 + g_i)^t \tag{3.9}$$

$$I_i^p(t) = J_i^d(t) + A_i^d(t) \tag{3.10}$$

$$X_i^p(t) = C_i^p(t) + G_i^p(t) + I_i^p(t). \tag{3.11}$$

3.2.4 Actual Production

Similarly for actual production,

$$X_i(t) = \min [X_i^p(t), (X_i^M(t)] \tag{3.12}$$

$$U_i(t) = 1 - [u_i X_i(t) / L_i^{eu}(t)] \tag{3.13}$$

$$Q_i(t) = v_i X_i(t) / K_i(t) \tag{3.14}$$

$$F_i(t) = X_i(t) / X_i^p(t) \tag{3.15}$$

$$C_i(t) = F_i(t) \, C_i^p(t) \tag{3.16}$$

$$G_i(t) = F_i(t) \, G_i^p(t) \tag{3.17}$$

$$I_i(t) = F_i(t) \, I_i^p(t). \tag{3.18}$$

3.2.5 Demand

Unemployment benefits are determined in the same way as in the P.M.:

$$H_i(t) = h W_{oi} u_i [X_i^{FE}(t) - X_i(t)]. \tag{3.19}$$

Demand for consumption goods in the interregional version again depends on the level of output, past consumption and unemployment benefits, but an additional coefficient, c_{ij}, is needed, to indicate what fraction of its consumption demand region j wishes to import from region i. The demand of region j for region i's consumption goods can then be written as

$$C_{ij}^d(t) = c_{ij}\{a_{1j}X_j(t) + a_{2j}C_j^r(t-1) + H_j(t)\}. \tag{3.20}$$

Here, C_j^r stands for consumption goods received by region j, or actually

54

sold to region j. C_j^r is the regional equivalent of C^s in (2.20) of the P.M. In an n-region model there will be $n \times n$ coefficients c_{ij}, together forming a matrix $[c]$, whose column entries add up to one. Treating these trade coefficients, c_{ij}, as parameters rather than variables can only be done if it is assumed that the trade patterns among regions are stable over the time span for which I want our model to hold. But then, models which employ parameters will only remain valid as long as the parameters remain constant in value, and in that sense most models will be short-term rather than long-term models.

Employing fixed trade parameters implies that within the consumption goods production sector there is specialization among regions. That is, I do not think of consumption goods as homogeneous, even though I am using only one consumption function, but I let the matrix of trade coefficients $[c]$ be indicative of the pattern of specialization that exists among regions. Such a pattern exists, of course, in reality: regions are differently endowed with natural resources, have different productive factor endowments, and in modified Heckscher-Ohlin terms, each region specializes in producing goods that use relatively more of its abundant factor.[1] Admittedly, some industries are 'foot-loose', that is, they can operate equally well at any location in an economy. When the demand for goods produced by such an industry exceeds supply in a particular region, imports from other regions might result if the same goods are produced in other regions. In Section 7.5 I shall cope with this 'trade overflow' by assuming that deviations from the fixed trade pattern are allowed to take place if demand for a region's products exceed its supply of them.

At this point it is useful to comment on the differences between interregional input–output matrices and the trade matrices I employ.[2] Both have in common that they give interregional trade patterns. Interregional input–output analysis, however, gives these trade patterns on a much more disaggregated level, that is for each industry, and for inter-industry demand as well as for final demand. Our two matrices, one for consumption goods production, the other for capital goods production, only relate to final goods, and would therefore be less difficult to implement.

My method of dealing with interregional trade implies that only imports and exports of final goods affect the interrelationships between regions. I have to be aware, however, of the distortions which this simplification will produce. The interregional trade of raw materials and semi-finished goods certainly is instrumental in propagating cyclical movements, but in our model the only input factors which are traded are capital goods (at least before they are installed). Analytically, I can do away with the interregional trade of non-final products by relying again on the assumption that resource endowments have led to a certain production pattern among regions such that no interregional trade of raw materials and semi-finished products has to take place. Phrasing this differently: production in the I.M. is assumed to be resource oriented rather than market oriented.

Obviously, the interregional version of the P.M. is only a first step. In a further stage it would be desirable to introduce raw materials and semi-finished products as separate output categories, and also to disaggregate final demand for consumption and capital goods into the final demand for industry output on the two-digit SIC-level. At present, however, data requirements would make the implementation of these disaggregated inter-regional trade matrices an enormous task.

Total demand for a region's consumption goods is obtained by summing over the buying regions:[3]

$$C_i^d(t) = \sum_j C_{ij}^d(t). \tag{3.21}$$

The equations for desired capital stock and desired private investment are similar to those of the P.M.:

$$K_i^*(t) = \min \left[v_i e^2 X_i^p(t-1), \, v_i e^2 X_i^{FE}(t-1) \right] \tag{3.22}$$

$$J_i^*(t) = \max \left\{ 0, \, b_i \left[K_i^*(t) - (1 - r_i) \, K_i(t) \right] \right\}. \tag{3.23}$$

For the second private-demand component, private investment demand, I again need a coefficient that indicates what fraction of its investment demand region j wishes to import from region i. This coefficient is k_{ij}. Again there will be $n \times n$ of these coefficients in an n-region economy. All assumptions made with respect to the consumption goods trade coefficient c_{ij} also apply to k_{ij}. Region j's demand for region i's capital goods then is given by

$$J_{ij}^d(t) = k_{ij} \left\{ (1 - q_j) \, J_j^*(t-1) + q_j J_j^*(t) \right\}. \tag{3.24}$$

The total demand for region i's capital goods is

$$J_i^d(t) = \sum_j J_{ij}^d(t). \tag{3.25}$$

Public investment will take place directly in region i itself. No trading takes place:

$$A_i^d(t) = A_{oi}(1 + g_i)^t + \max \left[0, \, w_i X_i^{FE}(t-1) - X_i(t-1) \right]. \tag{3.26}$$

3.2.6 Actual Sales

Actual sales of consumption goods by a region are determined in the same way as in the P.M.:

$$C_i^s(t) = \min \left[C_i(t) + V_i(t), \, C_i^d(t) \right]. \tag{3.27}$$

In addition to region i's total sales of consumption goods to all regions, the value of consumption goods sold to each particular region can be determined as follows:

$$C_{ij}^s(t) = [C_i^s(t)/C_i^d(t)] \, C_{ij}^d(t). \tag{3.28}$$

Here, the subscript i again refers to the producing region; j to the receiving region.

Total sales of output is the sum of consumption goods (private and public) and capital goods (private and public) sold:

$$X_i^s(t) = C_i^s(t) + G_i(t) + I_i(t). \tag{3.29}$$

3.2.7 Realized Demand

The counterpart of the variable C_i^s, standing for total value of consumption goods sold by region i, is the new variable C_i^r, standing for realized demand, or total value of consumption goods received by region i.[4] This value is obtained by summing the values of consumption goods sold to region i by the producing regions:

$$C_i^r(t) = \sum_j C_{ji}^s(t). \tag{3.30}$$

Investment received by region i, or I_i^r, is written as the sum of private investment sold to region i by the producing regions, multiplied for each producing region by its production realization coefficient F. To this sum is added public investment demand in region i times the production realization coefficient:

$$I_i^r(t) = \sum_j F_j(t) \, J_{ji}^d(t) + F_i(t) \, A_i^d(t). \tag{3.31}$$

3.2.8 Capital Stock and Inventory Next Period

The two stock equations are identical to those of the P.M.:

$$K_i(t+1) = (1-r_i) \, K_i(t) + I_i^r(t) \tag{3.32}$$

$$V_i(t+1) = V_i(t) + C_i(t) - C_i^s(t). \tag{3.33}$$

3.2.9 Balance of Trade

Knowing the values of consumption goods and capital goods sold and received by region i, I can write its balance of trade:

$$B_i(t) = C_i^s(t) + I_i(t) - C_i^r(t) - I_i^r(t). \tag{3.34}$$

All variables on the right-hand side of this equation include goods that do not cross regional borders; however, they cancel out against each other.

3.3 Summary of the Model

Supply

$$L_i^{eu}(t) = l_i N_{oi}(1 + p_i + m_i)^t \tag{3.1}$$

$$X_i^{FC}(t) = K_i(t)/v_i \tag{3.2}$$

$$X_i^{FE}(t) = L_i^{eu}(t)/u_i \tag{3.3}$$

$$X_i^M(t) = \min\left[X_i^{FC}(t),\ X_i^{FE}(t)\right] \tag{3.4}$$

Planned production

$$C_i^a(t) = eC_i^d(t-1) \tag{3.5}$$

$$V_i^*(t) = f_i C_i^a(t) \tag{3.6}$$

$$V_i^p(t) = s_i\left[V_i^*(t) - V_i(t)\right] \tag{3.7}$$

$$C_i^p(t) = C_i^a(t) + V_i^p(t) \tag{3.8}$$

$$G_i^p(t) = G_{oi}(1 + g_i)^t \tag{3.9}$$

$$I_i^p(t) = J_i^d(t) + A_i^d(t) \tag{3.10}$$

$$X_i^p(t) = C_i^p(t) + G_i^p(t) + I_i^p(t) \tag{3.11}$$

Actual production

$$X_i(t) = \min\left[X_i^p(t),\ X_i^M(t)\right] \tag{3.12}$$

$$U_i(t) = 1 - \left[u_i X_i(t)/L_i^{eu}(t)\right] \tag{3.13}$$

$$Q_i(t) = v_i X_i(t)/K_i(t) \tag{3.14}$$

$$F_i(t) = X_i(t)/X_i^p(t) \tag{3.15}$$

$$C_i(t) = F_i(t)\,C_i^p(t) \tag{3.16}$$

$$G_i(t) = F_i(t)\,G_i^p(t) \tag{3.17}$$

$$I_i(t) = F_i(t)\,I_i^p(t) \tag{3.18}$$

Demand

$$H_i(t) = h W_{oi} u_i\left[X_i^{FE}(t) - X_i(t)\right] \tag{3.19}$$

58

$$C_{ij}^d(t) = c_{ij}\{a_{1j}X_j(t) + a_{2j}C_j^r(t-1) + H_j(t)\} \tag{3.20}$$

$$C_i^d(t) = \sum_j C_{ij}^d(t) \tag{3.21}$$

$$K_i^*(t) = \min\left[v_i e^2 X_i^p(t-1),\ v_i e^2 X_i^{FE}(t-1)\right] \tag{3.22}$$

$$J_i^*(t) = \max\{0,\ b_i[K_i^*(t) - (1-r_i)\,K_i(t)]\} \tag{3.23}$$

$$J_{ij}^d(t) = k_{ij}\{(1-q_j)\,J_j^*(t-1) + q_j J_j^*(t)\} \tag{3.24}$$

$$J_i^d(t) = \sum_j J_{ij}^d(t) \tag{3.25}$$

$$A_i^d(t) = A_{oi}(1+g_i)^t + \max\left[0,\ w_i X_i^{FE}(t-1) - X_i(t-1)\right] \tag{3.26}$$

Actual sales

$$C_i^s(t) = \min\left[C_i(t) + V_i(t),\ C_i^d(t)\right] \tag{3.27}$$

$$C_{ij}^s(t) = \left[C_i^s(t)/C_i^d(t)\right] C_{ij}^d(t) \tag{3.28}$$

$$X_i^s(t) = C_i^s(t) + G_i(t) + I_i(t) \tag{3.29}$$

Realized demand

$$C_i^r(t) = \sum_j C_{ji}^s(t) \tag{3.30}$$

$$I_i^r(t) = \sum_j F_j(t)\,J_{ji}^d(t) + F_i(t)\,A_i^d(t) \tag{3.31}$$

Capital stock and inventory next period

$$K_i(t+1) = (1-r_i)\,K_i(t) + I_i^r(t) \tag{3.32}$$

$$V_i(t+1) = V_i(t) + C_i(t) - C_i^s(t) \tag{3.33}$$

Balance of trade

$$B_i(t) = C_i^s(t) + I_i(t) - C_i^r(t) - I_i^r(t) \tag{3.34}$$

3.4 Simulations of the Model

In this section a number of computer runs of the I.M. will be discussed. Instead of having to select values for parameters and lagged endogenous variables for one region or national economy, I am now dealing with *n* regions. This implies *n* times as many parameter values, and in addition, knowledge about the trade relationships between the regions as laid down in the trade matrices [c] (consumption goods), and [k] (capital goods).

In choosing the parameter values I shall proceed along the lines followed in Chapter 2. That is, values will be assigned that are thought to be empirically plausible for western economies. It is not within the scope of this study to test the I.M. (or for that matter the P.M.) for an existing economy; our goal is rather to look at the interregional patterns of economic activity that result for different parameter values.

To simulate the model I first have to choose n, the number of regions for which to simulate. For actual applications n can be any number, but for an analytical exercise the simulated time series must be interpretable. Three regions can display enough interrelationships, with these interrelationships still being interpretable, and three is the number of regions I have chosen throughout this study. The more distinct the regions are from each other, the easier the interpretation of model runs will be. In Section 3.4.1 the characteristics ascribed to the three regions are given. For better comparison with the P.M. the technical and behavioural parameters for each region have been made equal to those for the P.M. economy, so that the only differences between regions result from their specialization in the production of consumption and capital goods, and from the interregional allocation of government expenditure. Section 3.4.2 describes the interregional base run; Section 3.4.3 presents additional simulations with different parameter values. I stress here that no normative meaning has to be associated with the parameter values of what has been termed the base run. The base run, using realistic parameter values, serves only as a particular model implementation around which parameter value changes will be made in Section 3.4.3. The arbitrariness of the choice of trade parameters and government expenditure parameters is emphasized by the circumstance that the cyclical pattern that is generated for one of the regions with these parameters is rather peculiar, as will be seen in Section 3.4.2.

3.4.1   Three Regions

As far as economic fluctuations are concerned three types of economic activities take place in the I.M.:

(a)   The production of consumption goods, which follows movements in output.

(b)   The production of capital goods, which is governed by the acceleration principle and the prime cause of economic fluctuations.

(c)   Government expenditures, which are in part contracyclical, and in part growing autonomously. Interpretability of the computer simulations can be facilitated considerably by concentrating a particular type of activity in one region. That is what actually has been done. Since the number of types of activity matches the number of regions, each region can be the main production centre of one type of activity. In our three region set-up region 1 is chosen to be the region in which most (non-cyclical) government activities are concentrated, region 2 the region which produces most consumption goods, while region 3 is the main producer of capital goods.

A great number of different trade matrices can be reconciled with this general outline. The pair below, chosen for the base run, is just one possibility:

$$[c] = \begin{bmatrix} .4 & .2 & .2 \\ .4 & .5 & .4 \\ .2 & .3 & .4 \end{bmatrix}; \qquad [k] = \begin{bmatrix} .4 & .2 & .1 \\ .1 & .1 & .1 \\ .5 & .7 & .8 \end{bmatrix}.$$

Again, the coefficients c_{ij} and k_{ij} are the fractions of consumption and investment demand respectively, that region j wishes to import from region i. The column entries in both matrices add up to one, the sum of the relative import and production shares per region. A comparison of the row entries is only valid if all regions demand equal amounts of consumption goods and of capital goods. If this happens, region 1 will produce 8/30 of the total private consumption goods production, region 2, 13/30 and region 3, 9/30. Of the total private production of capital goods region 1 will then produce 7/30, region 2, 3/30 and region 3, 20/30. Usually demand among regions will not be equal, nor will the production capacity, so production shares will deviate from the numbers above. Region 2, however, easily remains the largest producer of consumption goods, region 3 the largest producer of capital goods.

The base-run vector with initial levels of government consumption has to reflect that region 1 has most government activities within its borders. The vector

$$G_o = \begin{bmatrix} 36 \\ 10 \\ 8 \end{bmatrix}$$

gives region 1, 2/3 of all government consumption in the initial period.[5] This share will not change much with time as government expenditures in all regions grow at the same rate ($g_i = .04$).

Government investment will be assumed to be distributed equally among regions, the rationale being that government investment is related to population size and growth and that the expenditure takes place in the receiving region. Since all our regions are given the same population characteristics (this again for reasons of comparability with the P.M. runs), they all can claim the same amount of government investment. For the base run this amount is chosen to be 3 in the initial period, or:

$$A_o = \begin{bmatrix} 3 \\ 3 \\ 3 \end{bmatrix}.$$

The values assigned to all other parameters and parametric constants are identical for all regions and the same as those of the P.M. I repeat them here in vector notation.

Values assigned to parameters

$$a_1 = \begin{bmatrix} .45 \\ .45 \\ .45 \end{bmatrix} ; \quad a_2 = \begin{bmatrix} .30 \\ .30 \\ .30 \end{bmatrix} ; \quad b = \begin{bmatrix} .60 \\ .60 \\ .60 \end{bmatrix} ; \quad e = \begin{bmatrix} 1.04 \\ 1.04 \\ 1.04 \end{bmatrix} ;$$

$$f = \begin{bmatrix} .125 \\ .125 \\ .125 \end{bmatrix} ; \quad g = \begin{bmatrix} .04 \\ .04 \\ .04 \end{bmatrix} ; \quad h = \begin{bmatrix} .30 \\ .30 \\ .30 \end{bmatrix} ; \quad l = \begin{bmatrix} .40 \\ .40 \\ .40 \end{bmatrix} ;$$

$$m = \begin{bmatrix} .03 \\ .03 \\ .03 \end{bmatrix} ; \quad p = \begin{bmatrix} .01 \\ .01 \\ .01 \end{bmatrix} ; \quad q = \begin{bmatrix} .40 \\ .40 \\ .40 \end{bmatrix} ; \quad r = \begin{bmatrix} .027 \\ .027 \\ .027 \end{bmatrix} ;$$

$$s = \begin{bmatrix} .60 \\ .60 \\ .60 \end{bmatrix} ; \quad u = \begin{bmatrix} 10 \\ 10 \\ 10 \end{bmatrix} ; \quad v = \begin{bmatrix} 2.5 \\ 2.5 \\ 2.5 \end{bmatrix} ; \quad w = \begin{bmatrix} 1.00 \\ 1.00 \\ 1.00 \end{bmatrix} ;$$

Values assigned to parametric constants

$$N_o = \begin{bmatrix} 2500 \\ 2500 \\ 2500 \end{bmatrix} ; \quad W_o = \begin{bmatrix} .075 \\ .075 \\ .075 \end{bmatrix}.$$

The last group of data that has to be fed to the computer to start the simulations are the initial values of some endogenous variables: $C_i^d(0)$, $C_i^r(0)$, $X_i^p(0)$, $X_i(0)$, $J_i^*(0)$, $K_i(1)$ and $V_i(1)$. The values of these variables will again be identical among regions, with the exception of the values of $C_i^d(0)$ and $V_i(1)$, which will have to account for the fact that the three regions produce unequal amounts of consumption goods. As I stated before, the overall long-term behaviour of the simulated economy is not affected by the choice of these initial values.[6] They do matter in the initial periods of the simulation, but for that reason I do not include the first periods of the simulations in the discussion of the computer runs. In vector notation the initial values are:

$$C^d(0) = \begin{bmatrix} 55 \\ 85 \\ 60 \end{bmatrix}; \qquad C^r(0) = \begin{bmatrix} 65 \\ 65 \\ 65 \end{bmatrix}; \qquad X^p(0) = \begin{bmatrix} 100 \\ 100 \\ 100 \end{bmatrix}; \qquad X(0) = \begin{bmatrix} 100 \\ 100 \\ 100 \end{bmatrix};$$

$$J^*(0) = \begin{bmatrix} 18 \\ 18 \\ 18 \end{bmatrix}; \qquad K(1) = \begin{bmatrix} 260 \\ 260 \\ 260 \end{bmatrix}; \qquad V(1) = \begin{bmatrix} 8 \\ 12 \\ 8 \end{bmatrix}.$$

3.4.2 The Base Run

I indicated before that the base run of the I.M. is just a simulation made with realistic parameters (after all, the purpose of the computer run is to simulate the real world). Here, I shall examine in some detail the time paths generated with the base-run parameters, and subsequently compare these time paths with those generated with slightly different parameter values. Key figures of the base run plus variations are brought together in Table 3.1. Figure 3.1 gives the time paths of the u.r.s of the base run and other selected runs. Since the u.r. is a relative measure it is preferred over output as an indicator of economic activity. Graphically it is much easier to compare u.r.s than absolute levels of output.

Table 3.1

Interregional Model Simulations (Base Run and Variations)

Run	Variation	U low-high	Q low	F low	CL	P.M. Run
		1.1–3.0	1.00	.97		
1716	base run	1.3–2.1	1.00	.97	9	1604
		5.5–8.9	.95	1.00	+2	
		2.4–3.0	1.00	.97		
1704	$b = .5$	2.6	1.00	.93	10	1613
		6.9–9.2	.96	1.00	+2	
		0.0–3.4	.96	.98		
1720	$b = 1.0$	0.0–3.1	.96	.99	12	1633
		0.0–12.9	.88	.86		
		1.8–2.1	1.00	.92		
1705	$a_1 = .48; a_2 = .30$	1.8–2.1	1.00	.88	11/12	1617
		1.1–4.8	.98	.94		

Table 3.1 (continued)

Run	Variation	U low-high	Q low	F low	CL	P.M. Run
1715	$a_1 = .48; a_2 = .32$	2.0	1.00	.91	—	
		2.0	1.00	.87	—	1635
		1.6–2.2	1.00	.97	12/14	
1706	$v = 2$	3.9–4.0	.99	1.00		
		2.9	1.00	1.00	—	1627
		13.2	.74	1.00		
1708	$v = 3$	2.4	1.00	.92		
		2.4	1.00	.91	—	1628
		2.4	1.00	.93		
1717	$A_o = 0$	2.1–5.5	1.00	.94		
		2.5–5.1	1.00	.93	15	1601
		1.9–9.3	.94	.90		
1719	$A_o = 6$	0.6–1.2	.99	.99	10	
		0.4	1.00	.98	—	1605
		7.2–9.0	.94	1.00	10^{+2}	
1709	$w = 0$	2.6–10.0	.98	.86		
		2.4–10.2	.97	.88	17	1608
		2.6–22.4	.91	.70		
1718	$A_o = 0; w = 0$	4.7–10.8	1.00	.87		
		4.8–12.6	1.00	.88	28	1603
		4.7–19.0	.97	.73		
1701	$h = .5$	1.6–1.7	1.00	.98	—	
		1.7	1.00	.93	—	1615
		4.7–7.4	.97	1.00	$8/10^{+2}$	
1703	$G_o \begin{bmatrix} 30 \\ 9 \\ 15 \end{bmatrix}$	4.9–6.1	.98	.99		
		1.4–3.2	1.00	.97	15/16	1604
		0.9–4.7	.98	.92		

Table 3.1 (continued)

Run	Variation	U low-high	Q low	F low	CL	P.M. Run
1710	$G_o = \begin{bmatrix} 18 \\ 18 \\ 18 \end{bmatrix}$	13.5–14.3 1.7– 2.0 1.0– 6.3	.88 1.00 .96	1.00 .89 .95	11	1604
1714	$G_o = \begin{bmatrix} 27 \\ 0 \\ 27 \end{bmatrix}$	8.4–8.5 7.5–7.6 2.1	.97 .98 1.00	1.00 1.00 .90	—	1604
1721	$G_o = \begin{bmatrix} 42 \\ 12 \\ 9 \end{bmatrix}$	2.0 1.8 5.5	1.00 1.00 .99	.90 .92 1.00	—	1622
1702	$G_o = \begin{bmatrix} 38 \\ 10 \\ 15 \end{bmatrix}$	2.1 2.1 2.1	1.00 1.00 1.00	.93 .92 .92	—	1622
1712	$G_o = \begin{bmatrix} 21 \\ 21 \\ 21 \end{bmatrix}$	11.8 2.1 1.9	.94 1.00 1.00	1.00 .86 .95	—	1622
1713	$G_o = \begin{bmatrix} 30 \\ 8 \\ 7 \end{bmatrix}$	7.1 4.1 13.2	.98 1.00 .92	1.00 1.00 1.00	—	1621

Explanation

1. For each *computer run* the key figures are given for regions 1, 2, and 3, in this order.
2. If in the column *Variation* the variation is given only once, it applies to all regions.
3. If the *cycle length* is identical for all regions, it is given only once.
4. See further the *Explanation* following Table 2.1.

A glance at Figure 3.1 shows that the u.r.s of both regions 1 and 2 (the 'government expenditure region' and the 'consumption region' respectively) are very low. They vary between 1 and 3 %. On the other hand,

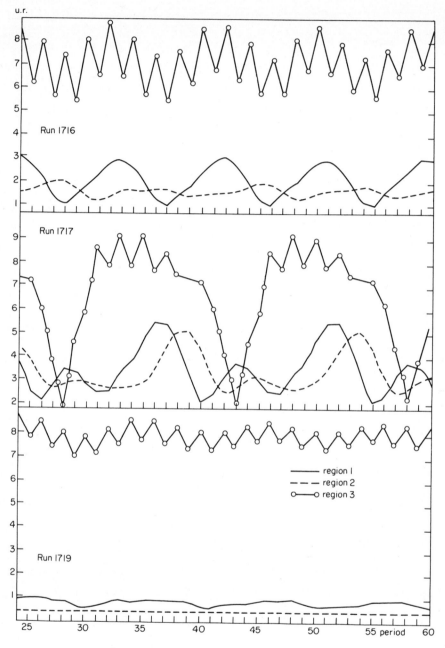

Figure 3.1 Interregional Model Runs

unemployment in the 'investment region' (region 3) is on a much higher level and also varies more, namely between 5.5% and 8.9%. The values of Q and F explain these differences somewhat. In regions 1 and 2, Q equals 1 in all periods while F is below 1 in most periods, indicating that not all planned production can be realized. For region 3 the reverse is true: here F never drops below 1 while Q seldom equals 1. So the picture is one of excess demand and low u.r.s in two of the three regions, while the third region, already most sensitive to cyclical fluctuations, has excess capacity and excess supply of labour most of the time.

The time paths between periods 24 and 60 give the impression that the amplitudes of the unemployment cycles are fairly constant. To observe the behaviour of the model in the very long term, a number of simulations, including the base run, were performed for periods 1 to 140. It then turns out that the range of u.r.s for region 1 stays the same in this longer simulation, that for region 2 is reduced from 1.3–2.1% to 1.4–2.0%, and that for region 3 from 5.5–8.9% to 6.0–8.3%. The base-run cycles are therefore slightly damped.

The length of the cycle in all three regions is nine periods. In addition to this main cycle, region 3 features a shorter two-period subcycle with an amplitude of 2 unemployment percentage points.[7] Compared with the base run of the P.M. which has the same parameter values as this base run, the length of the cycle has been reduced from 14 periods to nine periods. Furthermore, the peak and trough periods for the three regions do not coincide. Region 2 reaches its peak three periods later than region 1, which is a considerable lag when the cycle length is 9. The peaks and troughs of regions 1 and 3 do occur at the same time, with the understanding that region 3's subcycle prevents a perfect coincidence of peaks and troughs during each cycle.

3.4.3 Parameter Variations

In this section I shall again try to draw some conclusions from the simulations I ran with selected sets of parameter values, just as I did this for the P.M. in Chapter 2. Our evaluation will proceed along the same lines as in the previous chapter, that is, type of growth (cyclical v. steady state), the amplitude and the length of cycles (if cycles are generated), and in addition the propagation of cycles are the criteria through which I shall compare the different runs. Table 3.1 summarizes the parameter variations.

The partition of the national economy in three regional economies that each have their own share in the national production of consumption and capital goods, means that the parameter variations, such as I made them in the previous chapter and again in this chapter, will affect the regional economies depending on their production structure. The regional distribution of the production factors and of the demand for products is the key to the explanation of cyclical behaviour in the I.M. economy, and it is on this distribution and how it affects cyclical behaviour that I shall focus attention.

The base-run distribution of economic activities was one in which two regions (1 and 2) are experiencing high levels of activity (and therefore low u.r.s) and fairly mild fluctuations, the latter since the main part of their output is stable consumption output. The third region has a smaller overall production share (and therefore higher u.r.s), but also a heavier fluctuating economy because it happens to produce two-thirds of the total production of unstable private-investment output. So the distribution of national production clearly favours regions 1 and 2. They operate so close to the ceilings of their economies that a small increase in demand for their products will virtually eliminate fluctuations (as in runs 1705 and 1719), or even give steady-state growth (as in runs 1715 and 1701) at very low u.r.s. In all four examples region 3 has a higher unemployment level and a larger range of u.r.s than the other two regions. It will benefit from changes that increase the level of demand in the other regions, but obviously not as much as from changes that directly increase the demand for its own products, such as for instance an increase in v will (run 1708).

Runs 1715, 1719 and 1701 show that in an interregional model in which the regions have their own stocks of productive capacity and in which no migration takes place, it is possible for some regions to experience steady-state growth against either the upper boundary or the lower boundary of the economy, while other regions grow cyclically. Only when demand is raised sufficiently everywhere will all regions grow at the steady-state rate against the upper buffer (runs 1708 and 1702). Steady-state growth as such is not necessarily a desirable outcome. It might be caused by an excess supply of government investment, which is not responsive to the gap between desired and actual capital stock, but rather inspired by the existing levels of unemployment or by the need to carry out long-term projects—which might not be needed at the time they are carried out. In such a situation steady-state growth will be growth along the floor of the economy in one (runs 1721 and 1712), or more regions (runs 1706, 1714 and 1713), depending on the distribution of economic activities.

The runs with different distributions of government consumption (G_o) are interesting in that they give some insight into how the government might accomplish a more equal distribution of employment over the regions, using the reallocation of government consumption as a tool of economic policy. Every economy will have government activities that are 'foot-loose', services that can function equally well in all regions. Moving some of these services from excess-demand regions (such as region 1) to excess-supply regions (such as region 3) could result in more interregional equality, as far as the average u.r.s are concerned. Runs 1716 (the base run), 1703, 1710 and 1714 are all carried out with more or less random distributions of $\sum G_{oi} = 54$; runs 1721, 1702 and 1712 with random distributions of $\sum G_{oi} = 63$. These runs show that it is possible to reduce or even eliminate fluctuations by reallocating a given initial amount of government consumption. In the case of run 1714, however, this means steady-state growth with considerable interregional inequality in unemployment. If the policy maker's first concern is stable growth he will increase non-cyclical demand in the regions that are most susceptible to cycles, in order to reduce fluctuations in these regions. An over-all increase in government spending can eliminate cycles altogether in all regions without interregional inequalities in unemployment (run 1702), but even then there are enough distributions that will produce stability with inequality (runs 1721 and 1712). Very often, when the total amount of government expenditure is a political datum and interregional equality is the goal, a certain amount of fluctuations will have to be accepted, This, of course, provided that investment behaviour in the economy is inherently cyclical, which I assume to be the case throughout this study.

The effectiveness of the capacity and employment ceilings in our model makes the cycle length different from that in a model without buffers. This is true for the P.M. It is also true for the I.M., but in the latter case the number of buffers has tripled with respect to that of the P.M. economy. And with the distribution of economic activities being as it is in the base run and many of the other runs of Table 3.1, cycle lengths should be expected to differ from those of comparable P.M. runs. Most comparisons find the I.M. run to have the shorter cycle, most likely because of the impact which excess-demand regions 1 and 2 have on the over-all cycle length (which by the way will be the same for all regions, barring subcycles as in the base run). However, there are exceptions, for example, I.M. runs 1717 and 1718 generate longer cycles than their P.M. counterparts, because it takes the capital goods producing region 3 longer to close the gap between desired and actual capital stock than it takes all national productive capacity pooled together (as in the P.M.) to do this in the absence of government investment. On the other hand, the cycle length will drop from 16 to nine periods when a given amount of government consumption demand is more and more concentrated in one or two regions (runs 1703, 1710 and 1716), where the comparable P.M. base run gave a 14-period cycle.

In general, the particular distribution of economic activities is the key to the explanation of the cycle lengths, relative to those of the P.M. The conclusions with respect to the cycle length in a one-region model that I drew in the previous chapter (Section 2.4.3) still hold, but when an interregional distribution of economic activities enters the picture the new cycle lengths will largely depend on the particular distribution with which the model is simulated.

Next to the average levels of regional unemployment, the amplitude or the range of u.r.s over a cycle would probably be the cause of most concern to the regional policy makers. In subsequent chapters I shall devote a great deal of attention to the possibilities of controlling the amplitudes. With private investment being the most volatile output component, the amplitude of the u.r.s in a region will be determined by the share of investment in the regional output. And given the distribution of investment output the amplitudes will be larger the more oscillatory investment behaviour is.

Does the cycle originate somewhere and then spread over the rest of the economy? In a discrete macro-economic model it is the structure of the economy combined with particular parameter values that make the time paths oscillatory or not. Economists agree that usually private investment is the most volatile element in the economy, so that when cycles are generated one can point at investment as being the cause of the fluctuations. In a discrete interregional model there is the added element of an interregional distribution of economic activities. The individual region having a more fluctuating output than other regions is thus producing relatively more capital goods than other regions. In the extreme case of one region producing all capital goods and producing only capital goods one could indeed say that the cycle originates in that region. It does not seem correct, however, to explain the cyclical fluctuations in a multiregion economy in the causal terms of our question above. Fluctuations are the result of the behaviour of economic agents. The cycles are there because of this behaviour, which supposedly is the same in all regions. It is the industrial composition which makes the regions experience different cyclical amplitudes and which makes some regions lead and others lag behind the movements of aggregate economic activity. I mentioned that in the base run (but it holds for other runs too), region 2 is lagging three periods behind both regions 1 and 3. The explanation for this is that regions 1 and 3 are both producers of capital goods, while region 2 hardly is. The accelerator effect leads to a faster recovery in regions 1 and 3 than in region 2 after a depression or recession. *Vice versa*, region 2 reaches its peak when regions 1 and 3 have already started the downward move, since the demand for consumption goods (of which region 2 is the main producer) is affected by past consumption patterns.

Finally, I want to explain the two-period subcycle that appears in region 3 in a number of runs (1716, 1704, 1719 and 1701). This subcycle is caused by the one-period lag in contracyclical government investment. Equation (3.26) is specified such that a high level of unemployment during a particular period is followed by an increase in contracyclical investment in the next period, which makes unemployment go down. This decrease in unemployment is then followed by a decrease in government spending, which leads to a higher level of unemployment again, and so on.[8] Since the contracyclical investment coefficient is the same for all three regions ($w_i = 1$ or 0), the question is why region 3 is the only region in which the subcycle appears.

For an answer to this question Table 3.1 must again be consulted. In all there are four runs with a subcycle; the minimum value of F_3 is 1. This means that the capacity ceilings of region 3 are never active in these runs, and therefore the subcycle generated by contracyclical investment is never interrupted. Note that output in regions 1 and 2 of the I.M. economy is either too close to the ceilings (which means a minimum $F < 1$), or too close to the floor (which means a minimum $F = 1$ but also steady-state or close to steady-state growth),[9] to let the subcycle happen. Remember also that none of the simulations of the P.M. with $w = 1$ generated the subcycle, precisely because all P.M. simulations were made with parameter values such that planned output would hit a ceiling at least once during a cycle.

Notes

[1] Modified Heckscher-Ohlin terms, since the Heckscher-Ohlin proposition spoke of 'exporting' instead of 'producing' goods. See Richardson [1969, p. 290].

[2] For a discussion of interregional input–output analysis see for instance W. Isard [1960, Chapter 8 and especially pp. 316-26].

[3] Note the distinction between demand for region i's consumption goods, C^d, and total demand for consumption goods by region i's citizens, which is $\sum_j C^d_{ji}$.

[4] C^r_i gives the 'realization' of a variable for which I did not introduce a separate symbol, namely demand for consumption goods by region i. This variable would have to be defined as $\sum_j C^d_{ji}$. I did define C^d_i, demand for region i's consumption goods. The 'realization' of this variable is given by C^s_i, the value of consumption goods actually sold, where $C^s_i \leq C^d_i$. There is a third way, in which I can compare plans/demand and realizations. That is by comparing the planned production of consumption goods, C^p_i, with the actual production of consumption goods, C_i. Similar comparisons can be made for capital goods, with the only differences resulting

from the fact that capital goods are produced to order, not to stock, so that I_i is equal to the not separately introduced variable I_i^s.

[5] The location of the administrative capital of a nation has usually been determined in the past by non-economic motivations. Our vector G_o indicates that the administrative capital of the country could be in region 1, but that on the state or provincial level government consumption takes place as well (for instance: education).

[6] See the comments on the values of lagged endogenous variables in Section 2.4.1.

[7] Because of this subcycle the main cycle of region 3 actually is alternatively 8 or 10 periods long.

[8] Contracyclical policy does not necessarily reduce cyclical behaviour in terms of the periodicity of cycles! See W. J. Baumol [1961].

[9] Run 1710 is an example in which one region (region 1) operates close to steady-state growth and with a minimum $F=1$. Actually, region 1 does have a two-period subcycle which, however, is interrupted during the early periods of each downswing phase, and therefore not recorded in Table 3.1.

4 National Averages of the Interregional Model Simulations

4.1 Introduction

How do the simulations of the I.M. compare with the P.M. simulations? In the previous chapter I made some comparisons between the time series of single regional economies and time series of P.M. simulations. What I wish to do now is compare the national averages of the I.M. with the variables of the P.M. in comparable model simulations. Basically this means comparing the national variables of an economy in which the production factors labour and capital goods are not allowed to cross the regional borders[1] (so that regional bottle-necks may develop), with the national variables of an economy in which all production factors can move freely throughout the nation.

One has to realize that any comparison between the national averages of the I.M. and the variables of the P.M. is made for the particular set of trade matrices and initial levels of government expenditure that I chose for our I.M. simulations. As discussed in the previous chapter, that particular choice led for most simulations to excess demand in two of the three regions, and excess supply in the third region.

In Table 4.1 I have brought together the national averages of all simulations of Chapter 3 and confronted them with simulations of Chapter 2. This table is discussed in Section 4.2. In Section 4.3 I shall discuss the length of the cycles in our models and compare these with historically observed cycles.

4.2 National Averages of the Interregional Model Simulations and Comparable Prototype Model Simulations

The national averages of the I.M. base run (run 1716) show that the range of u.r.s has been reduced in comparison with the unemployment series of the P.M. base run (run 1604). In addition, the minimum values of both the national Q and the national F are larger in run 1716 than in run 1604. The cycle length for the aggregated economy is the same as for the regional economies, and as before, these regional cycles are shorter than the P.M. cycles. The two-period cycle of region 3 appears also in the national cycle.

73

Table 4.1
National Averages of Interregional Model Simulations

I.M. Run	P.M. Run	Variation	National Averages I.M. Run				P.M. Run			
			U low-high	Q low	F low	CL	U low-high	Q low	F low	CL
1716	1604	base run	2.8– 4.5	.99	.98	9	1.0– 5.5	.97	.94	14
1704	1613	$b = .5$	4.0– 4.9	.99	.97	10	2.1– 5.4	.99	.93	15
1720	1633	$b = 1.0$	0.0– 6.1	.94	.94	12	0.0– 6.8	.94	.89	13
1705	1617	$a_1 = .48$ $a_2 = .30$	1.7– 2.8	.99	.91	11/12	2.1	1.00	.91	—
1715	1635	$a_1 = .48$ $a_2 = .32$	1.9– 2.1	1.00	.91	14	2.3	1.00	.90	—
1706	1627	$v = 2$	6.7	.90	1.00	—	8.1	.95	1.00	—
1708	1628	$v = 3$	2.4	1.00	.92	—	2.5	1.00	.92	—
1717	1601	$A_o = 0$	2.7– 6.2	.98	.93	15	1.9– 6.8	.98	.90	13
1719	1605	$A_o = 6$	2.8– 3.4	.98	.99	10	1.7– 4.8	.97	1.00	14
1709	1608	$w = 0$	2.8–13.9	.97	.81	17	2.0–19.2	.93	.74	17
1718	1603	$A_o = w = 0$	4.9–13.7	.99	.82	28	4.0–23.5	.94	.70	15
1701	1615	$h = .5$	2.7– 3.6	.99	.97	10	1.1– 4.0	.99	.94	13
1703	1604	$G_o = 30/9/15$	2.6– 4.6	.99	.96	15/16	1.0– 5.5	.97	.94	14
1710	1604	$G_o = 18/18/18$	5.5– 7.4	.95	.94	11	1.0– 5.5	.97	.94	14
1714	1604	$G_o = 27/0/27$	6.0	.98	.96	—	1.0– 5.5	.97	.94	14
1721	1622	$G_o = 42/12/9$	3.1	1.00	.94	—	2.1	1.00	.93	—
1702	1622	$G_o = 38/10/15$	2.1	1.00	.92	—	2.1	1.00	.93	—
1712	1622	$G_o = 21/21/21$	5.3	.98	.93	—	2.1	1.00	.93	—
1713	1621	$G_o = 30/8/7$	8.2	.97	1.00	—	8.2	.97	1.00	—

See *Explanation* following Table 3.1.

The comparison of the two base runs clearly demonstrates that national averages can be misleading. As with all averages, they conceal the peculiarities of the individual observations from which the national averages are computed. Take for instance the unemployment figures. They show us that our national economy is fairly stable and that the level of unemployment is fairly low. What is not apparent, however, is that in one region unemployment varies between 5.5 and 8.9% in the course of a cycle, which means a higher level of unemployment with less stability for that particular region. Similarly, the national c-u.r. hides the fact that two out of three regions operate at full capacity all the time. Also, if the ratio between actual output and planned production is an indication of inflationary pressure, the national F gives too optimistic a picture of this pressure, as the lowest regional F is averaged out.

Obviously, the existence of these discrepancies between national and regional data would not represent any new information for a regional economist. Regional economics has developed into a separate branch of economics, among other reasons because economists became aware of the fact that production factors are not perfectly mobile between regions, as the neo-classicists assumed. In a comparison of the P.M. and the aggregate I.M. the perfect-mobility assumption of neo-classical economics is confronted with what Meyer calls 'the economics of resource immobility'.[2] The question of which model gives more desirable outcomes is secondary to the question of which of the two extremes is a better description of reality. An interregional model is a vast improvement over a national model such as the P.M. is. With its assumptions of perfect immobility and rigid trade patterns it remains an extreme, however, and later in this study I shall relax some of these extreme assumptions by allowing migration and flexible trade patterns. One result of neo-classical theory that I did relax right from the beginning in both the P.M. and the I.M., is steady-state growth. It is indeed a corner-stone of our approach that steady-state growth will only result under special conditions. Growth with fluctuations is the normal outcome, steady-state growth a limiting case.

In Section 2.4.3 I expressed the notion that fluctuations will occur if there is room for the economy to fluctuate. If total demand presses output against the capacity ceilings steady-state growth will result. In general more room for fluctuations can be expected in an economy in which resources are perfectly mobile (such as the P.M. economy), than in an economy which is partitioned into separate regional economies (such as the I.M. economy). The former can use its resources more fully when they are needed, i.e. during the upswing phase, but the other side of the picture is that the extra production of capital goods during the upswing phase leads to more excess capacity, a smaller production of private capital goods and higher unemployment during the contractionary phase.

I expect the I.M. economy, therefore, to be more stable than the P.M. economy. Indeed, there are only two examples in Table 4.1 in which the range of national average u.r.s in the I.M. run is larger than the range of u.r.s in the comparable P.M. run. These are runs 1705 and 1715, both with increased marginal propensities to consume. The fluctuations in these runs originate from region 3, which has excess supply of capacity where the two other regions have excess demand for capacity. In the P.M. equivalents of these runs the economy as a whole has an excess demand for capacity and is growing against the ceiling at the steady-state rate. Both runs 1705 and 1715 confirm the 'fluctuations if there is room for fluctuations' rule: region 3 of the I.M. alone has more room for fluctuations than the comparable P.M. economy as a whole.

While perfect mobility of resources will most likely lead to larger national fluctuations, by the same reasoning it will give lower average u.r.s in most cases. Large pockets of unemployment such as may develop in an economy with separated markets are less likely in an economy with mobile resources. Differences in the national u.r. between the P.M. economy and the I.M. economy, of course, depend on the distribution of economic activities in the I.M. economy, but the more uneven this distribution is, the more likely it is that the latter will have a higher national average u.r. This is most clearly demonstrated by the runs with varying distributions of $\sum G_{oi}$. Runs 1710, 1714, 1721 and 1712 all have national rates that are distinctly higher than their P.M. counterparts. Only when the distribution of government consumption is designed to complement the regional production structures as given by the trade matrices, such that equal production levels will result, will the P.M. and the I.M. average u.r. be the same (runs 1702 and 1713).[3]

Summarizing the differences between the national averages of the I.M. simulations and the P.M. simulations, I can state that in general:
(a) The P.M. economy will generate larger fluctuations than the I.M. economy.
(b) The P.M. economy will have lower national average u.r.s than the I.M. economy.
(c) Interregional inequalities in unemployment will be smaller in the P.M. economy than in the I.M. economy.

All three conclusions become stronger, the more uneven the interregional distribution of economic activities in the I.M. is. Conclusion (c) is a direct consequence of the perfect-mobility assumption of the P.M. Note that perfect labour mobility as such does not necessarily lead to equal u.r.s among regions at all times, as the simulations with the migration version of the I.M. in Chapter 8 will show.

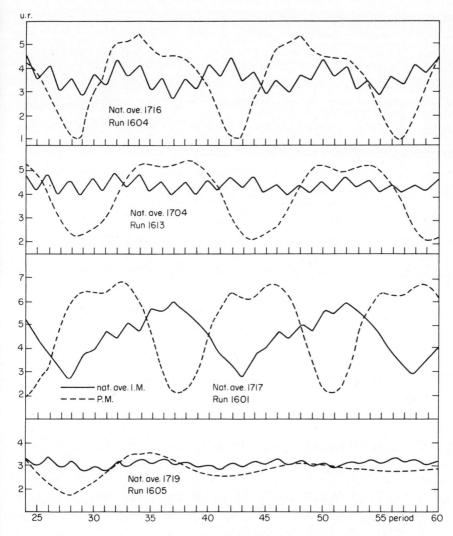

Figure 4.1   National Averages of Interregional Model Runs
and Comparable Prototype Model Runs

4.3 The Length of the National Cycle

When I specified the dynamic relationships in the P.M. and when I selected values for the parameters with a time dimension, I assumed that the length of the time period was one year. Hence the length of the cycle would also be measured in years. Turning now to the cycles generated by the P.M. and the I.M., this would mean that our cycles roughly vary between nine and 17 years, with the national cycles of the I.M. generally being somewhat shorter than those of the P.M.

This range of periodicities does not make it easy to put our cycles in any of the categories distinguished by business cycle theorists. In cycle literature, usually a distinction is made between these four types:
(a) The NBER or inventory cycle, averaging about 40 months.
(b) The major or Juglar cycle, associated with changes in fixed business investment, a 10-year cycle.
(c) The 20-year Kuznets or building cycle.
(d) The 40-year Kondratieff cycle.
In length our cycles are in between the major or Juglar cycle and the Kuznets cycle: too long to be major cycles, too short to be called Kuznets cycles. Does this mean that the dynamic specification of our model is wrong? Instead of jumping to a quick conclusion let me offer some possible explanations for this poor fit.

In the first place, the 40-month NBER cycle, which is the only generally recognized cycle in the post-war years, and which is caused by inventory fluctuations, is ruled out as an outcome of our simulations by the mere fact that our models are specified as annual, not quarterly models. In our concept, inventory investment tends to aggravate the long cycle somewhat, but is not able to generate its own subcycle. In reality, inventory investment is more volatile in the short term than fixed business investment, because divergencies between the actual and the desired inventory can be corrected more quickly than gaps between actual and desired capital stock.[4]

In the second place, our models do not distinguish between residential construction and other fixed business investment as the two components of fixed business investment. Actually, our variable 'private investment' is 'other fixed business investment' more than anything else, while autonomous investment is meant to include government controlled residential construction. This means that the Kuznets or building cycle, which finds considerable support in empirical work,[5] will not be generated by our models.

Dismissing the Kondratieff cycle as being mainly a cycle in prices,[6] the only remaining cycle that could be generated is the Juglar cycle associated

78

with fluctuations in fixed business investment. It should be clear that this is what our cycles are. The fluctuations in our models do indeed arise from the postulated investment behaviour. In fact, private investment is the only output component that can generate cycles by itself. Inventory investment and contracyclical government investment can change the amplitude and also the length of the cycle, but in our models they are led by the movements in fixed business investment.

If this is the case, it is important to discuss why our cycles are longer than the postulated 10 years of the Juglar cycle. R. C. O. Matthews, who suggests that the 20-year building cycle 'is the only systematically periodic element in the record of fluctuations in the U.S., apart from the short inventory cycle',[7] offers this explanation:

It appears that *generally* its [fixed investment other than building] fluctuations are pulled into conformity with those of the building cycle, and in contrast to inventory investment, it does not show *regular* independent fluctuations. Possible reasons for this are (a) that the inherent tendency of other fixed investment is to fluctuate in cycles not much shorter than the building cycle or (b) that building and the investment associated with it are quantitatively predominant or (c) that other classes of investment are more readily pulled into conformity with building than building is with them because they are more sensitive to changes in national income.[8]

And: 'it is possible that other fixed investment, if left to itself, would be more inclined to fluctuate in shorter waves'.[9] Of course, the building cycle itself varies in length. The absolutely periodic cycle does not exist, and Matthews observes that 'the regularity of the twenty-year period that has actually occurred is almost certainly partly fortuitous and owes a significant amount to the influence of wars'.[10]

These quotations imply that the 'pure' non-building investment cycle would have a length of, let us say, 12 to 18 years, depending on the volatility of investment behaviour, and this range would very well match our findings. Matthews' explanation also implies that the non-building investment cycle is unlikely to appear in the historical records, pulled into line as it is with the longer building cycle.

Now that I have come to grips with the range of periodicities generated by the model simulations, two intriguing questions concerning the lengths of cycles remain. One is: How have productive capacity ceilings historically affected business cycles? The other: What effect have regional bottle-necks had on the predictive performance of national econometric models?

Matthews and Evans point out that the historical record of past cycles is not very favourable to the view that cycles have been the reason of turning points,[11] that is, there is no clear evidence that the upswing phase of a cycle is turned into a downswing as soon as the ceiling is hit. But recall that this is not the way the ceilings work in our models. The typical pattern generated by the P.M. is an economy which grows along the capacity ceiling during most of the upswing phase. There is a capacity shortage all the way. This version of the ceiling hypothesis is not implausible at all. Again we turn to Matthews:

> The evidence is more favorable to the notion that the instability of the upswing is confined to its early stages and that some sort of ceiling is in operation for most of the upswing. The term ceiling is really rather a misnomer in this version of the hypothesis, since there is no question of anything like an absolute barrier to growth; what happens is merely that once the recovery has got beyond a certain point and some of the excess supply of labour and idle capacity has been absorbed, there is a sufficient number of supply inelasticities to act as a brake and convert the upswing from an unstable explosive one to one that will presently reverse itself. No striking manifestations of increased scarcity of factors of production in the vicinity of the upper turning point need then be expected. The positive evidence in favor of this version of the hypothesis is that there has been a fairly clear and general tendency for the level of activity to rise more rapidly in the earliest phase of cyclical upswings—their first quarter or less—than in their later phases. What this evidence suggests is, of course, merely that some check to expansion is felt at an early stage of the upswing on account of lessened elasticity of supply. It does not directly help to establish that such a check is an inherently necessary condition of the downturn, which is really the distinctive feature of the ceiling hypothesis.[12]

We could not explain the working of the ceiling in our own model better than Matthews has done it here.

If Matthews' suppositions are correct, supply inelasticities do play an important role in shaping the cycle. Are these capacity restrictions felt nation-wide, or are they more often regional bottle-necks? Historically, the effect which ceilings had on the behaviour of output during the upswing phase can be traced in a qualitative manner, but how would an econometric model of a national economy, that includes a capacity ceiling, take regional capacity constraints into account? As we have seen it is very well possible that the national c-u.r. is below one, while at the same time some regions are operating at full capacity. The national model, assuming perfect mobility of resources would overlook these regional bottle-necks. The consequence of this could be that the national model would generate cycles that are longer than actually observed cycles. That at least was the typical pattern I found in this chapter when we compared the national perfect-mobility model with the interregional model and its uneven distribution of economic activities.

Looking at the record for the United States there are no indications that well-known econometric models such as the Wharton-EFU model or the Brookings model have made errors in forecasting turning points because of overlooked regional bottle-necks. The Wharton-EFU model, for instance, has been simulated for the 12-year period 1952–1964, without intervening adjustments, and the model simulated cyclical fluctuations that closely corresponded with actual turning points.[13] It should be pointed out here that, in order to determine actual output, the Wharton model does contain a capacity utilization variable that is related to full capacity output. Apparently, using a national c-u.r. was sufficient to simulate the turning points fairly accurately. Yet the fact remains that perfect mobility of production factors is an implicit assumption of every national econometric model that contains a supply sector.

It might be that the United States post-war economy has not operated close enough to its capacity ceilings to warrant the inclusion of an elaborate supply side in econometric models,[14] but the story might be a different one for western European countries such as Switzerland, France, Germany, the Netherlands, the United Kingdom and Scandinavian countries. These countries have experienced relatively low unemployment rates and high capital utilization rates during most of the post-war years, yet with sometimes considerable interregional differences. It might very well be that for these countries (interregional) econometric models which do recognize the limited mobility of productive resources would have a better forecasting ability than the traditional national models. Unfortunately, the limited availability of regional and interregional data in most countries still makes it extremely difficult to test interregional econometric models.

Notes

[1] In the I.M. capital goods are traded, but once installed in a particular region cannot be shifted any more.

[2] J. R. Meyer [1963, p. 26]. The 'economics of resource immobility', Meyer says, 'might be a reasonably accurate, though less than fully comprehensive, description of regional economics'.

[3] Is it possible for the I.M. to generate lower average u.r.s than the P.M.? It is, but only because of peculiarities in the formulation of our models.

It happens if one region of the I.M. economy has a positive inventory all the time while other regions and the comparable P.M. economy as a whole do not. Technically, the inventory will be positive all the time if F never drops below $1/(1+sf)$, which is .9302 in the base run. This is the case with region 3's F in run 1715. On the other hand, the P.M. run and regions 1 and 2 in run 1715 have F's that are below .9302 in steady state. The same thing happens in run 1708.

There is another situation in which the economy of resource immobility gives a lower national average u.r. than its perfect-immobility counterpart, but it takes an uneven distribution of economic activities to accomplish this. Run 1706, with $v = 2$, is a case in point. As Table 4.1 shows, the national average rate for the I.M. is 6.7%, compared with an 8.1% rate for the P.M. But also note that the c-u.r.s are .90 and .95 respectively.

The variable Q drops below one during steady-state growth only because of government investment, which does not respond to the market demand for capital goods. The Q's tell us that this way much more capital goods are created in the I.M. economy than in the economy of the P.M. The main beneficiary of the production of these unused capital goods is region 3, whose private production is extremely low when $v = 2$. The larger the gap between private production and full employment output, the more effective government contracyclical investment is in reducing unemployment. So even while region 3 has by far the highest u.r. (13.2% v. 3.9 and 2.9% for the other two regions) the national average rate is lower than that of the P.M. Had the levels of activity in the I.M. been more evenly distributed, the national u.r.s would have been closer together.

[4] See R. C. O. Matthews [1959, p. 210].

[5] R. A. Gordon [1961, p. 240] mentions A. Burns, B. Thomas, M. Abramowitz and particularly S. Kuznets as the economists who have done the most important empirical work suggesting the existence of the 20-year cycle.

[6] See R. A. Gordon [1961, pp. 237-9].

[7] Matthews [1959, p. 212]. Matthews rejects the 10-year cycle for the United States on the grounds that the circumstances that surrounded it 'were so diverse that it is difficult to regard them as the manifestations of a regular cyclical tendency' (Matthews [1959, p. 211]).

[8] Matthews [1959, p. 213].

[9] Matthews [1959, p. 225].

[10] Matthews [1959, p. 213].

[11] Matthews [1959, p. 157] and Evans [1969, p. 418].

[12] Matthews [1959, pp. 157-8]. Despite the evidence, there are only a few econometric models that include a capacity ceiling. The Dutch Central Planning Bureau model is one of them.

[13] Evans [1969, p. 598].

[14] Evans [1969, pp. 504-5] argues that for the United States the demand equations hold the key to accurate forecasts, although he recognizes that 'in 1947 and 1956 bottlenecks in capital equipment were a major deterrent to increased output' (Evans [1969, p. 599]).

5 Trends in the Prototype Model

5.1 Introduction

In Chapter 3 I gave the characteristics of the two kinds of steady-state growth that were simulated by the P.M. as well as by the I.M.: 'upper' steady-state growth was characterized by a planned production that always exceeds the maximum possible production, with the ratio between X^p and X^M constant; 'lower' steady-state growth has X^M always exceeding X^p, and constant ratios between planned production and full capacity and full employment output respectively. The distinction between steady-state growth along the ceiling and steady-state growth along the floor is a basic one in our models as it shows that because of capacity restrictions on the one hand and the existence of built-in stabilizers on the other, both economies that are facing excess demand and economies with excess supply of production factors can grow at the same steady-state rate. In this chapter a third type of steady-state growth will be discussed, namely, both 'upper' and 'lower' steady-state growth. That is the case of full capacity, full employment growth where at all times planned output, full employment output and full capacity output are equal to each other. In neoclassical growth theory this unique steady-state solution is known as the Golden Age,[1] and that is how I shall refer to it.

As mentioned before, steady-state growth for our models will only be the result of special conditions. In terms of describing the state of an economy, however, steady-state growth has the clear advantage of easy characterization: all rates are constant. It is much more difficult to characterize an economy that grows with fluctuations: ranges of u.r.s, c-u.r.s, production realization rates and growth rates exist where single rates would be preferable. Especially in applying economic policy it is desirable to have key figures that give the underlying trends around which the economic variables fluctuate. Knowing these trend figures would enable us to assess by how much, for instance, government expenditure would have to be changed to reach certain trend levels of economic activity.

Is there a way to find these underlying rates? Statistically speaking there certainly is. Every introductory statistics textbook contains chapters that tell us how to classify economic time series into four elements: the trend, the cyclical fluctuations, the seasonal variations and the irregular variations. For the analytical P.M. I have adopted a different method of separating the trend from the other types of economic change. This method, which is described in Section 5.2 and in more detail in the Appendix to this chapter, allows us to determine the trend values of the economy regardless of whether the economy generates fluctuations or not. That is, the method provides us with the same steady-state values of U, Q and F as the P.M. did in cases in which it actually generated steady-state growth; on the other hand, it gives us trend values for U, Q and F when a set of parameter values generates fluctuations.

If steady-state growth is the outcome, the trend rates are also the steady-state rates; if the economy is growing with fluctuations, the trend rates are the long-term characteristics of the economy. The four main types of trends that are distinguishable for the P.M. serve as a classification of steady-state growth types as well. Two of these four types (Golden Age growth being one) are unique in the sense that their trend rates are necessarily at the same time steady-state rates (see Section 5.3). The hypothetical case of Golden Age growth is discussed separately in Section 5.4. Finally, Section 5.5 discusses the outcomes our trend determining method gave for different sets of parameter values.

This chapter deals with trends in the P.M. only. It is conceivable to apply our method to the regions of the I.M. as well. Per region the same classification could be made as for the P.M., and the I.M. with different sets of parameter values could be solved for its long-term behaviour. I shall not go through this very cumbersome procedure.[2] Instead, the trend determining method will be used for solving problems of regional economic policy, in particular for determining which regional distribution of a given amount of government expenditure will minimize unemployment, under the condition that the trend rates of unemployment are identical for all regions. This is done in Chapter 6.

5.2   The Trend Determining Method

Since I have assumed that all exogenous variables grow at the same rate, g, the trend rate of growth will automatically also be g.[3] To find out now what the relative trend level of output will be, I must solve the P.M. for the unemployment rate, U, the capital utilization rate, Q, and the production realization rate, F, by 'forcing' the trend rate of growth on the model; i.e. all equations and reduced-form equations connecting variables at different points of time are translated into equations in which all lags and leads are eliminated, by assuming that all variables (except U, Q and F) grow at the rate g. For instance, equation (2.20) will be written as: $C^d(t) = a_1 X(t) + a_2 \cdot (1/e) C^s(t) + H(t)$; equation (2.27) as $eK(t) = (1-r) K(t) + I(t)$. In these equations e again equals $(1+g)$.

In solving the model in this way a number of equations are met in which

84

inequalities determine the actual specification of the equation. These equations are (2.4), (2.12), (2.21), (2.22), (2.24) and (2.25). To get an exhaustive list of types of trends I must combine all possible specifications and solve the model for all these combinations. It turns out that seven trend types and subtypes can be distinguished. These are listed in the following section. The solution for the trend values of U, Q and F (written as $\bar{U}$, $\bar{Q}$, and $\bar{F}$) is then obtained as follows.

I reduce the model to two equations in which $\bar{X}(t)$ is written as a function of $\bar{Q}$, $\bar{F}$ and parameters only. One equation has $\bar{X}(t)$ as the sum of planned production components, the other has $\bar{X}(t)$ as a function of productive capacity. Then, depending on the type of trend for which I am solving the model, I will either get two equations in two unknowns ($\bar{Q}$ and $\bar{F}$) or one quadratic equation in one unknown ($\bar{Q}$ or $\bar{F}$), the latter equation by setting the two equations in $\bar{X}(t)$ equal to each other. The solution for $\bar{U}$ is subsequently derived using $\bar{Q}$ and $\bar{F}$. Altogether I obtain seven sets of equations for $\bar{U}$, $\bar{Q}$ and $\bar{F}$, one for each trend type or subtype. In the Appendix to this chapter the solution procedure is given for all types.

The next step is to determine what type of trend belongs to a particular set of parameter values. Since *a priori*, I do not know the answer there is only one way to find this out, and that is by checking all possibilities. I obtain seven sets of numerical solutions for $\bar{U}$, $\bar{Q}$ and $\bar{F}$ and lift out the correct one by eliminating those that contradict the assumptions of the particular trend type. Invariably our trend determining method eliminates all sets of solutions but one, which then is concluded to be the type that belongs to the particular set of parameter values for which I was solving. The next section will show how the mutually exclusive character of the trend types distinguished, makes it possible to find the correct type for each set of parameter values in this way.[4]

5.3   Types of Trends

At any time, actual output X, in the P.M. will be equal to either planned production, X^p, or full capacity output, X^{FC}, or full employment output X^{FE}.[5] The trend or long-term state of the P.M. economy with respect to ceiling and floor can be fully described by the variables $\bar{U} = 1 - [\bar{X}(t)/X^{FE}(t)]$, $\bar{Q} = \bar{X}(t)/\bar{X}^{FC}(t)$, and $\bar{F} = \bar{X}(t)/\bar{X}^p(t)$, with the u.r. and c-u.r. indicating the gap between output and ceiling, the production realization rate indicating whether or not any ceiling is hit at all.

If $\bar{Q} < 1$, and $\bar{U} > 0$, $\bar{F}$ will have to be equal to one. The $\bar{Q} < 1$ then means that the time path of output is equal to the floor path since only government investment can keep $\bar{Q}$ below one. This trend type I have labelled type 1. If, in addition, the time path of output is a steady-state growth path, I refer to it as 'lower' steady-state growth.

On the other hand, if $\bar{F}<1$, I can distinguish between different types and subtypes. With the production realization rate being less than one, either $\bar{Q}=1$, or $\bar{U}=0$. The former case I have labelled type 2, the latter, type 3. Both types can be divided up in a number of subtypes. In the first place, when $\bar{F}<1$, $\bar{Q}=1$, $\bar{U}>0$ it makes a difference whether $\bar{X}^p(t)<X^{FE}(t)$ or $\bar{X}^p(t)\geq X^{FE}(t)$, and also whether $\bar{V}(t)>0$, or $\bar{V}(t)=0$. The long-term relationship between X^p and X^{FE} determines which version of equation (2.21) holds; a long-term $V=0$ technically implies that $\bar{F}\leq 1/(1+sf)$.[6] Since it is highly unlikely to find a combination of parameter values that will give $\bar{X}^p(t)<X^{FE}(t)$ and at the same time a long-term $V=0$, I can distinguish three subtypes of type 2:

$$\bar{V}(t)>0,\ \bar{X}^p(t)<X^{FE}(t) \tag{2a}$$

$$\bar{V}(t)>0,\ \bar{X}^p(t)\geq X^{FE}(t) \tag{2b}$$

$$\bar{V}(t)=0,\ \bar{X}^p(t)\geq X^{FE}(t) \tag{2c}$$

Table 5.1

Types of Trends

Type and Subtype	Output	$\bar{U}$	$\bar{Q}$	$\bar{F}$	$\bar{V}(t)$	$\bar{X}^p(t)$ v. $X^{FE}(t)$
1	$\bar{X}(t)=\bar{X}^p(t)$	>0	<1	1	>0	$\bar{X}^p(t)<X^{FE}(t)$
2	$\bar{X}(t)=\bar{X}^{FC}(t)$	>0	1	<1		
2a					>0	$\bar{X}^p(t)<X^{FE}(t)$
2b					>0	$\bar{X}^p(t)\geq X^{FE}(t)$
2c					0	$\bar{X}^p(t)\geq X^{FE}(t)$
3	$\bar{X}(t)=X^{FE}(t)$	0	<1	<1		$\bar{X}^p(t)\geq X^{FE}(t)$
3a					>0	
3b					0	
4 (Golden Age)	$\bar{X}(t)=\bar{X}^p(t)=\bar{X}^{FC}(t)=X^{FE}(t)$	0	1	1	>0	$\bar{X}^p(t)=X^{FE}(t)$

(See also Appendix to Chapter 5.)

In applications it is easy to distinguish subtype 2c from 2a and 2b, since $\bar{V}(t)=0$ will mean that $\bar{F}<1/(1+sf)$ ($=.9302$ with the base-run parameter values). But how to decide whether a set of numerical values of $\bar{U}$, $\bar{Q}$ and $\bar{F}$ indicates 2a or 2b? The answer is: if $\bar{X}^p(t)<X^{FE}(t)$ (indicating 2a), then $[\bar{X}(t)/\bar{X}^p(t)]>[\bar{X}(t)/X^{FE}(t)]$, or $\bar{F}>(1-\bar{U})$; *vice versa* if $\bar{X}^p(t)\geq X^{FE}(t)$ (indicating 2b), then $\bar{F}\leq(1-\bar{U})$. Even simpler: if 2a holds then $(\bar{F}+\bar{U})>1$; if 2b holds then $(\bar{F}+\bar{U})=1$.

Type 3, which has $\bar{U}=0$, $\bar{Q}<1$ and $\bar{F}<1$, will only be possible for $\bar{X}^p(t)\geq X^{FE}(t)$, but depending on whether $\bar{F}>1/(1+sf)$ or $\bar{F}\leq1/(1+sf)$, the long-term V will be positive or zero. Hence two subtypes can be distinguished:

$$\bar{V}(t)>0 \tag{3a}$$

$$\bar{V}(t)=0 \tag{3b}$$

'Upper' steady-state growth (steady-state growth along the ceiling) will be of either type 2 or type 3. Simulations that are of type 3, however, are necessarily steady-state growth simulations: with $\bar{X}^p(t)\geq X^{FE}(t)$, output will be continuously pressed against the ceiling.

The trend rates of type 4, Golden Age growth, are at the same time 'upper' as well as 'lower' steady-state rates. Because of its unique nature Golden Age is discussed separately in the next section.

All trend types and subtypes are tabulated in Table 5.1. The solutions of the P.M. for $\bar{U}$, $\bar{Q}$ and $\bar{F}$, for each trend type and subtype, plus the derivations of these solutions are given in the Appendix to this chapter.

5.4 The Golden Age

Golden Age growth, that is, full employment and full capacity growth at the steady-state rate is purely accidental, even in a certainty model. But: 'it sets a hypothetical but useful standard against which other models can be assessed'.[7] In this section I should like to make such an assessment. First, treating G_o and A_o as variables instead of parameters and using the parameter values of the P.M. base run, I want to find the values of G_o and A_o that would make the P.M. a Golden Age model. The importance of doing this is that in the context of national economic policy, Golden Age growth represents an 'optimum optimorum'; although unattainable in real life, policy makers can set it against policy alternatives that are within reach, or just against 'random' situations. In this pre-policy phase of our study, the second thing I will do here is compare Golden Age growth, type 4 of our classification, with the other three types of trends.

In the next chapter I will pick up Golden Age growth again, but then to use it as an absolute standard of economic policy.

Golden Age growth implies $\bar{X}^p(t)=\bar{X}(t)=X^{FE}(t)=\bar{X}^{FC}(t)$, $\bar{U}=0$, $\bar{Q}=1$, $\bar{F}=1$. Forcing steady-state growth on the P.M. and removing all lags I obtain the following equations that together constitute planned production. From (2.1), (2.3), (2.5) to (2.8), (2.13), (2.16), (2.19), (2.20), (2.25) and (2.28):

$$\bar{C}^p(t)=[1+sf-s^2f/(e-1+s)]\,[a_1/(1-a_2/e)]\,\bar{X}(t). \tag{5.1}$$

From (2.14), (2.21) to (2.23):

$$\bar{J}^d(t)=[qb+(1-q)b/e]\,[v(e-1+r)]\,\bar{X}(t). \tag{5.2}$$

From (2.9):

$$\bar{G}^p(t)=G_o(1+g)^t. \tag{2.9}$$

From (2.14):

$$\bar{A}^d(t)=A_o(1+g)^t. \tag{5.3}$$

From (2.2), (2.4), (2.9), (2.11), (2.12), (5.1) to (5.3):

$$\bar{X}(t)=\{[1+sf-s^2f/(e-1+s)]\,[a_1/(1-a_2/e)] \\ +[qb+(1-q)b/e]\,[v(e-1+r)]\}\,\bar{X}(t)+(G_o+A_o)\,(1+g)^t, \tag{5.4}$$

or

$$[1-\{\cdots\}]\,\bar{X}(t)=(G_o+A_o)\,(1+g)^t. \tag{5.5}$$

Since $\bar{X}(t)=X^{FE}(t)=(lN_o/u)\,(1+g)^t$:

$$[1-\{\cdots\}]\,lN_o/u=G_o^*+A_o^*.^{8} \tag{5.6}$$

On the other hand, from (2.10), (2.14), (2.15), (2.18), (2.21) to (2.24) and (2.27):

$$[\{1-[qb+(1-q)b/e]\}\cdot v(e-1+r)]\,\bar{X}(t)=A_o(1+g)^t, \tag{5.7}$$

and because $\bar{X}(t)=lN_o/u(1+g)^t$:

$$[\cdots]\,lN_o/u=A_o^*. \tag{5.8}$$

Given the values of all parameters and parametric constants except G_o and A_o, I can first compute the Golden Age value of A_o from (5.8), and

88

then that of G_o from (5.6). All parameters and parametric constants appear in (5.6) and (5.8), except W_o, w and h, three parameters that are only relevant when unemployment is positive. The lagged endogenous variables, whose values we need to start a simulation, do not appear in the two Golden Age equations.

The role of autonomous investment is made clear on comparing (5.2) and (5.7). Autonomous investment complements private investment, the latter's output share being $[qb+(1-q)b/e]\,[v(e-1+r)]$, the former's share being $\{1-[qb+(1-q)b/e]\}\,[v(e-1+r)]$. Actually, (5.7) and (5.8) state the condition which A_o has to fulfil in order to make $\bar{Q}$ equal to one. Total investment as a share of total output is $v(e-1+r)$, that is the capital–output ratio times the sum of growth rates and depreciation rate, a familiar result from growth theory. For our parameter values the investment–output ratio is .1675.

What determines private investment's share of total investment? This share is $b[q+(1-q)/e]$, or the adjustment coefficient times a weighted average of 'this period' and 'next period', the weight q depending on how fast plans are executed. Autonomous investment will be zero if $b[q+(1-q)/e]=1$, which will only happen if both b and q assume their maximum value, or in other words, if the gap between desired and actual capital stock is completely and immediately closed. The value of $b[q+(1-q)/e]$ in the base run is .586, which means that in that case non-cyclical investment would in the long term constitute more than 41% of total investment.

Setting total Golden Age output at 100, A_o^* will be 6.9319 and G_o^* 19.7103. The complete breakdown of output is as follows:

Private consumption	63.2432
Inventory investment	0.2965
Government consumption	19.7103
Private fixed investment	9.8181
Government investment	6.9319
	100.0000

With G_o and A_o being the only variable parameters, the Golden Age distinguishes itself from other types of trends in that it features the only possible G_o and A_o that will bring full employment and full capacity growth simultaneously with equilibrium in the product market. The other three types can be evaluated in terms of G_o and A_o relative to the Golden Age. Type 1, with $\bar{Q}<1$, has relatively too much A_o and too little G_o. Type 2 is the opposite of type 1: too little A_o and too much G_o. When both G_o and A_o exceed their Golden Age values, the trend rates will be steady-state rates and of type 3. In general, the actual growth path will be cyclical when there is room for fluctuations and when the structural parameters are such that cycles can result. A high enough b (such as $b = .6$) combined with a G_o and A_o that are both below their Golden Age value will certainly create a cyclical output path.

5.5 Trend Values of Prototype Model Simulations

In this section I shall return to the P.M. simulations of Chapter 2 and see for some of the runs we discussed there to what type of trend they belong. Since it is relatively easy (and in terms of computer money, also cheap) to test other sets of parameter values for which I did not generate time series in Chapter 2, I also experimented with different combinations of G_o and A_o to find how these would be classified according to our method.[9] The different combinations of parameter values for which I did compute the trend values are listed in Table 5.2. The combinations have their own computer number, but for these sets which were tested in Chapter 2, the P.M. run number is also mentioned.

Table 5.2
Trend Values of Prototype Model Simulations

Run	P.M. Run	Variation	Type and Subtype	Trend Values		
				$\bar{U}$	$\bar{Q}$	$\bar{F}$
1916	1604	base run	2a	3.44	1.000	.997
1911	1621	$G_o = 15$	1	8.22	.970	1.000
1901		$G_o = 19$	2a	2.00	1.000	.986
1902		$G_o = 20$	2b	1.89	1.000	.948
1903	1622	$G_o = 21$	2c	2.06	1.000	.925
1904		$G_o = 22$	2c	2.12	1.000	.917
1905		$G_o = 23$	2c	2.18	1.000	.909
1906		$G_o = 24$	2c	2.25	1.000	.901
1918	1607	$G_o = 15; A_o = 0$	1	8.73	.986	1.000
1907	1601	$G_o = 18; A_o = 0$	2a	4.17	1.000	.980
1908		$G_o = 19; A_o = 0$	2b	2.94	1.000	.965
1909		$G_o = 20; A_o = 0$	2c	3.20	1.000	.928
1910		$G_o = 21; A_o = 0$	2c	3.27	1.000	.920
1912		$A_o = 5$	1	3.07	.992	1.000
1913	1605	$A_o = 6$	1	2.90	.987	1.000
1914		$A_o = 9$	1	2.40	.972	1.000

Table 5.2 (continued)

Run	P.M. Run	Variation	Type and Subtype	$\bar{U}$	$\bar{Q}$	$\bar{F}$
				Trend Values		
1915		$A_o=15$	1	1.38	.943	1.000
1919	1613	$b = .5$	2a	3.91	1.000	.986
1920	1612	$b = .7$	1	3.16	.995	1.000
1921	1633	$b =1.0$	1	2.66	.980	1.000
1927		$b = .7; A_o=0$	2a	3.73	1.000	.990
1929		$b = .8; A_o=0$	2a	3.39	1.000	.998
1931		$b =1.0; A_o=0$	1	3.00	.990	1.000
1945	1608	$A_o=3; w=0$	2a	4.48	1.000	.973
1937	1603	$A_o=0; w=0$	2a	5.40	1.000	.951
1939		$b = .7; A_o=0; w=0$	2a	4.68	1.000	.968
1941		$b = .8; A_o=0; w=0$	2a	4.14	1.000	.981
1943		$b =1.0; A_o=0; w=0$	2a	3.39	1.000	.998
1932		$a_1=.46; G_o=15; A_o=0$	2a	6.62	1.000	.999
1933		$a_1=.48; G_o=15; A_o=0$	2b	3.05	1.000	.950
1934		$a_1=.50; G_o=15; A_o=0$	2c	3.34	1.000	.909
1935		$h=.4; G_o=15; A_o=3$	1	7.46	.995	1.000
1936		$h=.5; G_o=15; A_o=3$	2a	6.52	1.000	.998

Explanation

1. *Trend types*
   Type 1: $\bar{U}>0, \bar{Q}<1, \bar{F}=1; \bar{V}(t)>0, \bar{X}^p(t)<X^{FE}(t)$.
   Type 2: $\bar{U}>0, \bar{Q}=1, \bar{F}<1$;
                        subtype 2a: $\bar{V}(t)>0, \bar{X}^p(t)<X^{FE}(t)$
                        subtype 2b: $\bar{V}(t)>0, \bar{X}^p(t)\geq X^{FE}(t)$
                        subtype 2c: $\bar{V}(t)=0, \bar{X}^p(t)\geq X^{FE}(t)$.

2. See also *Explanation* following Table 2.1.

From the computer outputs brought together in Table 5.2 I conclude that:

(a) The fluctuations of unemployment in the P.M. runs are not exactly symmetrical around the trend rate of unemployment. Generally, $\bar{U}$ will be a little higher than the arithmetic average of the range of u.r.s found for a particular P.M. run. For instance, the base run $\bar{U}$ is 3.44% where the range of u.r.s in run 1604 gave 1.0–5.5% (arithmetic average: 3.25%). I shall come back to this asymmetry in Chapter 6.

(b) The classification of the economy moves from type 1 ($\bar{X}(t)=\bar{X}^p(t)<$

$X^{FE}(t)$, $\bar{V}(t) > 0$), to subtype 2a ($\bar{X}(t) < \bar{X}^p(t) < X^{FE}(t)$, $\bar{V}(t) > 0$), subtype 2b ($\bar{X}^p(t) \geq X^{FE}(t)$, $\bar{V}(t) > 0$), and finally to subtype 2c ($\bar{X}^p(t) \geq X^{FE}(t)$, $\bar{V}(t) = 0$) as consumptive expenditures increase. This sequence holds for private consumption (runs 1932 to 1934), and contracyclical consumption (runs 1935 and 1936), as well as for autonomous government consumption (runs 1911, 1901 to 1903). Raising consumptive demand when the economy is of subtype 2c means a rise in the trend rate of unemployment. Subtype 2c is characterized by zero inventory all the time, i.e. by an $\bar{F} \leq 1/(1+sf) = .9302$, and in terms of $\bar{U}$ an economy is better off when $\bar{F}$ is above the no-inventory point than when consumption demand makes it drop below.[10]
(c)   Raising autonomous investment reduces the trend rate of unemployment, but the effectiveness of A_o gets smaller the higher the investment becomes. Capital goods are produced that are not needed by the economy. In addition, the higher that A_o is, the less the incentive that exists for private investment. The trend level of private investment without any public investment at all will never be too high, but both contracyclical and autonomous public investment can force the trend level of Q below one. When $\bar{Q}$ drops to or below .935, the trend level of private investment will be zero.[11] Disregarding the heavier fluctuations that come with it and looking only at long-term trends, a higher b is an alternative for higher autonomous investment. Both reduce $\bar{U}$. Compare, for instance, run 1912 with run 1920, or run 1912 with run 1931.
(d)   One unit of autonomous consumption does not affect the economy in the same way that one unit of autonomous investment does; the impact of one marginal unit of either autonomous consumption or investment depends on the proportionate levels of the two, given the level of non-autonomous expenditure. For instance, the combination $G_o = 21/A_o = 3$ (run 1903) gives a higher level of activities than $G_o = 18/A_o = 6$ (run 1913), even though the total amount of autonomous expenditure is the same in both cases.

5.6   Conclusion

Concluding this chapter I want to stress what our trend determining method achieves, and what it does not. It does give a way to characterize an economy in a few key numbers, these numbers being the trend or long-term figures for unemployment, capital utilization and planned-production realization. It does not indicate how the actual u.r.s, c-u.r.s and production realization rates will fluctuate around their long-term values, or for that matter, whether they will fluctuate at all. In other words, the method gives no insight into the cyclical behaviour of an economic system for which a particular set of parameter values holds.

The trend values I compute for U, Q, and F should not in general be interpreted as 'normal' or 'equilibrium' values. If the economy is cyclical, equilibrium values do not exist. Cycles then are the normal situation. Even steady-state growth generally does not imply an equilibrium position, as steady-state growth in our models may be the result of permanent excess demand in the product market. Gordon [1961] explains the difference between 'trend' and 'equilibrium' very lucidly:

An equilibrium position implies a position of rest, a balance of forces such that no further change would take place in the absence of new disturbances. Does the secular trend trace out such a moving equilibrium position, portraying how the economy would behave in the absence of forces making for cyclical instability? The answer is clearly in the negative. Since trends result from the action of secular forces in a world that is cyclically unstable, we do not know what the secular movement in particular series would have looked like in the absence of cyclical change. The present structure of the economy is a product of, among other things, past cyclical instability and the expectation that fluctuations will continue in the future. Computed trends do not tell us how economic series would have behaved in the absence of cyclical disturbances. If cyclical change were to cease, a projection of past trends would certainly not tell us at what level total output or the production of particular industries would come to rest. It is therefore not correct to think of the trend, or of any particular position between cyclical low and high points, as representing an equilibrium position which would prevail in the absence of those forces that create business cycles.[12]

The trend determining method is not a statistical method, but an analytical method, developed for the P.M. which is an analytical certainty model. The principle of forcing steady-state growth conditions upon a model, however, can also be applied to consistent econometric models. The main advantage of our method of obtaining long-term averages for an economic system over statistical methods of obtaining measures of location, is precisely that it does away with the necessity to look for an appropriate measure of location. Questions like: 'How are we going to weight the different u.r.s recorded during a cycle?' do not bother us with this method. The choice of values of lagged endogenous variables does not affect our trend outcomes (which are determined by parameters only), although they do affect the actual u.r.s in the early periods of the simulations. The method is unambiguous about the type of trend that holds for a particular set of parameter values, as it immediately falsifies the $\bar{U}$s, $\bar{Q}$s, and $\bar{F}$s that do not satisfy the characteristics of a trend type.

Appendix: Trend Values of U, Q and F

Abbreviations

In the derivation of the trend values of U, Q and F for the different types of trends, the abbreviations listed overleaf will be used:

$$A = (1 + sf) (a_2/e)$$
$$B = qb + (1 - q) b/e$$
$$C = (e - 1 + r) v$$
$$D = Bve$$
$$E = Bve + 1/e$$
$$G = Bv(1 - r)$$
$$H = Bv(1 - r) + 1/e$$
$$J = 1 + sf - (s^2 f)/(e - 1 + s)$$
$$K = l N_o/u$$
$$L = (1 + sf) (a_1 - h W_o u)$$
$$M = (1 + sf) (h W_o u)$$
$$N = (a_1 - h W_o u)/(1 - a_2/e)$$
$$P = (h W_o u) (1 - a_2/e)$$
$$R = (1 - r)/(e - 1 + r)$$
$$S = (e - 1) (1 + sf) + s$$

Trend type 1 $(\bar{U} > 0, \bar{Q} < 1, \bar{F} = 1, \bar{V}(t) > 0, \bar{X}^p(t) < X^{FE}(t))$

If $w = 1$

Planned production:

$$\bar{C}^p(t) = JN\bar{X}(t) + JPX^{FE}(t) \tag{5.9}$$

$$\bar{J}^d(t) = (D - G/\bar{Q}) \, \bar{X}(t) \tag{5.10}$$

$$\bar{G}^p(t) = G_o (1 + g)^t \tag{2.9}$$

$$\bar{A}^d(t) = (1/e) \, [X^{FE}(t) - \bar{X}(t)] + A_o (1 + g)^t. \tag{5.12}$$

From (5.9) to (5.11) and (2.9), and since $\bar{X}^p(t) = \bar{X}(t)$:

$$\bar{X}(t) = \frac{[(JP + 1/e) K + G_o + A_o] (1 + g)^t}{1 - JN - D + G/\bar{Q} + 1/e}. \tag{5.12}$$

Output as a function of full capacity output:

$$\bar{X}(t) = \frac{[(l/e) K + A_o] (1 + g)^t}{C/\bar{Q} - D + G/\bar{Q} + 1/e}. \tag{5.13}$$

Equating (5.12) and (5.13):

$$\bar{Q} = \frac{[(C + G) JP + C (1/e)] K + (C + G) G_o + CA_o}{[(D - 1/e) JP + (1 - JN) (1/e)] K + (D - 1/e) G_o + (1 - JN) A_o} \tag{5.14a}$$

$$\bar{U} = 1 - \frac{1/e + A_o/K}{(C + G)/\bar{Q} - D + 1/e}. \tag{5.15a}$$

94

If $w=0$

$$\bar{Q}=\frac{(C+G)\,JPK+(C+G)\,G_o+A_o}{DJPK+DG_o+(1-JN)\,A_o} \tag{5.14b}$$

$$\bar{U}=1-\frac{JP+(G_o+A_o)/K}{1+G/\bar{Q}-D-JN}.$$

Trend type 2 $(\bar{U}>0,\ \bar{Q}=1,\ \bar{F}<1)$

Subtype 2a $[\bar{V}(t)>0,\ \bar{X}^p(t)<X^{FE}(t)]$

If $w=1$

Planned production:

$$\bar{C}^p(t)=\frac{SN}{(e-1)+\bar{F}s}\,\bar{X}(t)+\frac{SP}{(e-1)+\bar{F}s}\,X^{FE}(t) \tag{5.16}$$

$$\bar{J}^d(t)=(D-\bar{F}G)\,\bar{X}^p(t) \tag{5.17}$$

$$\bar{G}^p(t)=G_o\,(1+g)^t \tag{2.9}$$

$$\bar{A}^d(t)=(1/e)\,[X^{FE}(t)-\bar{X}(t)]+A_o\,(1+g)^t. \tag{5.11}$$

From (5.16), (5.17), (2.9) and (5.11), and since $\bar{X}(t)=\bar{F}\bar{X}^p(t)$:

$$\bar{X}^p(t)=\frac{\left\{\left[\dfrac{SP}{(e-1+\bar{F}s)}+(1/e)\right]K+G_o+A_o\right\}(1+g)^t}{1-\dfrac{SN\bar{F}}{(e-1+\bar{F}s)}-D+\bar{F}H}. \tag{5.18}$$

Output as a function of full capacity output:

$$\bar{X}^p(t)=\frac{[(1/e)\,K+A_o]\,(1+g)^t}{C-D+\bar{F}H}. \tag{5.19}$$

Equating (5.18) and (5.19), $\bar{F}$ is found by solving the quadratic equation:

$$sHG_o\,\bar{F}^2+\{(e-1)\,HG_o+s[(C-1)\,(1/e)\,K+(C-D)\,G_o+(C-1)\,A_o]$$
$$+S[N\{(1/e)\,K+A_o\}+PHK]\}\,\bar{F}$$
$$+(e-1)\,[(C-1)\,(1/e)\,K+(C-D)\,G_o+(C-1)A_o] \tag{5.20a}$$
$$+(C-D)\,SPK=0.$$

$$\bar{U}=1-\bar{F}\left[\frac{1/e+A_o/K}{C-D+\bar{F}H}\right]. \tag{5.21a}$$

If w = 0

$$sHG_o\bar{F}^2 + \{(e-1)\,GG_o + s\,[(C-D)\,G_o + (C-1)\,A_o] \\ + S\,(NA_o + PGK)\}\,\bar{F} + (e-1)\,[(C-D)\,G_o \\ + (C-1)\,A_o] + (C-D)\,SPK = 0 \tag{5.20b}$$

$$\bar{U} = 1 - \bar{F}\left[\frac{(SP)/(e-1+\bar{F}s) + (G_o + A_o)/K}{1 - (\bar{F}SN/(e-1+\bar{F}s) - D + \bar{F}G}\right]. \tag{5.21b}$$

Subtype 2b $[\bar{V}(t) > 0,\ \bar{X}^p(t) \geq X^{FE}(t)]$

If w = 1

Planned production:

$$\bar{C}^p(t) = [SN/(e-1+\bar{F}s)]\,\bar{X}(t) + [SP/(e-1+\bar{F}s)]\,X^{FE}(t) \tag{5.16}$$

$$\bar{J}^d(t) = DX^{FE}(t) - G\bar{X}(t) \tag{5.22}$$

$$\bar{G}^p(t) = G_o\,(1+g)^t \tag{2.9}$$

$$\bar{A}^d(t) = (1/e)\,[X^{FE}(t) - \bar{X}(t)] + A_o\,(1+g)^t. \tag{5.11}$$

From (5.16), (5.22), (2.9) and (5.11), and since $\bar{X}(t) = \bar{F}\bar{X}^p(t)$:

$$\bar{X}(t) = \frac{\bar{F}\,\{[E + SP/(e-1+\bar{F}s)]\,K + G_o + A_o\}\,(1+g)^t}{1 - \bar{F}\,\{[SN/(e-1+\bar{F}s)] - H\}}. \tag{5.23}$$

Output as a function of full capacity output:

$$\bar{X}(t) = \frac{\bar{F}\,(EK + A_o)\,(1+g)^t}{C + \bar{F}H}. \tag{5.24}$$

Equating (5.23) and (5.24), $\bar{F}$ is found by solving the quadratic equation:

$$sHG_o\bar{F}^2 + \{(e-1)\,HG_o + s\,[(C-1)\,EK + CG_o + (C-1)\,A_o] \\ + S\,[N(EK+A_o) + PHK]\}\,\bar{F} + (e-1)\,[(C-1)\,EK \\ + CG_o + (C-1)\,A_o] + CSPK = 0. \tag{5.25a}$$

$$\bar{U} = 1 - \bar{F}\left[\frac{E + A_o/K}{C + \bar{F}H}\right]. \tag{5.26}$$

If w = 0

$$SGG_o\bar{F}^2 + \{(e-1)\,GG_o + s\,[(C-1)\,DK + CG_o + (C-1)\,A_o] \\ + S\,[N(DK+A_o) + PGK]\}\,\bar{F} + (e-1)\,[(C-1)\,DK \\ + CG_o + (C-1)\,A_o] + CSPK = 0. \tag{5.25b}$$

Subtype 2c $[\bar{V}(t)=0,\ \bar{X}^p(t)\geq X^{FE}(t)]$

If $w=1$

Planned production:

$$\bar{C}^p(t)=[L/(1-A\bar{F})]\ \bar{X}(t)+[M/(1-A\bar{F})]\ X^{FE}(t) \qquad (5.26)$$

$$\bar{J}^d(t)=DX^{FE}(t)-G\bar{X}(t) \qquad (5.22)$$

$$\bar{G}^p(t)=G_o\,(1+g)^t \qquad (2.9)$$

$$\bar{A}^d(t)=(1/e)\,[X^{FE}(t)-\bar{X}(t)]+A_o\,(1+g)^t. \qquad (5.11)$$

From (5.26), (5.22), (2.9) and (5.11), and since $\bar{X}(t)=\bar{F}\bar{X}^p(t)$:

$$\bar{X}(t)=\frac{\bar{F}\{[M/(1-A\bar{F})+E]\ K+G_o+A_o\}\,(1+g)^t}{1-\bar{F}[L/(1-A\bar{F})-H]}. \qquad (5.27)$$

Output as a function of full capacity output:

$$\bar{X}(t)=\frac{\bar{F}(EK+A_o)\,(1+g)^t}{C+\bar{F}H}. \qquad (5.24)$$

Equating (5.27) and (5.24), $\bar{F}$ is found by solving the quadratic equation:

$$\begin{aligned}AHG_o\,\bar{F}^2+\{CA-A-L)\,A_o&-(H-CA)\,G_o\\ -[(1-C)\,EA+(LE+MG)]\,K\}\,\bar{F}&\\ +(1-C)\,A_o-CG_o-[CM-(1-C)\,E]\,K&=0.\end{aligned} \qquad (5.28a)$$

$$\bar{U}=1-\bar{F}\left[\frac{E+A_o/K}{C+\bar{F}H}\right]. \qquad (5.26)$$

If $w=0$

$$\begin{aligned}AHG_o\,\bar{F}^2+\{(CA-A-L)\,A_o&-(G-CA)\,G_o-[(1-C)\,DA\\ +(LD+MG)]\,K\}\,\bar{F}&+(1-C)\,A_o-CG_o\\ -[CM-(1-C)\,D]\,K&=0.\end{aligned} \qquad (5.28b)$$

Trend type $3\,(\bar{U}=0,\ \bar{Q}<1,\ \bar{F}<1)$

Subtype 3a $[\bar{V}(t)>0,\ \bar{X}^p(t)\geq X^{FE}(t)]$

Planned production:

$$\bar{C}^p(t)=J\,(N+P)\,X^{FE}(t) \qquad (5.29)$$

$$\bar{J}^d(t)=(D-G/\bar{Q})\,X^{FE}(t) \qquad (5.30)$$

$$\bar{G}^p(t)=(G_o/K)\,X^{FE}(t) \qquad (5.31)$$

$$\bar{A}^d(t) = (A_o/K)\, X^{FE}(t). \tag{5.32}$$

From (5.29) to (5.32), and since $\bar{X}^p(t) = (1/\bar{F})\, X^{FE}(t)$:

$$1/\bar{F} = J(N+P) + D - G/\bar{Q} + (G_o + A_o)/K. \tag{5.33}$$

Output as a function of full capacity output:

$$X^{FE}(t) = \left[\frac{\bar{Q}\bar{F}(D + A_o/K)}{C + G\bar{F}}\right] X^{FE}(t), \tag{5.34}$$

or

$$\bar{Q} = \frac{C + G\bar{F}}{F(D + A_o/K)}.$$

Two equations, (5.33) and (5.35), in two unknowns $\bar{F}$ and $\bar{Q}$.

Subtype 3b $[\bar{V}(t) = 0,\ \bar{X}^p(t) \geq X^{FE}(t)]$

   Planned production:

$$\bar{C}^p(t) = [(L+M)/(1-A\bar{F})]\, X^{FE}(t) \tag{5.36}$$

$$\bar{J}^d(t) = (D - G/\bar{Q})\, X^{FE}(t) \tag{5.30}$$

$$\bar{G}^p(t) = (G_o/K)\, X^{FE}(t) \tag{5.31}$$

$$\bar{A}^d(t) = (A_o/K)\, X^{FE}(t). \tag{5.32}$$

From (5.30) to (5.32) and (5.36), and since $\bar{X}^p(t) = (1/\bar{F})\, X^{FE}(t)$:

$$1/\bar{F} = (L+M)/(1-A\bar{F}) + D - G/\bar{Q} + (G_o + A_o)/K. \tag{5.37}$$

Output as a function of full capacity output:

$$X^{FE}(t) = \left[\frac{\bar{Q}\bar{F}(D + A_o/K)}{C + G\bar{F}}\right] X^{FE}(t), \tag{5.34}$$

or

$$\bar{Q} = \frac{C + G\bar{F}}{F(D + A_o/K)}. \tag{5.35}$$

Two equations, (5.35) and (5.37), in two unknowns, $\bar{F}$ and $\bar{Q}$.
   Trend type 4, Golden Age growth, is discussed in Section 5.4.

Notes

[1] J. Robinson [1966].
[2] With the seven trend types and subtypes that I shall distinguish in Section 5.2, and with three regions, the number of combinations for which I would have to solve the trend values of U, Q and F would be $7^3 = 343$.
[3] Only in the absence of autonomous expenditures $(G_o = A_o = W_o = 0)$ and if in addition $w = 0$, will output steadily decline until a zero level is reached. In that case the natural rate of growth is zero.
[4] A check of our method was provided by the fact that in instances where the computer simulations of Chapter 2 gave steady-state values, the trend determining method came up with precisely the same trend values of U, Q and F.
[5] Formally the 'or's' in this statement should be replaced by 'and/or's', to account for the possibility that any two of the three variables $X^p(t)$, $X^{FC}(t)$ and $X^{FE}(t)$ are identical. This, of course, is accidental. Even more exceptional is $X(t) = X^p(t) = X^{FC}(t) = X^{FE}(t)$, which as a steady-state growth solution would be the Golden Age.
[6] One might argue that the same distinctions should be made for type 1. This is not true however. If $\bar{F} = 1$, X^p is always lower than X^{FE} (except in the Golden Age), and the long-term V is always positive.
[7] R. G. D. Allen [1967, p. 207].
[8] The Golden Age values of G_o and A_o are written as G_o^* and A_o^* respectively.
[9] The output of the trend-type computer programme I made consisted of only the values for $\bar{U}$, $\bar{Q}$ and $\bar{F}$. Once the solution method was programmed, additional sets of parameter values could be tested at very low additional costs.
[10] Note that this comparison is in terms of $\bar{U}$ only. The higher consumptive demand is, the smaller fluctuations will be, and so the rising $\bar{U}$ will at the same time bring smaller fluctuations or even no fluctuations at all.
[11] If $\bar{Q} < 1$, and $\bar{F} = 1$ (type 1), the trend level of private investment is: $[qb + (1-q)b/e] \, v \, [e - (1-r)/\bar{Q}] \, \bar{X}(t)$. With $e = 1.04$ and $r = .027$, a value for $\bar{Q}$ of approximately .935 will make private investment zero.
[12] R. A. Gordon [1961, pp. 256-7].

6 Optimal Distributions of Government Expenditure

6.1. Introduction

In the previous chapter I developed a method to determine trends for fluctuating economies as well as economies that are growing at steady-state rates. This method unambiguously classified each of the different implementations of the P.M. into one of seven trend types or subtypes. But since the regional economies are our main concern, the question that came to mind in Chapter 5 was: Can the trend determining method be applied to the I.M.? The answer was: It is conceivable, but it is a very cumbersome and time consuming operation. Instead of having to solve for seven different types and subtypes, I now theoretically would have to solve for the 343 $(=7^3)$ different combinations of types and subtypes that can possibly exist among three regions, and that only if I make the simplifying assumption of identical parameter values for all regions.

Of course, for testing simulations such as the ones discussed in Chapter 3 the actual number of combinations would be considerably reduced, to maybe ten or even less. For instance, in Chapter 3 the following pattern often recurred: regions 1 and 2 fully using their capital stocks, with unemployment being positive, which indicates trend type 2; region 3 operating below the ceiling, and therefore characterized by trend type 1. In the first Appendix to this chapter I shall work out the combination of subtype 2a for regions 1 and 2, and type 1 for region 3 as an example of how the trend determining model works for the I.M.

Solving for the regional $\bar{U}$s, $\bar{Q}$s and $\bar{F}$s for all kinds of combinations of trend types, however, is not the way I shall apply the trend determining method to the I.M. The way I will apply it instead is directly geared towards the purpose of this chapter, and relies heavily on some of the findings for the P.M. in the previous chapter. The purpose of this and the following chapters is to gain insight into how interregional distribution of economic activities can be improved, or more ambitiously, to find an optimal distribution of economic activities, when the goals of regional economic policy are in the first place interregional equality of unemployment at the lowest possible level ('interregional equity'), and secondly, stable growth ('stability'). In this chapter, government spending will be the instrumental variable to attain these goals; in the next two chapters

I shall investigate how changes in the trade pattern and migration respectively affect the interregional distribution of unemployment and the fluctuations of the regional output paths.

The plan for this chapter is as follows. First, in Section 6.2, I shall define the 'optimum optimorum' for the I.M.: Golden Age growth for all regions. Then, in Section 6.3, using the trend determining method I shall define optimality as interregional equality of trend rates of unemployment, subject to the condition that the total available amount of government spending is a datum. As will be seen, equality of trend rates does not necessarily give stability at the same time. The next section, 6.4, is devoted to the search for distributions of government expenditure that will reduce the amplitude of the fluctuations while still maintaining a fair degree of equity among regions. Finally, in Section 6.5, I shall present some conclusions.

6.2. The Golden Age[1]

Solving for regional government consumption (G_{oi}) and regional government investment (A_{oi}) under Golden Age growth will give an absolute measure, against which I can assess optimal distributions of government expenditure in cases when $\sum G_{oi}$ and A_{oi} are given.

With the values of all parameters and parametric constants identical for all regions and equal to the values I used for the P.M. base run, it should not surprise us that the Golden Age value of $\sum G_{oi}$ is three times G_o^*, and that A_{oi}^* equals A_o^*.[2] After all, the economics of the I.M. is the same as that of the P.M. If all regions are to operate at full employment, with in addition $\bar{Q}_i = \bar{F}_i = 1$, our only problem is to allocate three times G_o^* over the three regions. This problem is solved by reducing the I.M.—using the Golden Age assumptions—to two vector equations, one with $\bar{X}(t)$ as the sum of planned-production components, the other expressing $\bar{X}(t)$ as full capacity output. In the following equations all variables are vectors, all parametric terms are scalars. $[c]$ and $[k]$ are the consumption goods and capital goods trade matrices. $[1]$ is the identity matrix. The components of planned production are:

$$\bar{C}^p(t) = [1 + sf - (s^2f)/(e - 1 + s)] \, [a_1/(1 - a_2/e)] \, [c] \, \bar{X}(t) \tag{6.1}$$

$$\bar{J}^d(t) = [qb + (1 - q) \, b/e] \, [v(e - 1 + r)] \, [k] \, \bar{X}(t) \tag{6.2}$$

$$\bar{G}^p(t) = (1 + g)^t \, G_o^* \tag{6.3}$$

$$\bar{A}^d(t) = (1 + g)^t \, A_o^* . \tag{6.4}$$

Total planned production therefore is:

$$\bar{X}(t) = \{[1 + sf - (s^2 f)/(e - 1 + s)]\,[a_1/(1 - a_2/e)]\,[c]$$
$$+ [qb + (1 - q)\,b/e]\,[v(e - 1 + r)]\,[k]\}\,\bar{X}(t) + (1 + g)^t\,(G_o^* + A_o^*), \qquad (6.5)$$

or:

$$[[1] - \{\cdots\}]\,\bar{X}(t) = (1 + g)^t\,(G_o^* + A_o^*). \qquad (6.6)$$

Since $\bar{X}(t) = X^{FE}(t) = (1 + g)^t\,lN_o/u$:

$$[[1] - \{\cdots\}]\,lN_o/u = G_o^* + A_o^*. \qquad (6.7)$$

On the other hand, interpreting $\bar{X}(t)$ as full capacity output:

$$[\{1 - [qb + (1 - q)\,b/e]\}\,v(e - 1 + r)]\,\bar{X}(t) = (1 + g)^t\,A_o^*, \qquad (6.8)$$

and since $\bar{X}(t) = (1 + g)^t\,lN_o/u$:

$$[\cdots]\,lN_o/u = A_o^*. \qquad (6.9)$$

Equation (6.9) is (5.9) written three times, so:

$$A_o^* = \begin{bmatrix} 6.9319 \\ 6.9319 \\ 6.9319 \end{bmatrix}.$$

If this result is used to solve for G_o^*, equation (6.7) gives:

$$G_o^* = \begin{bmatrix} 35.3637 \\ 7.5210 \\ 16.2462 \end{bmatrix}.$$

As can easily be checked, $\sum G_{oi}^* = 59.1309$, which is three times the G_o^* of the P.M.

6.3. Optimal Distributions of Government Expenditure: Interregional Equity

6.3.1 *Interregional Equity as a Goal of Regional Economic Policy*

Richardson [1969, p. 365] argues that a rational regional policy should perform two broad functions: (a) It should help to promote growth in the national economy, (b) It should handle inequities resulting from large interregional disparities in indices of growth and welfare. For our model I assumed a ceiling growth rate which is constant and identical for all sectors of the economy. Interregional inequities, therefore, do not result from disparities in growth rates, but only from differences in the levels of activities and from the different susceptibility of regions to business fluctuations. With the maximum possible growth rate being an assumption instead of a target, the first goal of regional policy should be to achieve the highest possible level of activities for the total economy, subject to the condition that interregional differences in levels of activities be minimized. This goal I have labelled 'interregional equity'.

How to define 'level of activities' for an economy which grows with fluctuations? With contracyclical economic policy, the level of activities is output or unemployment in any given year, relative maybe to a desired or acceptable level of output or unemployment. Contracyclical policy measures in the form of government investment and unemployment benefits are included in both the P.M. and the I.M. as built-in stabilizers. When structural economic policy is the concern, as is the case in this chapter, the initial interest is in trend levels of output or unemployment. The trend determining method of Chapter 5 provided us with trend levels of U, Q and F, and for the purposes of this chapter I shall define 'level of activities' as the trend rate of unemployment. Using $\bar{U}$ rather than $\bar{X}(t)$ as our measure means that I can abstract the time period from the analysis.

I can express the first goal of structural regional policy as the following objective function:

min $\bar{U}$ (trend rate of national unemployment), subject to

$$
\begin{array}{ll}
\text{(i)} & \bar{U}_1 = \bar{U}_2 = \bar{U}_3 \\
\text{(ii)} & \bar{Q}_1 = \bar{Q}_2 = \bar{Q}_3 \\
\text{(iii)} & \bar{F}_1 = \bar{F}_2 = \bar{F}_3
\end{array}
\qquad (6.10)
$$

given

$$
\text{(a)} \ \sum_i G_{oi},
$$

and

$$
\text{(b)} \ A_{oi} \qquad (i = 1, 2, 3).
$$

Note that in this specification I do not only require that the trend rates of unemployment are identical among regions, but also that all regions have the same trend c-u.r.s and production realization rates. Note also that this specification does not contain a single condition regarding the amplitude of national or regional economic fluctuations. At this stage I am only concerned with trend levels; fluctuations do not affect the optimal distribution. With respect to our instrumental variables:

I have fixed the amount of government non-cyclical investment per region, so that government consumptive expenditure becomes the sole instrument of regional economic policy, although it too is subject to the condition that the total amount of government consumption that can be distributed over the regions, is given.

The reason for constraints (i), (ii), and (iii) is not only that in this way more interregional equality will be accomplished (even though the actual U_is, Q_is and F_is will still vary considerably because of the interregional distribution of the production of capital goods), but also because in this way full advantage can be taken of the findings of Chapter 5 and thereby immense amount of computational work saved. For if it is required that no interregional differences in trend levels exist I might as well go back to the national model, to see which $\bar{U}$, $\bar{Q}$, and $\bar{F}$ will result if all parameters and G_o are given. This is precisely what the trend determining method did. The problem for this chapter then becomes allocating this given amount of G_o (or three times that amount in the way that our parameter values were chosen) such that the national values for $\bar{U}$, $\bar{Q}$ and $\bar{F}$ are also the trend values of each region. Recall from Section 6.2 that this is also the way in which I stated the problem of finding the regional Golden Age values of government consumption.

6.3.2 An Example of How to Use the Trend Determining Method to Obtain an Optimal Distribution

To give an example of how the trend rates computed for the P.M. can be used for regional economic policy, let us take run 1907 of Chapter 5. Run 1907 gave the trend values of U, Q and F for the parameter values I used for P.M. run 1601 (see Table 5.2). These parameter values are equal to the base-run values, except that A_o is 0 instead of 3. As solutions for the trend rates, I found: $\bar{U}=4.17\%$, $\bar{Q}=1$ and $\bar{F}=.980$, which means that the type of trend is 2, subtype 2a. What I require now is that in the optimal solution for G_{oi} these trend rates hold for each of the three regions of the I.M. Again I remind the reader, that optimality is defined as a distribution of government consumption that will give each region this minimum trend rate of unemployment, in addition to a $\bar{Q}_i=1$, and an $\bar{F}_i=.980$. Optimality, given $\sum G_{oi}$ is indeed pareto-optimality: no region can improve its trend level of employment without hurting another region.

Given $\bar{U}_i$, $\bar{Q}_i$ and $\bar{F}_i$ and given the type of trend, the next step is to write the reduced-form equations of the I.M. for this type of trend, which comes down to writing the vector version of the reduced-form equations for the P.M., including the trade matrices. Actually, I did this in Section 6.2 for type of trend 4, Golden Age growth. Using vector notation for the variables and using the same abbreviations as in the Appendix to Chapter

5, for subtype 2a the reduced-form equation I need is:

$$\{(1/\bar{F})\,[1]-[SN/(e-1+\bar{F}s)]\,[c]-(D/\bar{F}-G)\,[k]$$
$$+(1/e)\,[1]\}\,\bar{X}_o=\{[SP/(e-1+\bar{F}s)]\,[c] \qquad (6.11)$$
$$+(1/e)\,[1]\}\,K+G_o+A_o.$$

In (6.11), $\bar{X}_o$ is the trend level of output in the initial period. Once I know $\bar{U}$, I know $\bar{X}_o$, since $\bar{U}=1-\bar{X}_o/K$.

Equation (6.11) is the interregional equivalent of (5.18). Note that I do not need the second reduced-form equation, in which output is expressed as a function of full capacity output, since A_o is not a policy variable, but a parameter in this case. The vector G_o is the only unknown in (6.11). Solving for G_o gives this optimal distribution:

$$G_o = \begin{bmatrix} 34.39 \\ 7.64 \\ 11.97 \end{bmatrix}.$$

Equations such as (6.11) can be written for all seven trend types and subtypes. They are brought together in the second Appendix to this chapter. For all types it is true that only the first of the two reduced-form equations is needed, if A_o is a parameter and not an instrument of economic policy. But even if A_o is our second instrumental variable I do not have to compute the optimal value of regional autonomous investment separately, since for each region this value will be identical to the optimal value for A_o in the (national) P.M., as long as I require equal trend rates for all regions.

6.3.3 Simulations with Optimal Distributions

Table 6.1 summarizes our quest for optimality as it was defined in (6.10). Some of the combinations of parameter values for which I computed the optimal distribution of government consumption have been used before in previous computer runs, others are new. All variations concern investment parameters, the reason being that I am mainly interested to see how different combinations of private and government investment (autonomous as well as contracyclical) would affect the optimal distribution of $\sum G_{oi}$, but also how they would affect the fluctuations around the equal regional trend levels. The runs are numbered 1725 to 1734. For the sake of comparability, where necessary, additional simulations were also made of the P.M. with the same variations in the investment parameters. These are summarized in Table 6.3.

What is most striking about the u.r.s in Table 6.1, is that optimal distributions of $\sum G_{oi}$ certainly do not lead to identical fluctuations for all

Table 6.1

Interregional Model Simulations with Optimal Distributions of Government Consumption

Run	Investment Parameters			G_o^*	I.M. Run			CL	Trend Rates			Compare With
	b	w	A_o		U low-high	Q low	F low		U	Q	F	
				34.39	2.6– 6.2	.99	.94					
1725	.6	1	0	7.64	2.2– 6.2	.99	.94	12	4.17	1.00	.98	1601,
				11.97	1.6– 9.3	.95	.83					1717
				35.95	4.7–12.2	1.00	.85					
1726	.6	0	0	10.23	4.7–13.7	1.00	.97	28	5.40	1.00	.95	1603,
				7.82	4.6–21.7	.96	.70					1718
				33.34	1.8– 4.2	.98	.98					
1727	.6	1	3.51	5.90	2.2– 4.4	.99	.98	16	3.32	1.00	1.00	1646
				14.76	0.7– 6.6	.95	.93					
				33.34	0.4– 9.1	.96	.88					
1728	.6	0	6.70	5.90	0.1– 9.4	.95	.91	18	3.32	1.00	1.00	1652
				14.76	0.2–19.4	.86	.69					
				34.39	1.4– 5.6	.97	.94					
1729	.7	1	0	8.01	1.4– 5.4	.98	.94	12	3.83	1.00	.99	1647
				11.60	0.5–10.4	.93	.83					
				35.74	2.7–16.6	.96	.78					
1730	.7	0	0	10.36	2.3–17.8	.97	.83	28	4.68	1.00	.97	1653
				7.90	2.9–33.9	.86	.51					
				33.82	0.9– 4.9	.97	.96					
1731	.7	1	1.92	7.01	1.0– 4.7	.97	.97	14	3.32	1.00	1.00	1648
				13.17	0.1– 9.0	.93	.88					
				33.82	0.2–10.7	.96	.85					
1732	.7	0	5.12	7.01	0.6–11.1	.94	.88	17	3.32	1.00	1.00	1654
				13.17	0.0–22.9	.85	.61					

See *Explanation* following Table 3.1.

regions. The amplitudes of the fluctuations differ quite a bit, among regions as well as for the different variations. But actually, this is what should be expected. Our economic policy does not affect the regional production structure as far as the production of capital goods is concerned. Region 3 is still the main producer of capital goods, and region 3 will be more susceptible to fluctuations than the other two regions. Especially when I as-

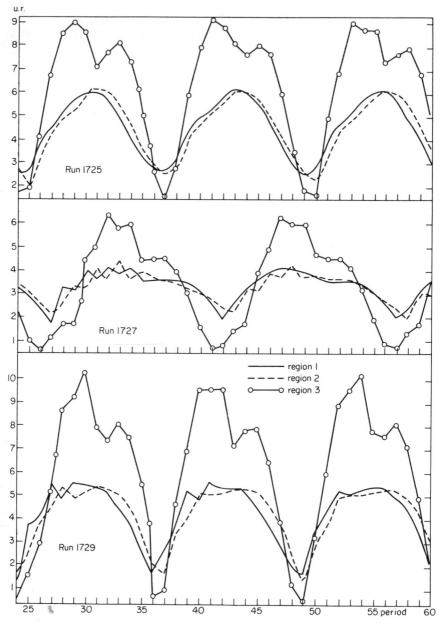

Figure 6.1 Interregional Model Runs with Optimal Distributions
of Government Consumption

sume that $w=0$ (no contracyclical investment), as in the even-numbered runs, the economy of region 3 oscillates severely. Fluctuations take place because there is room for them. With $\sum G_{oi}=54$, not enough production is generated to have steady-state growth, and when contracyclical investment is zero, a prime stabilizing force is taken away and the economies go through longer lasting and heavier fluctuating cycles.

Another striking outcome which appears in all simulations is that the differences in u.r.s between regions 1 and 2 on the one hand, and region 3 on the other, are much larger during the trough period than at the peak of the cycle. The capital goods producing region 3 experiences deeper troughs than the other two regions. This is especially true for the four simulations with $w=0$. Furthermore it turns out that the trend rate of unemployment is closer to the lowest recorded u.r. than to the highest (except in regions 1 and 2, when $w=1$). In other words, the cycles are asymmetrical around the trend. The explanation is that the trend level of economic activity is close enough to the full employment ceiling to prevent a full swing of the regional cycles during the upswing phase, and consequently the range of u.r.s will be smaller between peak and trend than between trend and trough. The asymmetrical cycle makes us aware of a special property of the trend as computed by our trend determining method. Our trend is not a statistical average of an observed cycle, but the centre line of the cycle as it would have been without ceilings.

Let us now turn more specifically to the parameter variations we experimented with. I commented on the effects of $w=0$. Making all investment private investment gives the highest possible fluctuations (runs 1726 and 1729), the amplitude being larger, the higher that b is. In general, of course, a higher b makes the system more cyclical. In our eight simulations A_o was zero or it assumed a value that both $\bar{F}$ and $\bar{Q}$ equal one, in all regions. Runs 1727, 1728, 1731 and 1732 show how this value increases if w becomes zero. Given the total amount of government consumption, the trend rate of unemployment becomes independent of the adjustment coefficient b, if I let A_o assume the value for which $\bar{F}_i=\bar{Q}_i=1$. A higher b simply means that A_o can be lower, or that a shift takes place from government autonomous to private non-autonomous investment. What the trend rate conceals, but what the actual rates show us, is that the shift to more private investment means heavier fluctuations.

In the regional policy set-up the task of government consumption is to complement the economic structure in the three regions as it follows from the parameter variations, such that the trend u.r. is identical for all regions. This complementary character can be most clearly demonstrated by looking at the optimal value of G_o for region 3. This value decreases if w goes from 1 to 0, since with $w=0$ region 3 stands to get more investment orders.

It slightly decreases if b is increased from .6 to .7, since in the long run a higher b will mean more private investment. The optimal value of G_{o3} remains the same if the elimination of contracyclical investment is compensated by a rise in A_o, because these are changes that affect only government investment. Actually, in this latter case the optimal distribution of $\sum G_{oi}$ as a whole remains the same, since non-private investment is produced in the region where it is needed.

It is interesting to compare the computer runs with optimal G_{oi}, with non-optimal runs of the I.M. Only in two cases is this possible, namely for runs 1725 and 1726, which can be compared with runs 1717 and 1718, that have the same set of parameter values but different distributions of G_o. Amazingly enough, the fluctuations in the optimal runs cover a wider range of u.r.s than the non-optimal runs, at least in regions 1 and 2. In all regions the optimal runs have equally deep or deeper troughs. Clearly, this comparison illustrates that the optimality criterion I used in this section does not reduce fluctuations.

Another comparison I can make is that between the national averages of the optimal I.M. runs and the P.M. runs with the same parameter values, just as I did in Chapter 4. Since some parameter variations were not tested before, I had to make additional runs cf the P.M. These runs, and the national averages of the optimal runs, are summarized in the upper part of Table 6.3. As indicated earlier, the comparison is actually one between an economy with immobile resources and an economy characterized by perfect mobility. In the latter, the concept of an optimal distribution of activities does not exist because the resources will be there where they are needed. As far as the time path of output during a business cycle is concerned, one expects higher peaks (or lower peak u.r.s), and deeper troughs (or higher trough u.r.s) in the economy with perfect mobility. This is what occurred in Chapter 4, and this is what we find here in most cases. For the three exceptions, all with $w=1$, and $A_o=0$ or A_o very low, the troughs are slightly deeper in the optimal runs (runs 1725, 1729 and 1731). I can explain these exceptions only by referring to the different amplitudes experienced by the three regions during the trough, and the different amounts of contracyclical investment to which this leads.[3]

6.3.4 Summary

I shall summarize the eight computer runs with an optimal distribution of government consumption as follows. It seems that the optimal policy, as defined in (6.10), perfectly complements the regional economic structure as it follows from the trade matrices, such that the trend rates of U, Q, and F will be the same in all regions. Taking the trend rates as a norm, however, does not allow us to take cyclical behaviour into consideration when the total amount of government consumption is given. As it turns out, the amplitudes of the fluctuations in the optimal runs are sometimes larger than those in comparable non-optimal runs (runs 1725, 1726 versus 1717, 1718). In all optimal runs the downward swings reach deeper than the upward swings are high. Reason for this asymmetry is the existence of ceilings in the economies. Otherwise the optimal policy does full justice to the oscillations that are implied by the economic characteristics of the regions, with region 3 having heavier fluctuations than the other regions because capital goods form a larger part of its regional product.

6.4. Adjusted Optimal Distributions: Equity Versus Stability

6.4.1 Equity Versus Stability

The previous section left us with somewhat of a dilemma: the choice between equity and stability. It is possible to allocate government consumption such that equal trend levels of output will result for all regions, but these trend levels are not close enough to full employment to free the economy from fluctuations. On the other hand, earlier experience (Chapter 3) shows that concentrating economic activities in a few regions will give these regions low u.r.s and stable or fairly stable growth, while the economies of the remaining regions have higher structural unemployment, but also stable growth because of the stabilizing influence of the low-unemployment regions.

Perfect stability, that is steady-state growth, is not difficult to accomplish, even when $\sum G_{oi} = 54$ and all parameter values are as in the base run. Run 1714 in Chapter 3 showed that allocating government consumption such that $G_{o1} = 27$, $G_{o2} = 0$, and $G_{o3} = 27$ led to steady-state growth, but also, of course, to inequity ($\bar{U}_1 = 8.4/8.5\%$, $\bar{U}_2 = 7.5/7.6\%$, $\bar{U}_3 = 2.1\%$). Steady-state growth with inequity means that some regions are growing along the ceiling (hence low u.r.s, $\bar{Q}_i = 1$ and $\bar{F}_i < 1$), while others grow along the floor (hence high u.r.s, $\bar{Q}_i > 1$ and $\bar{F}_i = 1$).

There is clearly a trade-off between equity and stability. Unless the government is willing, and able, to push up the level of economic activities to a point closer to full employment, so that there will be more of both (the absolute optimum being Golden Age growth), it will be a matter of give and take. In this section I shall take the equity point of view as a starting point, and from there on gradually reduce equity in favour of more stability, using the same total value of government consumption ($\sum G_{oi} = 54$) as in Section 6.2. How to obtain more stability while still maintaining the 'equality doctrine' as much as possible? As mentioned earlier, fixed business investment is the principal cause of instability in our model. With equal trend levels-of-output fluctuations will be severest

111

in the capital goods producing regions. It is therefore logical to shift government consumptive expenditure to the capital goods producing regions, to allow less room for fluctuations in those regions. More G_{oi} raises region i's floor level of expenditure, which will mean that the downward swings of the optimal runs of Section 6.3 will decrease in amplitude. Stated differently: part of the production space that was reserved for the production of capital goods will be occupied by G_{oi}, when government consumption is increased with respect to the optimal distribution of 6.3. Clearly, an increase in G_{oi} will raise the trend level of output in region i, but given $\sum G_{oi}$ it will necessarily leave one or more of the other regions with a lower trend level. This is the price paid for more stability.

6.4.2 The z-Method and an Example of How to Use It

The problem is now: by how much should government consumption increase in the capital goods producing regions? I shall solve this problem by introducing a coefficient z, which can vary between 0 and 1. This coefficient z gives the weight I attach to private investment in the trend version of our model. As mentioned, the trend level of private investment is an average level around which actual private investment would fluctuate if no buffers existed in the economy. Adopting a $z < 1$ means that I lower this average. I, so to speak, lower the centre of gravity of the private-investment time series, the idea being that, to be fair and stabilizing, a distribution of government consumption has to compensate the capital goods producing regions for the fact that fluctuations of output in these regions have deeper troughs than those of the other regions. With the lower weight attached to private investment, I then proceed by solving for what I shall call the 'adjusted optimal' distribution of $\sum G_{oi}$, in the same way as I did before. That is, again I take the P.M., solve for $\bar{U}$ and require that $\bar{U} = \bar{U}_i$, $\bar{Q} = \bar{Q}_i$, and $\bar{F} = \bar{F}_i$. Obviously, the new G_{oi} will be relatively higher, as region i's share in capital goods production increases. Also, the lower that z is, the higher the government consumption in the capital goods producing region will be, and the less room there will be for fluctuations in this region.

To clarify the procedure I followed, I shall again take trend subtype 2a as an example. The reduced-form equation for this type will now be written as:

$$\{(1/\bar{F})\,[1] - [SN/(e-1+\bar{F}s)]\,[c] - z(D/\bar{F} - G)\,[k] + (1/e)\,[1]\}\,\bar{X}_o$$
$$= \{[SP/(e-1+\bar{F}s)]\,[c] + (1/e)\,[1]\}\,K + G_o + A_o. \tag{6.12}$$

As can be seen from comparing (6.11) with (6.12), all I did was multiply the vector $(D/\bar{F} - G)\,[k]\,\bar{X}_o$ with a scalar z^4 to get the new reduced-form equation. The insertion of $z < 1$, however, has created two extra unknowns,

112

besides G_o. The values of $\bar{F}$ and $\bar{X}_o$ $[=(1-\bar{U})K]$, as I computed them from the P.M. are not valid any more. $\bar{X}_o$ will be lower, because of the underestimation of private investment in the trend equation, and $\bar{F}$ will change too. To get the correct $\bar{F}$ and $\bar{X}_o$ for each value of z, I should go back to the P.M. and compute them in the same way as I did before, but now with z included.[5] For our actual applications of the z-method I did not do this. Instead, I assumed that $\bar{F}$ would not change much, and used the already known value of $\bar{F}$ as an approximation. The value of the vector $\bar{X}_o$, and at the same time the distribution of $\sum G_{oi}$, was then found by trial and error, the desired distribution being the one that gave identical $\bar{X}_{oi}$s for all regions.

It should be stressed that this application of the z-method is an approximation. The lower that z is, the more the old and the new values of $\bar{F}$ will diverge and the less precise this approximation of the correct value will be. This puts restrictions on the range of values of z for which I can apply the method. Even when the correct $\bar{F}$ and $\bar{X}_o$ are computed these restrictions are there. For instance, as will be seen later, a $z=.7$ already can make the actual u.r.s in region 3 lower than those in regions 1 and 2. This can only happen because $\bar{X}_o$ is not the true trend level of output any more, but an adjusted trend. The point I want to make is that the z-method is not a method that optimizes the distribution of $\sum G_{oi}$ in the same way that the trend determining method did in Section 6.3. That is why I call the new distributions of government consumption 'adjusted optimal' distributions. They increase over-all stability by compensating the capital goods producing regions for the asymmetry of their cycles around the trend. If interregional equity is still our main goal of regional policy, it will be the interregional equality of actual average levels of unemployment that will determine the choice of the proper z. If I rank stability higher than equity (I cannot have both at the same time, given $\sum G_{oi}$ and A_{oi}), then I will have to look for a lower z. It is a matter of judgement which z to select. For low enough z the model will generate steady-state growth, but also considerable inequity.

6.4.3 Simulations with Adjusted Optimal Distributions

The computer runs with adjusted optimal distributions of $\sum G_{oi}$ are summarized in Table 6.2. Four runs were made with the parameter values of P.M., run 1601; five runs with the parameter values of run 1604, the P.M. base run. The only variations I experimented with were variations in z. National averages were computed for all nine runs. These are brought together in Table 6.3. From Table 6.2 it is clear that lowering z lowers the average rate of unemployment in region 3, and at the same time reduces the amplitude of the fluctuations in that region. On the other hand, in regions 1 and 2, which produce much less capital goods than region 3, a lower z causes milder fluctuations too, however with slightly higher average u.r.s.

Table 6.2

Interregional Model Simulations with Adjusted Optimal Distributions of Government Consumption

Run	P.M. Run	G_o^*	A_o	z	U low-high	Q low	F low	CL
1750	1601	33.71 6.37 13.92	0	.85	2.6–6.4 3.0–6.3 1.8–7.9	.98 .97 .96	.94 .95 .83	12/13
1744	1601	33.49 5.95 14.56	0	.80	3.0–6.4 3.5–6.4 1.9–7.4	.98 .98 .97	.95 .95 .83	12
1749	1601	33.28 5.53 15.19	0	.75	3.0–6.5 3.4–6.5 2.0–7.0	.98 .98 .97	.95 .95 .83	11
1743	1601	33.06 5.13 15.81	0	.70	3.0–6.7 3.0–6.5 2.1–6.4	.98 .98 .98	.95 .96 .83	10/11
1754	1604	33.31 5.82 14.87	3	.95	2.0–4.4 2.1–4.4 1.0–6.2	.98 .98 .96	.97 .98 .91	16
1753	1604	33.14 5.47 15.39	3	.90	2.1–4.4 2.5–4.5 0.9–5.7	.98 .98 .97	.98 .98 .91	16
1752	1604	32.96 5.15 15.89	3	.85	2.5–4.3 3.0–4.4 0.8–4.9	.98 .99 .97	.98 .98 .91	16
1748	1604	32.74 4.82 16.40	3	.80	2.9–4.4 3.4–4.6 0.9–4.7	.99 .98 .98	.98 .99 .91	16

Table 6.2 (continued)

Run	P.M. Run	G_o^*	A_o	z	U low-high	Q low	F low	CL
		32.41			3.6–4.3	.99	.99	
1747	1604	4.17	3	.70	4.0–4.6	.99	1.00	16
		17.42			1.1–3.9	1.00	.96	

See *Explanation* following Table 3.1.

Table 6.3

National Averages of Interregional Model Simulations with Optimal and Adjusted Optimal Distributions of Government Consumption

I.M. Run	P.M. Run	z	National Averages I.M. Run				P.M. Run			
			U low-high	Q low	F low	CL	U low-high	Q low	F low	CL
1725	1601	1	2.3– 7.0	.98	.90	12	1.9– 6.8	.98	.90	13
1726	1603	1	4.9–15.3	.99	.80	28	4.0–23.5	.94	.70	16
1727	1646	1	1.7– 4.9	.98	.96	15	0.9– 5.4	.97	.95	14/15
1728	1652	1	0.4–12.5	.93	.82	18	0.0–16.9	.91	.76	16/17
1729	1647	1	1.1– 6.9	.97	.90	12/13	1.0– 6.7	.97	.90	12/13
1730	1653	1	3.3–22.5	.93	.68	28	2.9–31.3	.86	.59	14
1731	1648	1	0.8– 6.1	.97	.93	14	0.4– 6.0	.97	.93	14
1732	1654	1	0.5–14.9	.92	.77	16	0.1–20.7	.89	.70	15
1750	1601	.85	2.5– 6.8	.98	.91	12/13	1.9– 6.8	.98	.90	13
1744	1601	.80	2.7– 6.5	.98	.91	12	1.9– 6.8	.98	.90	13
1749	1601	.75	3.0– 6.2	.98	.91	11	1.9– 6.8	.98	.90	13
1743	1601	.70	3.3– 5.9	.98	.91	10	1.9– 6.8	.98	.90	13
1754	1604	.95	1.9– 4.9	.98	.96	16	1.0– 5.5	.97	.94	14
1753	1604	.90	2.1– 4.7	.99	.96	16	1.0– 5.5	.97	.94	14
1752	1604	.85	2.3– 4.5	.99	.96	16	1.0– 5.5	.97	.94	14
1748	1604	.80	2.6– 4.2	.99	.96	16	1.0– 5.5	.97	.94	14
1747	1604	.70	3.1– 3.9	1.00	.97	16	1.0– 5.5	.97	.94	14

See *Explanation* following Table 3.1.

The changes in relative levels of unemployment are understandable since the adjusted optimal distribution of government consumption allocates more in region 3 and less in regions 1 and 2. The range of fluctuations in region 3 gets smaller for lower z because there is less and less room for fluctuations. This increased stability is then exported to regions 1 and 2, which are inherently stable, but which are affected by region 3's cycles through trade relationships.

The problem is now which value of z to choose. Starting at $z = .95$ or 1.00, the sequence of graphs in Figure 6.2 shows that for both sets of parameter values—1601 $(A_o = 0)$ and 1604 $(A_o = 3)$—the cycle of region 3 starts falling (falling because of the way in which I plotted unemployment), relative to those of regions 1 and 2, when I decrease z. At the same time all cycles flatten, that of region 3 the most. If I carry this process far enough, region 3's cycle will eventually be completely below the other two cycles: run 1747 with $z = .7$ is an example. In run 1743, with $z = .7$ for the 1601-economy, this has almost happened. Clearly, these are examples of an over-compensation for the capital goods producing region 3, examples in which interregional equity has been given up in favour of national and regional stability. If the goal is equity in the first place, with in addition a reasonable amount of stability, I shall have to look for a z in between those extreme values. Of the four runs with $A_o = 0$, run 1744 with $z = .8$ seems to come closest to the 'equity plus stability' ideal, although admittedly the fluctuations in region 3 are still over 5 unemployment percentage points. Of the remaining five runs with $A_o = 3$, run 1754 with $z = .95$ would probably give the best 'middle of the road' distribution of $\sum G_{oi}$. Again, however, the price paid for equity is a relatively high amplitude of the cycle of region 3.

Maybe the price tag of interregional equity is too high if I see what a lower z will accomplish. Again, for instance, take run 1754 and compare it with run 1747, the extreme case in which region 3's u.r. is always below the u.r.s of the other two regions. The obvious strong point of run 1747 is the high stability in all regions (the national u.r. varies between 3.1 and 3.9%); the weak point is the inequity: region 3 is favoured by the government at the expense of the other regions. Yet, it can be seen from the u.r.s of regions 1 and 2 that on average these are less than 1% higher than in run 1754, with its much heavier fluctuations (national u.r. range: 1.9–4.9%). It would seem then that the change from 1747 to 1754 means a greater gain for region 3 and in terms of over-all stability, then it is a loss for regions 1 and 2. Furthermore, the greater equality but lesser stability of run 1754 means lower minimum values of F (that is, stronger inflationary pressures).

Given these outcomes I am inclined to choose the more stable solution. A conclusive answer, however, expressed as a value for z, can only be given if an objective function is properly defined, with weights attached to each of our two goals of regional policy (and possibly to price stability as a third goal).

116

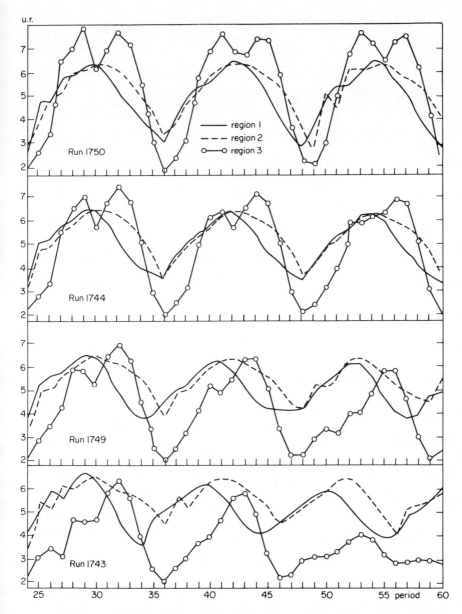

Figure 6.2　Interregional Model Runs with Adjusted Optimal
Distributions and $A_o = 0$

117

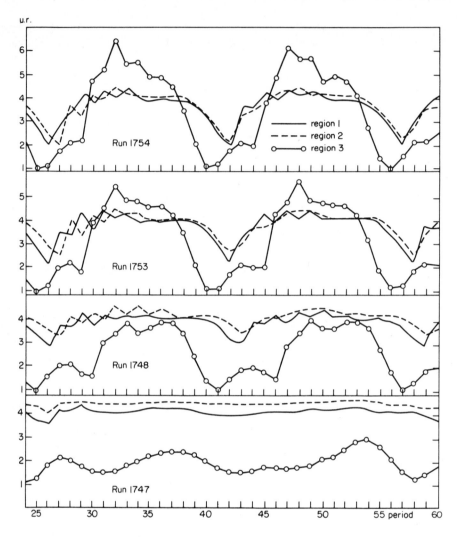

Figure 6.3　Interregional Model Runs with Adjusted Optimal
Distributions and $A_o = 3$

118

6.5 Conclusion

In this chapter I have developed a criterion for an optimal interregional distribution of a given amount of government expenditure. I defined optimality as equality of the trend rates of unemployment among regions. In the mathematical specification of optimality I included the inter-regional equality of $\bar{Q}_i$ and $\bar{F}_i$ in the objective function. When the trend rates of unemployment are required to be identical among regions, the problem of finding an optimal distribution of government expenditure is reduced to that of finding an optimal distribution of government consumption alone, since all regions can claim the same amount of government investment under this requirement.

Next to interregional equity, regional (and therefore also national) stability was adopted as the second goal of regional economic policy. In Section 6.3, equity was the only goal considered. In Section 6.4 I corrected the previously found optimal distribution of government consumption to obtain more stability, by under-representing the trend value of private investment, the most volatile output component. Those regions which produce more capital goods than others, received more government consumption in what I called the 'adjusted optimal' distribution.

The computer runs that were made with the optimal and adjusted optimal distributions of $\sum G_{oi}$ clearly showed it impossible to have both equity and stability at the same time, when the level of government consumption is given. Either of the two goals can be fully accomplished: there can be steady-state growth in all regions, with interregional differences in unemployment, or there can be equal trend levels of output for all regions, but with cycles. The instability of private investment is inherent in the model; I cannot get rid of it, unless I am willing to give up interregional equity. The only way to escape this dilemma is by raising the over-all level of expenditure such that the gap between the trend level of output and the ceiling is too small to allow cycles. It is also possible to adjust both government consumption and investment such that the 'optimum optimorum' will result in our certainty model: Golden Age growth.

It is interesting to note that there is a large number of possible solutions that will give steady-state growth in all regions, while there is only one distribution of $\sum G_{oi}$, the optimal distribution, that will give identical $\bar{U}_i$s, $\bar{Q}$s and $\bar{F}$s. In between these two extremes there is a number of adjusted optimal distributions of government consumption, for a range of values of the private-investment weighting coefficient z. Starting with the optimal distribution (which has z equalling unity) I can reduce the weight of private investment in the trend version of the model until an adjusted optimal distribution results that produces steady-state growth.

Weighting private investment less than fully does not give the true trend level, but a downward adjusted average. That is why the distributions of government consumption with $z<1$ were not called optimal, but rather adjusted optimal distributions: I use the term optimal only in connection with identical trend levels of $\bar{U}_i$, $\bar{Q}_i$ and $\bar{F}_i$ as the outcome for all regions. The virtue of the z-method is, however, that it enables us to compensate regions for the instability of private investment proportionally to the amount of capital goods they produce. Computer runs showed how equity can be traded for stability by decreasing the value of z. As far as this trade-off is concerned, it appeared that, by reducing z, more was gained in terms of a higher stability than was lost in the form of larger inter-regional differences in unemployment.

In the next chapters I shall look for additional or alternative ways to attain our two goals of equity and stability. In Chapter 7 I shall try to get an insight into how the trade matrices affect the stability of the system. In Chapter 8 I shall be looking for interregional equity when I allow migration to alter the thus far, fixed distribution of labour.

Appendix A: The Trend Determining Method for the Interregional Model

A typical outcome of the simulations of Chapter 3 was the following: full capacity utilization all the time for regions 1 and 2, with positive unemployment; less than full capacity utilization for region 3, also with positive unemployment. Furthermore: $X^P(t)<X^{FE}(t)$ and $V(t)>0$ most of the time for all regions. The types of trends for this outcome are: subtype 2a for regions 1 and 2, type 1 for region 3.

Below, this combination of trend types will be worked out to the point where I have reduced the trend version of the I.M. to three equations in three unknowns, the unknowns being $\bar{F}_1$, $\bar{F}_2$ and $\bar{Q}_3$. Once I know these rates the remaining trend rates can be computed from them.

The variables in the following equations are all vectors. The same abbreviations, denoted by capital letters, are used as in the Appendix to Chapter 5. The abbreviated letters are all scalars, except for K, which is a vector. The derivations below are for $w=1$.

Planned production

$$\bar{C}^P(t)=\begin{bmatrix} SN/(e-1+\bar{F}_1 s) & 0 & 0 \\ 0 & SN/(e-1+\bar{F}_2 s) & 0 \\ 0 & 0 & JN \end{bmatrix}\cdot[c]\,\bar{X}(t)$$

$$+\begin{bmatrix} SP/(e-1+\bar{F}_1 s) & 0 & 0 \\ 0 & SP/(e-1+\bar{F}_2 s) & 0 \\ 0 & 0 & JP \end{bmatrix}\cdot[c]\,X^{FE}(t), \qquad (6.13)$$

or, in abbreviated form

$$\bar{C}^p(t) = [\alpha]\,[c]\,\bar{X}(t) + [\beta]\,[c]\,X^{FE}(t). \qquad (6.13a)$$

$$\bar{J}^d(t) = [k] \cdot \begin{bmatrix} (1/\bar{F}_1)\,(D-G) & 0 & 0 \\ 0 & (1/\bar{F}_2)\,(D-G) & 0 \\ 0 & 0 & (D-G/\bar{Q}_3) \end{bmatrix} \cdot \bar{X}(t), \qquad (6.14)$$

or, in abbreviated form $\qquad \bar{J}^d(t) = [k]\,[\gamma]\,\bar{X}(t). \qquad (6.14a)$

$$\bar{G}^p(t) = (1+g)^t\,G_o \qquad (6.3)$$

$$\bar{A}^d(t) = (1/e)\,[X^{FE}(t) - \bar{X}(t)] + (1+g)^t\,A_o. \qquad (6.15)$$

From (6.13a), (6.14a), (6.3) and (6.15), and since[6] $\bar{X}^p(t) = [1/\bar{F}]\,\bar{X}(t)$:

$$[[1/\bar{F}] - [\alpha]\,[c] - [k]\,[\gamma] + (1/e)\,[1]]\,\bar{X}(t) = \\ (1+g)^t\,\{([\beta]\,[c] + (1/e)\,[1])\,K + [1]\,G_o + [1]\,A_o\}, \qquad (6.16)$$

or

$$\bar{X}(t) = (1+g)^t\,\{[\cdots]^{-1} \cdot ([\beta]\,[c] + (1/e)\,[1])\,K \\ + [\cdots]^{-1}\,G_o + [\cdots]^{-1}\,A_o\}. \qquad (6.17)$$

On the other hand, writing output as a function of full capacity output:[7]

$$\bar{X}(t) = (1+g)^t\,\bar{F} \begin{bmatrix} \dfrac{1}{C - \sum_1\,[(1/\bar{F}_1)\,D - G] + (1/e)\,\bar{F}_1} & 0 & 0 \\ 0 & \dfrac{1}{C - \sum_2\,[(1/\bar{F}_2)\,D - G] + (1/e)\,\bar{F}_2} & 0 \\ 0 & 0 & \dfrac{1}{C/\bar{Q}_3 - \sum_3\,[D - G/\bar{Q}_3] + (1/e)} \\ & & \cdot (1/e)\,K + A_o. \end{bmatrix} \cdot (1/e)\,K + A_o. \qquad (6.19)$$

Equating (6.17) and (6.18) will give three equations in three unknowns, the unknowns being $\bar{F}_1$, $\bar{F}_2$, and $\bar{Q}_3$.

Appendix B: Reduced-Form Equations for the Interregional Model When the Same Type of Trend Holds for All Regions

If all regions of the I.M. are characterized by the same type of trend and in addition by the same trend rates, the reduced-form equations I

121

developed for the P.M. can be readily transformed into reduced-form equations for the I.M. To solve for the optimal vector G_o under the above assumptions, I need only the first of the two reduced-form equations per trend type (that which expresses output as the sum of planned-production components), since A_o is either known or can be computed from the P.M. (see Section 6.3.2).

The notation below is as in the Appendix to Chapter 5. Again the abbreviated terms are all scalars, except K, which is a vector.

Trend type 1

$$\{[1] - JN[c] - (D - G/\bar{Q})[k] + (1/e)[1]\}\,\bar{X}_o =$$
$$\{JP[c] + (1/e)[1]\}\,K + G_o + A_o \qquad (6.19)$$

Trend type 2

Subtype 2a

$$\{(1...\bar{F})[1] - (SN/(e-1+\bar{F}s))[c] - (D/\bar{F} - G)[k] + (1/e)[1]\}\,\bar{X}_o =$$
$$\{(SP/(e-1+\bar{F}s))[c] + (1/e)[1]\}\,K + G_o + A_o \qquad (6.11)$$

Subtype 2b

$$\{(1/\bar{F})[1] - (SN/(e-1+\bar{F}s))[c] + G[k] + (1/e)[1]\}\,\bar{X}_o =$$
$$\{SP/(e-1+\bar{F}s))[c] + D[k] + (1/e)[1]\}\,K + G_o + A_o \qquad (6.20)$$

Subtype 2c

$$\{(1/\bar{F})[1] - (L/(1-A\bar{F}))[c] + G[k] + (1/e)[1]\}\,\bar{X}_o =$$
$$\{(M/(1-A\bar{F}))[c] + D[k] + (1/e)[1]\}\,K + G_o + A_o \qquad (6.21)$$

Trend type 3

Subtype 3a

$$(1/\bar{F})\,K = \{J(N+P)[c] + (D - G/\bar{Q})[k]\}\,K + G_o + A_o \qquad (6.22)$$

Subtype 3b

$$(1/\bar{F})\,K = \{((L+M)/(1-A\bar{F}))[c] + (D - G/\bar{Q})[k]\}\,K + G_o + A_o \qquad (6.23)$$

Trend type 4, Golden Age growth, is discussed in Section 6.2.

Notes

[1] See also Section 5.4.

[2] The * refers to the Golden Age value of the parametric constants.

[3] Although the direct relation between contracyclical investment and unemployment is linear, this is not the case once multiplier effects are taken into account: the amount of contracyclical investment generated by un-

employment in three regions is less than the amount generated by total unemployment, summed over the regions.

[4] A scalar because I weight each region's private investment identically.

[5] The corrected $\bar{F}$ and $\bar{X}_o$ can no longer be properly called trend values. By giving private investment a weight $z<1$ I am computing averages below the true trend. Their position with respect to the actual cycle will differ depending on the share of capital goods production in total regional output.

[6]
$$[1/\bar{F}]=\begin{bmatrix} 1/\bar{F}_1 & 0 & 0 \\ 0 & 1/\bar{F}_2 & 0 \\ 0 & 0 & 1/\bar{F}_3 \end{bmatrix} \text{ or in this case } \begin{bmatrix} 1/\bar{F}_1 & 0 & 0 \\ 0 & 1/\bar{F}_2 & 0 \\ 0 & 0 & 1 \end{bmatrix}.$$

[7]
In this equation, $[\bar{F}]=\begin{bmatrix} \bar{F}_1 & 0 & 0 \\ 0 & \bar{F}_2 & 0 \\ 0 & 0 & \bar{F}_3 \end{bmatrix} \text{ or in this case } \begin{bmatrix} \bar{F}_1 & 0 & 0 \\ 0 & \bar{F}_2 & 0 \\ 0 & 0 & 1 \end{bmatrix}$

and $\sum_i = \sum_j \bar{F}_j k_{ji}$.

7 Variations in the Trade Pattern

7.1 Introduction

At several places in this study I have emphasized that it is the industrial composition that causes regional differentials in cyclical behaviour. Thus I adhere to the industrial composition hypothesis, which holds that 'regional variations merely reflect the different weights of various industries in the industrial structure of the region'.[1] Differences in cyclical performance for reasons other than the industrial mix are not within the scope of this study, although admittedly specific regional factors might be of considerable importance in explaining regional cyclical differences. Different locations for instance might cause differences in costs and consequently different rates of growth for a certain industry, something which is assumed away by our model.[2] I shall only consider regional differentials caused by the industrial composition of the regions. In the I.M., the industrial composition is laid down in the trade matrices $[c]$ and $[k]$, and in the parametric constants, G_o and A_o. By the way in which I implemented these trade matrices in the previous chapters, one region (region 3) was endowed with the greater part of the capital goods production, and therefore unstable, while the other two regions had mainly stable industries and services within their borders. It is time now to see to what extent the regional outcomes as well as the national aggregates are affected by the particular implementation of the trade matrices. Can the economy be made more stable by changing the trade pattern? In regional economics texts, usually the desirability of introducing stable industries is stressed for regions that experience large fluctiations. This is the diversification argument (Engerman [1965, p. 295]). Section 7.4 will show how diversification affects our model, but before I test the I.M. for selected types of trade matrices, I shall, in Section 7.2, write the unconstrained versions of the P.M. and the I.M. as systems of first-order difference equations. That is, I shall write the models as if no buffers exist and as if all relationships between variables are linear. I shall then examine the system matrices of both unconstrained versions and see how interregional trade enters the economic system. The properties of the trade matrices alone are the subject of Section 7.3. In Section 7.5 I abandon the idea that trade between regions is entirely fixed according to the trade matrices. The I.M. is changed such that regions will satisfy unrealized production plans by importing from regions that have excess capacity. In this new version of the model the trade matrices $[c]$ and $[k]$ are average patterns around which the actual trade shares will flucutate. Finally, in Section 7.6 I offer some conclusions.

7.2 The Unconstrained Versions of the Prototype and Interregional Models as Systems of First-Order Difference Equations

As has been discussed earlier in this study, it is impossible to obtain an analytical solution for the P.M. or the I.M. because of the many inequalities and non-linearities in the two models. This was why I had to use the simulation technique to gain insight into the behaviour over a time interval of the national and regional economies, as described by the models. Only when I make the following assumptions can the two models be analytically solved, that is, written as a single higher-order difference equation or an equivalent system of first-order difference equations:

(a) No capacity or full employment constraints exist, i.e. $F(t)=1$ for all t. For the P.M. this means: equations (2.2) and (2.4) are deleted; (2.12) is changed into $X(t)=X^p(t)$. Full employment output as a concept is only used for computing unemployment benefits.

(b) Full employment output does not serve as an upper bound for the determination of desired capital stock as in (2.21) of the P.M.

(c) No non-negativity constraint exists for the desired-investment function. Equation (2.22) of the P.M. is changed into: $J^*(t)=b[K^*(t)- -(1-r)K(t)]$. This implies negative net investment if $K^*(t)<(1-r)K(t)$.

(d) $C^s(t)=C^d(t)$ for all t.

(e) w is either 0 or 1.

Actually, all these conditions would hold for trend type 1, which I discussed in Chapters 5 and 6, under steady-state growth conditions. Trend type 1 was characterized as: $\bar{U}>0$, $\bar{Q}<1$, $\bar{F}=1$, $\bar{V}(t)>0$ and $\bar{X}^p(t)<X^{FE}(t)$, and checking these characteristics with the first four assumptions above will show that trend type 1 satisfies these assumptions.[3] If an economy is of trend type 1 but not growing at the steady-state rate things are different, however. Depending on the amount of instability in the model the actual time path of output and its components will then fluctuate, and it is likely that during the course of a cycle the ceilings for instance will be active at least for one period, which immediately would violate assumption (a). Therefore, if the output path is fluctuating, it is only under the special condition of a trend type 1 economy growing without ever activating a ceiling, and with private investment always

126

being positive or zero that the assumptions above would hold, and that consequently output at time t in this economy could be written as a difference equation.

Despite the limited usefulness of the difference equation as an alternative way of exploring the properties of the two models, the analytical solution is helpful for another reason. That is that comparing the characteristic matrices, which I shall obtain for the unconstrained versions of the P.M. and the I.M. will show us where the trade relationships enter the characteristic matrices. From this some conclusions might be drawn as to the impact the trade matrices have on the stability of the economic system.

I shall solve both unconstrained models as systems of first-order difference equations. For the P.M., the equations I need are (assuming $w=1$):

$$C^p(t)=(1+sf)\,eC^d(t-1)-sV(t) \tag{7.1}$$

$$V(t)=C^p(t-1)+V(t-1)-C^d(t-1) \tag{7.2}$$

$$C^d(t)=a_2C^d(t-1)+(a_1-hW_ou)\,X(t)+hW_ouX^{FE}(t) \tag{7.3}$$

$$I^p(t)=(1-q)\,b\left[K^*(t-1)-(1-r)\,K(t-1)\right]+qb\left[K^*(t)\right. \\ \left.+(1-r)\,K(t)\right]-X(t-1)+X^{FE}(t-1)+A_o(1+g)^t \tag{7.4}$$

$$K(t)=(1-r)\,K(t-1)+I^p(t-1) \tag{7.5}$$

$$K^*(t)=ve^2X^p(t-1) \tag{7.6}$$

$$X(t)=C^p(t)+I^p(t)+G_o(1+g)^t. \tag{7.7}$$

Using the following abbreviations:

$$\alpha=(1+sf)\,e+s$$
$$\beta=b(1-r)\,(1-qr)$$
$$\gamma=a_1-hW_ou,$$

and making the necessary substitutions, the system matrix becomes:

$$
\begin{array}{l}
C^p(t) \\
V(t) \\
C^d(t) \\
I^p(t) \\
K(t) \\
K^*(t) \\
X(t)
\end{array}
\left[
\begin{array}{ccccccc}
-s & -s & \alpha & 0 & 0 & 0 & 0 \\
1 & 1 & -1 & 0 & 0 & 0 & 0 \\
-\gamma s & -\gamma s & (\alpha\gamma+a_2) & -\gamma qb(1-r) & -\beta\gamma & \gamma(1-q)\,b & \gamma qbve^2 \\
0 & 0 & 0 & -qb(1-r) & -\beta & (1-q)\,b & qbve^2-1 \\
0 & 0 & 0 & 1 & (1-r) & 0 & 0 \\
0 & 0 & 0 & 0 & 0 & 0 & ve^2 \\
-s & -s & \alpha & -qb(1-r) & -\beta & (1-q)\,b & qbve^2-1
\end{array}
\right] . \tag{7.8}
$$
$$
\begin{array}{ccccccc}
& C^p(t-1) & V(t-1) & C^d(t-1) & I^p(t-1) & K(t-1) & K^*(t-1) & X(t-1)
\end{array}
$$

127

In this 7×7 matrix, the columns one and two are identical, and the first and fourth row add up to row seven. Therefore the resulting seventh degree characteristic polynomial will have at least one zero root. This simplification, however, is not going to help much, since no general solution can be obtained for a characteristic polynomial that exceeds the fourth degree. Furthermore, the system matrix lacks a desirable property such as non-negativity, which would allow us to use the Perron-Frobenius theorems for non-negative square matrices.[4] Such matrices have among their characteristic roots one particular root, which is real and not exceeded in modulus by any other root of the system.

Since this dominant root will determine the long-term course of the economy, the stability problem would be solved by knowing the value of this largest real root, and computer programmes exist that can find this root. But since our characteristic matrix contains several negative entries no such readily obtainable solutions are available. Stability tests such as the Schur theorem[5] state stability conditions for higher-order difference equations. It would be too cumbersome, however, to study the characteristic equation qualitatively through these tests. The only alternative then is to devise algorithms to solve the characteristic polynomial for selected parameter values.[6] This, however, would be a time-consuming process too, and because of the limited applicability of the solutions that would be obtained in that way, I did not go into this.

If I make the same assumptions as for the P.M., and in addition assume that the regions all have identical parameter values, the equivalent of (7.8) for the I.M. will be:

$$
\begin{array}{c}
C^p(t) \\
V(t) \\
C^d(t) \\
I^r(t) \\
K(t) \\
K^*(t) \\
X(t)
\end{array}
\begin{bmatrix}
-s & -s & \alpha[c] & 0 & 0 & 0 & 0 \\
1 & 1 & -[c] & 0 & 0 & 0 & 0 \\
-\gamma s & -\gamma s & (\alpha\gamma[c]+a_2) & -\gamma[k]\, qb(1-r) & -\gamma[k]\,\beta & \gamma[k]\,(1-q)\,b & \gamma[k]\, qbve^2 \\
0 & 0 & 0 & -qb(1-r) & -\beta & (1-q)\,b & qbve^2-1 \\
0 & 0 & 0 & 1 & (1-r) & 0 & 0 \\
0 & 0 & 0 & 0 & 0 & 0 & ve^2 \\
-s & -s & \alpha[c] & -[k]\, qb(1-r) & -[k]\,\beta & [k]\,(1-q)\,b & [k]\, qbve^2-1
\end{bmatrix}.
$$
$$\qquad C^p(t-1) \quad V(t-1) \quad C^d(t-1) \quad I^r(t-1) \quad K(t-1) \quad K^*(t-1) \quad X(t-1) \tag{7.9}$$

With the number of regions being three, each entry in this matrix is actually a 3×3 submatrix. Altogether there are 7×7 of these submatrices. Each submatrix is either the scalar multiple of a trade matrix, or just a scalar matrix, or the sum of both.

If the solution of the characteristic polynomial of the P.M. is difficult to obtain, this 21×21 system matrix looks even less attractive. The first two columns of the partitioned matrix are again identical, which would reduce the order to 16 at least, but because of the trade interactions the first and the fourth row do not add up to row seven. If, however, relationships could be established between the 7×7 P.M. matrix and the 7×7 partitioned I.M. matrix, this would take us a long way in solving the stability problem for the I.M. As will be seen below, the trade matrices possess desirable features. The question then is: can I say anything at all about the roots of the I.M. system matrix given the properties of the trade matrices, if I already know the roots of the P.M. system matrix? A positive answer would be of considerable importance, not only for our I.M., but for any business cycle model in which interregional trade enters in a similar fashion. It would mean that first I would have to write the national version of an interregional model and find the characteristic roots of the national system, and then bring in interregional trade to arrive at a conclusion about the cyclical behaviour of the interregional system. Unfortunately, however, no theorems exist in matrix algebra that would enable us to establish such relationships between the P.M. system matrix and the partitioned I.M. system matrix.[7] Only in the simplest case, that of the Metzler-Goodwin-Chipman interregional model written as a first-order difference equation, is it possible to assess the influence of the trade matrix directly. This case will be worked out in the next section.

Once I accept the impossibility of developing useful theorems on the interaction of the trade matrices and the national system matrix, the only road open is that of again using the simulation technique. In Section 7.4 I shall report on the simulations I made of the I.M. with different selected trade matrices, and without the assumptions that made it an unconstrained model.

7.3 The Properties of the Trade Matrices

The interregional trade matrices $[c]$ and $[k]$ are necessarily column stochastic, that is, they are non-negative, square matrices with column entries adding up to one. These desirable properties mean that a number of theorems by Perron and Frobenius are particularly relevant for the trade matrices:

One, by Frobenius, stating that the characteristic roots of a matrix $[\alpha]$ are in absolute value less than, or equal to $\min(\beta, \gamma)$, where $\beta = \max \beta_i$ (β_i = sum of absolute values of the ith row), and $\gamma = \max \gamma_j$ (γ_j = sum of absolute values of the jth column).[8]

The well-known Perron-Frobenius theorems for non-negative square matrices that can be strengthened if the matrix is indecomposable and if the matrix is strictly positive (which necessarily means indecomposability). These matrices have a dominant root, such that:

(a)   this root is real and non-negative (or positive and non-repeated, if the matrix is indecomposable),

(b)   no other root has a modulus exceeding the dominant root (or, if the matrix is strictly positive: the dominant root exceeds the modulus of every other root).[9]

For any characteristic root λ_i of our trade matrices these theorems imply $0 \leq \lambda_i \leq 1$, in other words, the trade matrices as such are non-explosive.[10] But again, unfortunately, this does not permit us to draw any conclusions with respect to the stability of an interregional system matrix such as (7.9). Only in the first-order difference equation case when the trade matrix is at the same time the interregional system matrix, is over-all non-explosiveness implied.

I shall work out now two of the simplest interregional models. One is the first-order difference equation model to which I just referred (which is not a business cycle model), and the other is an interregional variant of the multiplier-accelerator model, which can be reduced to a second-order difference equation. This second model was presented before in Section 1.4.4, as the first of four models in Airov's 1963 summary article.

Using Airov's terminology,[11] the first model might be designated:

The Metzler-Goodwin-Chipman multiplier model
  In matrix notation:

$$C(t) = a_1 [c] X(t-1) \tag{7.10}$$

$$X(t) = C(t) + \bar{I}. \tag{7.11}$$

In this model the production of capital goods is exogenous (which is indicated by the bar on the variable I). No interregional shipments of capital goods take place. Capacity and full employment constraints are assumed away. I also assume that all regions have the same marginal propensity to consume a_1. Substituting (7.10) into (7.11) gives this non-homogeneous first-order difference equation:

$$X(t) = a_1 [c] X(t-1) + \bar{I}. \tag{7.12}$$

The stability of this system depends on the characteristic equation that I can derive from the matrix $a_1 [c]$. Since $[c]$ has column entries adding up to one, the matrix $a_1 [c]$ has column entries adding up to a_1. This means, according to the theorems I mentioned above, that each characteristic root is non-negative and less than, or equal to a_1. So, if $a_1 < 1$, the system is stable.[12]

130

In matrix notation again:

$$C(t) = a_1 [c] X(t-1) \tag{7.13}$$
$$I(t) = v[k] \{X(t-1) - X(t-2)\} + \bar{I}.^{13} \tag{7.14}$$

Investment here consists of an endogenous and an exogenous part. The former is traded, the latter not, just as government investment in the I.M. is not traded. The difference equation is now of the second order:

$$X(t) = (a_1 [c] + v[k]) X(t-1) - v[k] X(t-2) + \bar{I}. \tag{7.15}$$

Introducing $Z(t) = X(t-1)$, this second-order difference equation can be written as two first-order equations:

$$\begin{bmatrix} X(t) \\ Z(t) \end{bmatrix} = \begin{bmatrix} \{a_1 [c] + v[b]\} - v[k] \\ [1] \qquad 0 \end{bmatrix} \begin{bmatrix} X(t-1) \\ Z(t-1) \end{bmatrix} + \begin{bmatrix} \bar{I} \\ 0 \end{bmatrix}. \tag{7.16}$$

Compare (7.16) now with the equivalent equation for the national version of the multiplier-accelerator model:

$$\begin{bmatrix} X(t) \\ Z(t) \end{bmatrix} = \begin{bmatrix} (a_1 + v) & -v \\ 1 & 0 \end{bmatrix} \begin{bmatrix} X(t-1) \\ Z(t-1) \end{bmatrix} + \begin{bmatrix} \bar{I} \\ 0 \end{bmatrix}. \tag{7.17}$$

In (7.17), X, Z and I are scalars instead of vectors.

The cyclical properties of the national multiplier-accelerator model can be ascertained fairly easily, not because the system matrix possesses any nice properties, but simply because the characteristic equation is a simple second-order equation. Once I turn to the interregional version however, things are no longer as simple. The 2×2 system matrix then becomes a $2n \times 2n$ matrix, or for $n=3$, a 6×6 matrix. This 6×6 matrix lacks the desirable features that could help us give a quick answer to the stability question. In this particular case, writing the characteristic equation of (7.17) will still be feasible, because of the low number of regions and the quadrant of zeros in the system matrix. For larger n, however, and for other second-order difference equation models even that becomes a time-consuming task.

Building more sophisticated economic models will very likely increase the order of the difference equation and make the cyclical behaviour of the economy more difficult to ascertain. The P.M. and the I.M. are evidence of the difficulties I face when I attempt to arrive at some general conclusions concerning the stability of our economic systems, even when I simplify these systems such that they fit the mould of the difference equation solution method. This all leads to simulation as the only feasible method of investigating to what extent the trade matrices affect the cyclical behaviour of the regional and national economies.

7.4 Variations in the Trade Matrices

In this section I want to report on three different kinds of experiments which I conducted with the I.M. For the first group of experiments I simulated the I.M. with the base-run parameter values, and with government consumption and government autonomous investment distributed equally over the regions for certain symmetrical trade patterns (7.4.1). The second group concerned computer runs with (adjusted) optimal distributions of government consumption, and trade patterns such that a region has the same constant share of the national market as well as all regional markets for a certain product (7.4.2). Finally, using this same trade pattern I varied the regional shares with private investment being zero all the time, which means that any fluctuations that do occur in the simulations cannot be caused by private investment (7.4.3).

7.4.1 Symmetrical Trade Patterns

Giving the regions equal shares of government consumption and investment ($G_{oi} = 18$, $A_{oi} = 3$) and using the base-run parameter values, I simulated the I.M. with the following 'well-behaved' symmetrical trade patterns:

$$[c] = [k] = \begin{bmatrix} (1-2\beta) & \beta & \beta \\ \beta & (1-2\beta) & \beta \\ \beta & \beta & (1-2\beta) \end{bmatrix}, \text{ where } 0 < \beta < \tfrac{1}{2}. \tag{I}$$

In this set-up each region exports equal percentages of its total production to its two leading partners. Two subcases can be distinguished:
   (a)   production for internal use is equal to or larger than export production: $(1-2\beta) \geq 2\beta$, or $0 < \beta \leq \tfrac{1}{4}$,
   (b)   production for internal use is smaller than export production: $(1-2\beta) < 2\beta$, or $\tfrac{1}{4} < \beta < \tfrac{1}{2}$.

Both cases lead to identical time paths for all regions. Hence it does not make any difference whether a region exports 90% of its total output (and consequently also imports 90% of its expenditures, assuming identical spending parameters), or just 10%. Not surprisingly, the time path generated is that of the P.M. base run: the range of u.r.s is 1.0–5.5%, the lowest Q .97, the lowest F .94, and the cycle length 14 periods.

$$[c] = [k] = \begin{bmatrix} (1-\beta) & \beta & 0 \\ \beta & (1-2\beta) & \beta \\ 0 & \beta & (1-\beta) \end{bmatrix}, \text{ or } \begin{bmatrix} (1-2\beta) & \beta & 0 \\ 2\beta & (1-2\beta) & 2\beta \\ 0 & \beta & (1-2\beta) \end{bmatrix}, \tag{II}$$

where $0 < \beta < \tfrac{1}{2}$.

These are examples of 'well-behaved' trade matrices when three regions are located in a row geographically, trading only with the adjacent region(s). Simulating with matrices such as these produces the same extreme values of U, Q and F as under I, with slight differences (in the order of .1% unemployment) between the 'middle' region and the other two during the course of a cycle.

$$[c] = [k] = \begin{bmatrix} 1 & 0 & 0 \\ 0 & (1-\beta) & \beta \\ 0 & \beta & (1-\beta) \end{bmatrix}, \text{ where } 0 < \beta < 1. \qquad \text{(III)}$$

Here is the case of one region being isolated while the other two trade. The time path of region 1's economy is, of course, the base-run time path of the P.M. Slight differences with the other two regions may again occur during the course of a cycle.

Of course, more 'well-behaved', symmetrical trade matrices can be devised. The three types with which I simulated the I.M. suggest that as long as interregional trade takes place in a similar symmetrical way, regions will be alike, cyclically speaking. The not surprising outcomes, however, are of limited value since all trade patterns imply that the national production of consumption and capital goods is perfectly distributed over the three regions.

Specialization takes place, but if it does, it does so in a perfect way, so that no region is better off than another. Output levels will only be different if I mix consumption goods trade matrices of a certain type with capital goods trade matrices of another type such that concentrations of production take place.

7.4.2 *Identical Regional and National Production Shares*

Another type of specialization with which I shall deal next is that in which regions hold certain shares of the market for certain goods, these shares being the same nationally as in each region. In our macro-model these goods will be either consumption goods or capital goods. The trade matrices will be of this general form:

$$\begin{bmatrix} \alpha & \alpha & \alpha \\ \beta & \beta & \beta \\ (1-\alpha-\beta) & (1-\alpha-\beta) & (1-\alpha-\beta) \end{bmatrix},$$

where $0 < \alpha < 1$, $0 < \beta < 1$, $(\alpha+\beta) < 1$.

In empirical work this trade pattern might serve as a useful first approximation when regional shares in national output are known but a breakdown per region is not available. Using these same shares to determine imports from, and exports to, other regions is the most neutral assumption that can be made when no data are available that indicate otherwise.

I have used various numerical combinations of these trade matrices, to simulate the I.M. with adjusted optimal distributions of government consumption, allocating the same total initial amount as in Chapter 6 ($\sum G_{oi}=54$) and again using the z-method to accomplish smaller fluctuations (see 6.4.2). Table 7.1 gives a summary of my findings. The national averages for these simulations are in Table 7.2. All runs are with the base-run parameters, i.e. $A_{oi}=3$. Five runs were made with $z=.7$ (which, as we recall from Chapter 6, gave u.r.s for region 3 that were always lower than those for the other two regions in the adjusted

Table 7.1

Interregional Model Simulations with Selected Trade Matrices and Adjusted Optimal Distributions of Government Consumption

	Trade Matrices							
Run	[c]	[k]	G_o^*	z	U low-high	Q low	F low	CL
	.3 .3 .3	.3 .3 .3	24.88		1.1–5.6	.98	.96	
1755	.4 .4 .4	.2 .2 .2	8.32	.7	2.1–5.5	.97	.97	15
	.3 .3 .3	.5 .5 .5	20.80		1.0–5.3	.97	.93	
		.3 .3 .3	24.88		1.8–4.6	.98	.97	
1756	id.	.1 .1 .1	10.36	.7	3.9–5.0	.99	.99	15/16
		.6 .6 .6	18.76		1.1–4.0	.98	.94	
		.2 .2 .2	27.15		3.2–4.3	.99	.99	
1757	id.	.1 .1 .1	10.24	.7	4.3–4.8	.99	1.00	16
		.7 .7 .7	16.61		1.2–3.4	1.00	.95	
		.1 .1 .1	28.96		4.5–4.6	.99	1.00	1.00
1758	id.	.1 .1 .1	10.36	.7	4.4–4.5	1.00	1.00	—
		.8 .8 .8	14.68		1.7	1.00	.97	
	.4 .4 .4	.2 .2 .2	8.32		3.0–4.6	.99	.99	
1760	.4 .4 .4	.1 .1 .1	10.36	.7	4.0–4.9	.99	1.00	15
	.2 .2 .2	.7 .7 .7	35.32		1.1–3.7	.98	.95	
	.3 .3 .3	.3 .3 .3	25.00		1.0–5.4	.98	.95	
1764	.4 .4 .4	.2 .2 .2	8.69	.8	1.5–5.3	.97	.96	14/15
	.3 .3 .3	.5 .5 .5	20.31		1.1–6.0	.96	.93	

Table 7.1 (continued)

Run	[c]	[k]	G_o^*	z	U low-high	Q low	F low	CL
1765	id.	$\begin{bmatrix} .3 & .3 & .3 \\ .1 & .1 & .1 \\ .6 & .6 & .6 \end{bmatrix}$	25.00 11.04 17.96	.8	1.5–4.3 3.1–4.9 1.1–5.0	.98 .98 .97	.96 .98 .93	15
1766	$\begin{bmatrix} .3 & .3 & .3 \\ .4 & .4 & .4 \\ .3 & .3 & .3 \end{bmatrix}$	$\begin{bmatrix} .2 & .2 & .2 \\ .1 & .1 & .1 \\ .7 & .7 & .7 \end{bmatrix}$	27.40 10.93 15.67	.8	2.8–4.4 3.4–4.7 1.1–3.9	.99 .99 .98	.98 .99 .94	16
1767	id.	$\begin{bmatrix} .1 & .1 & .1 \\ .1 & .1 & .1 \\ .8 & .8 & .8 \end{bmatrix}$	29.70 11.03 13.27	.8	3.7–4.4 3.6–4.4 1.3–3.5	.99 .99 .99	.99 .99 .95	17

Trade Matrices

See *Explanation* following Table 3.1.

Table 7.2

National Averages of Interregional Model Simulations with Selected Trade Matrices and Adjusted Optimal Distributions of Government Consumption

I.M. Run	[c]	[k]	G_o^*	z	U low-high	Q low	F low	CL
	Regional Shares				National Averages I.M. Run			
1755	.3/.4/.3	.3/.2/.5		.7	1.5–5.1	.98	.95	15
1756	id.	.3/.1/.6		.7	2.5–4.4	.99	.97	15/16
1757	id.	.2/.1/.7		.7	3.1–4.1	1.00	.98	16
1758	id.	.1/.1/.8		.7	3.6	1.00	.99	—
1760	.4/.4/.2	.2/.1/.7	See Table 7.1	.7	2.8–4.3	.99	.98	15
1764	.3/.4/.3	.3/.2/.5		.8	1.4–5.4	.98	.95	14/15
1765	id.	.3/.1/.6		.8	2.1–4.7	.99	.96	15
1766	id.	.2/.1/.7		.8	2.6–4.2	.99	.97	16
1767	id.	.1/.1/.8		.8	3.1–4.1	1.00	.98	17
comp. P.M. Run:								
1604					1.0–5.5	.97	.94	14

See *Explanation* following Table 3.1

optimal situation), and four runs with $z = .8$. Otherwise, the only variations I made concerned the trade matrices.

Runs 1755 to 1758 (with $z = .7$) and runs 1764 to 1767 (with $z = .8$) combine constant regional shares in the production of consumption goods (.3/.4/.3) with a sequence of capital goods production shares in which this production sector is increasingly concentrated in one region, region 3. The adjusted optimal distribution of $\sum G_{oi}$ adjusts itself to this concentration by allocating less government consumption in region 3, the larger that region 3's investment share becomes. Tables 7.1 and 7.2 show that the national economy becomes more stable, the larger that region 3's investment share is. In general it is true for this model that a concentration of production in a few regions will have a stabilizing effect, by bringing the output level closer to the capacity ceilings in those regions. This stabilizing effect propagates itself through the economy to make all regions more stable. The extreme case is 'upper' steady-state growth in the regions of concentration, and 'lower' steady-state growth in the others. Run 1714 in Chapter 3 was an example of this. Part of the explanation of the higher stability, however, is the coefficient z. The smaller z, the more that capital goods producing regions will be compensated for the fluctuations they suffer from, and the more concentrated capital goods production is, the more effective the compensation. Actually, a $z = .7$ clearly over-compensates when capital goods production is as concentrated as in runs 1757 and 1758, to the point that interregional equity is given up in favour of stability.

Run 1760, which features the only variation in consumption goods production shares, can be compared with run 1757. It is interesting to see which impact a change in the production shares has on the adjusted optimal distribution of $\sum G_{oi}$. It can be seen that stability is not increased by taking away consumption from region 3, despite a higher optimal G_{o3}.

7.4.3 Identical Regional and National Production Shares and Steady-State Growth

Simulating the I.M. with the base-run parameters, but with $G_{oi} = 0$ will bring regional output down to a level at which private investment is zero all the time in all regions, unless the concentration of production is such that in one or more regions still some private investment is invoked. Keeping $J_i^*(t) = 0$ for all t has the advantage that the prime cause of fluctuations is eliminated so that simulations with a quick convergence to steady state can be expected. The speed of this will depend on the choice of values for the lagged endogenous variables.

Runs 1768 to 1772 were made so that this expectation could be confirmed. Using the trade matrices variations of runs 1755 to 1760, the

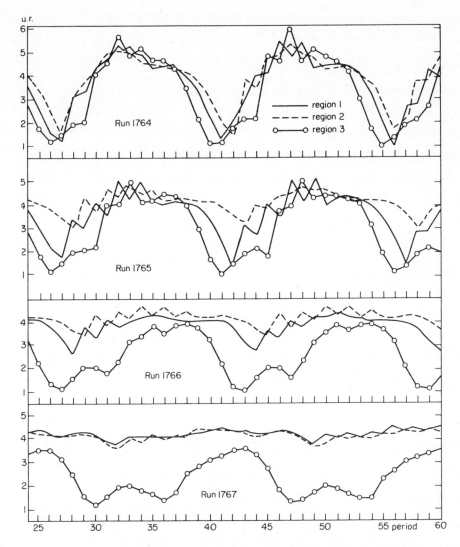

Figure 7.1   Interregional Model Runs with Selected Trade Matrices and
Adjusted Optimal Distributions of Government Consumption

output time paths of the three regions converge to steady state in all five runs, steady state being a fact around period 60. This convergence process takes place in the form of two-period cycles with the largest fluctuations occurring in the region with the lowest level of activities. Since private investment is zero all the time, the matrix $[k]$ does not affect the regional levels of output any more. It does, however, affect the amplitude of the fluctuations such that the more uneven the distribution of private investment is, the larger the range of u.r.s is. Compare, for instance, runs 1768 and 1771 in Table 7.3. In region 1, which together with region 3 has the lowest level of activities, the u.r. amplitude at periods

Table 7.3

Interregional Model Simulations with Selected Trade Matrices
and $G_o = 0$

Run	[c]			[k]			U low-high	Q low	F low	CL	National Average U
1768	.3 .3 .3 .4 .4 .4 .3 .3 .3			.3 .3 .3 .2 .2 .2 .5 .5 .5			18.3–28.1 10.0–19.3 23.0–23.5	.50 .78 .51	1.00 1.00 1.00	2	20.4
1769	id.			.3 .3 .3 .1 .1 .1 .6 .6 .6			18.3–28.1 10.9–18.0 22.1–24.5	.50 .79 .51	1.00 1.00 1.00	2	20.4
1770	id.			.2 .2 .2 .1 .1 .1 .7 .7 .7			17.3–29.0 10.9–18.3 21.1–25.5	.50 .79 .51	1.00 1.00 1.00	2	20.4
1771	id.			.1 .1 .1 .1 .1 .1 .8 .8 .8			16.2–30.1 11.0–18.2 19.9–26.7	.49 .80 .50	1.00 1.00 1.00	2	20.4
1772	.4 .4 .4 .4 .4 .4 .2 .2 .2			.2 .2 .2 .1 .1 .1 .7 .7 .7			7.7–21.1 14.0–15.0 25.0–39.3	.77 .83 .33	1.00 1.00 1.00	2	20.4
1774	.4 .2 .2 .4 .5 .4 .2 .3 .4			.4 .2 .1 .1 .1 .1 .5 .7 .8			25.6–26.7 11.2–11.5 21.8–23.3	.44 .95 .53	1.00 1.00 1.00	2	20.0

See *Explanation* following Table 3.1.

24 and 25^{14} increases from 9.8% in run 1768 (shares: .3/.2/.5) to 13.9% in run 1771 (shares: .1/.1/.8).

The two-period cycle that appears in runs 1768 to 1772 was also found in the I.M. base run and some of the other runs discussed in Chapter 3. In Section 3.4.3 I stated that this cycle could be generated if the contracyclical investment coefficient w was equal to 1, and if the output level was such that at all times $F=1$ would hold. In runs 1768 to 1772 these conditions are satisfied by all three regions.

Although conceivably the two-period cycle could also be generated by the national P.M., here it is only an interregional phenomenon. If national averages of our runs are taken, it will be found that from period 17 on, the national u.r. is at its steady-state level ($\bar{U}=20.4\%$), regardless of the distribution of economic activities. That is, while the regions go through considerable fluctuations, the national figures show a perfectly stable economy! Actually, the two-period cycles of the individual regions compensate each other in such a way that the national average time path is identical to the time path generated by the comparable P.M. run with $G_o=0$ and $A_o=3$.

Things are a little different if I take the base-run trade matrices with $G_{oi}=0$ (run 1774 in Table 7.3). Again, there is the two-period cycle in all regions, converging to steady state, but the convergence is completed before period 60. Again, the national u.r. is at its steady-state level in the early periods of the simulation, but now this steady-state level is 20.0% instead of 20.4% unemployment, while private investment is positive. The explanation for these differences is that the base-run trade matrices allocate so much production in region 2, that autonomous and contracyclical investment alone do not provide enough capacity to carry out all production plans. Hence a positive $J_2^*(t)$, which leads to production of capital goods in all regions according to region 2's import pattern. And hence the lower steady-state u.r.

7.5 Simulations with Flexible Trade Patterns

Thus far the I.M. has been a model in which interregional trade was fixed according to the trade matrices $[c]$ and $[k]$. Among other things, the fixed-trade coefficients implied that regions would not attempt to satisfy unrealized demand by importing from regions with excess productive capacity, when their usual trading partners would be unable to meet all demand. In this section I shall relax the fixed-trade assumption and make the trade pattern more flexible by allowing this pattern to vary according to the regional differences in productive capacity. I shall assume that deviations from the trade pattern as given by $[c]$ and $[k]$ are allowed if in that way more regional demand for consumption and capital goods can be satisfied than otherwise would have been the case.[15]

There are several ways to make the trade pattern more flexible in our model, but the simplest is by changing the 'actual production' part of the I.M. The main part of such a change in the model is an allocative mechanism that channels excess demand and distributes it over the excess-supply regions in proportion to the relative size of excess demand and excess supply.[16] Applying this relative-size rule, the new 'actual production' section becomes:

$$X_i(t) = \min\left[X_i^P(t),\, X_i^M(t)\right] \tag{3.12}$$

$$E_i(t) = X_i^P(t) - X_i^M(t) \tag{7.18}$$

$$E^d(t) = \sum_i \max\left[0,\, E_i(t)\right] \tag{7.19}$$

$$E^s(t) = \sum_i \max\left[0,\, -E_i(t)\right] \tag{7.20}$$

$$X_i'(t) = X_i(t) + \max\left\{0,\, -E_i(t)\left[E^d(t)/E^s(t)\right]\right\}, \\ \text{if } E^d(t) < E^s(t) \tag{7.21a}$$

$$X_i'(t) = X_i^M(t),\ \text{if } E^d(t) \geq E^s(t) \tag{7.21b}$$

$$U_i(t) = 1 - \left[u_i X_i'(t)/L_i^{eu}(t)\right] \tag{7.22}$$

$$Q_i(t) = v_i X_i'(t)/K_i(t) \tag{7.23}$$

$$F_i(t) = 1,\ \text{if } E^d(t) < E^s(t) \tag{7.24a}$$

$$F_i(t) = \left[X_i(t) + \max\left\{0,\, E_i(t)\left[E^s(t)/E^d(t)\right]\right\}\right]/X_i^P(t), \\ \text{if } E^d(t) \geq E^s(t) \tag{7.24b}$$

$$C_i(t) = F_i(t)\, C_i^P(t) \tag{3.16}$$

$$G_i(t) = F_i(t)\, G_i^P(t) \tag{3.17}$$

$$I_i(t) = F_i(t)\, I_i^P(t). \tag{3.18}$$

Here, E_i is the excess demand for region i's productive capacity,

E^d is the sum of positive regional excess demand,

E^s is the sum of negative regional excess demand, and

X_i' is the output after excess productive capacity has been employed in region i to satisfy excess demand from other regions.

The allocative mechanism operates as follows:

First, excess demand and excess supply are computed, per region and for the economy as a whole [(7.18) to (7.20)].

Output in the regions that do have excess productive capacity will then be adjusted upwards if there are regions that have excess demand. If $E^d(t) > E^s(t)$, all regions will operate at full capacity. Otherwise output will go up in the excess-supply regions proportionally to the size of regional excess supply [see (7.21a) and (7.21b)].

Once I know corrected output, $X_i'(t)$, I can compute the rates $U_i(t)$, $Q_i(t)$ and $F_i(t)$. The latter rate will be unity in all regions if total excess demand is smaller than total excess supply. If $E^d(t) > E^s(t)$, $F_i(t)$ will be determined by the fraction of unrealized production plans that can be realized through production in excess supply regions [(7.22) to (7.24b)].

It is possible to compute the distribution of additional production in terms of the receiving region, that is, to correct the 'actual sales' part of the I.M. to cope with flexible trade. It is also conceivable to implement the trade matrices as they actually will be in every period, but because of the computational difficulties that would be involved I have refrained from producing these by-products,[17] which are not necessary for simulating the flexible-trade model.

Four of the I.M. simulations of Chapter 3 were again carried out, but now with flexible trade (runs 2301 to 2304). In addition, three runs were made with adjusted optimal distributions of government consumption (runs 2305, 2306 and 2308). See Table 7.4 for the presentation of these runs. In general the flexible-trade economy will be more cyclical: during a boom fewer resources will be left unused, and more capital goods will be produced, but this will imply more excess capacity during a depression. And indeed, the simulations show that invariably the ranges of u.r.s become larger and that the minimum values of Q and F become smaller in the flexible-trade simulations. In addition, steady-state growth becomes growth with fluctuations again (run 2304). The adjusted optimal runs ($z < 1$), too, differ from their fixed-trade equivalents, although the differences are smaller, the closer z is to 1 (runs 2306 and 2308). The reason for this is that an optimal distribution (that is, one with $z = 1$) will bring more equity in terms of the variable F. It is only when some regions have an $F < 1$, while for others $F = 1$ at the same time, that a higher national output can be materialized through additional trade. The regional Fs will differ more from each other when z is lower, or for that matter, the more the distribution of government consumption deviates from the optimum.

The summary of Table 7.4 does not give the whole picture. For example, it fails to show that cycles can be subdivided into a long expansionary phase and a very short contractionary phase (on the average four periods long). Better utilization of productive resources sustains the expansion

Table 7.4

Interregional Model Simulations with Flexible Trade Patterns

Run	I.M. Run	w	G_o	A_o	z	U low-high	Q low	F low	CL	U low-high	CL
			36			1.0–3.6	.98	.96		1.1–3.0	
2301	1716	1	10	3		1.1–3.3	.99	.95	14	1.3–2.1	9
			8			0.0–11.8	.91	.91		5.5–8.9	
			36			2.1–6.5	.98	.91		2.1–5.5	
2302	1717	1	10	0		2.2–6.0	.98	.92	13/14	2.5–5.1	15
			8			0.8–12.3	.93	.86		1.9–9.3	
			36			4.7–11.8	1.00	.86		4.7–10.8	
2303	1718	0	10	0		4.8–13.3	1.00	.88	28	4.8–12.6	28
			8			4.6–19.7	1.00	.72		4.7–19.0	
			42			1.2–2.9	1.00	.88		2.0	
2304	1721	1	12	3		1.1–2.9	1.00	.91	9	1.8	—
			9			0.0–12.4	.99	.79		5.5	
			32.41			0.2–6.1	.96	.95		3.6–4.3	
2305	1747	1	4.17	3	.7	3.4–4.9	.98	.99	14	4.0–4.6	15
			17.42			0.4–5.0	.98	.93		1.1–3.9	
			33.14			1.1–5.9	.96	.96		2.1–4.4	
2306	1753	1	5.47	3	.9	2.4–4.8	.99	.98	15	2.5–4.5	16
			25.39			0.8–5.8	.95	.92		0.9–5.7	
			33.49			3.4–7.0	.98	.96		3.0–6.4	
2308	1744	1	5.95	0	.8	3.3–6.6	.98	.95	13	3.5–6.4	12
			14.56			1.4–9.0	.96	.82		1.9–7.4	

For other key figures of the comparable I.M. runs see Tables 3.1 and 6.1. See also *Explanation* following Table 3.1.

of the economy, while contracyclical investment keeps the depression relatively short. Run 2303, with $w=0$, is of course an exception.

Despite the better utilization of productive resources the average level of unemployment in regions 1 and 2 is higher when trade is flexible. It is region 3 that benefits from the flexibility. On comparing for instance, the time series of the I.M. base run (run 1716) with those of run 2301, this is evident. While F_3 equals 1 all the time in 1716, it drops below 1 during the early expansionary periods of run 2301. In addition, region 3's average u.r. is lower in run 2301 than in run 1716. So again there is the familiar trade-off between stability and interregional equity. Flexible trade patterns give more equity at the expense of over-all stability.

Finally, I want to remind the reader of an implicit assumption I am making when I allow flexible trade patterns. In our model, region 3 is the region that benefits from the additional trade by producing goods that originally were ordered from regions 1 and 2. The assumption I have to make is that region 3 has the resources to produce these goods. One reason for assuming fixed-trade coefficients in the I.M. was that regions are endowed with different resources, which precludes the production of certain goods in certain regions. Flexible trade then is only possible when the products involved are those from 'foot-loose' industries.

7.6 Conclusion

The trade matrices and their impact on the stability of the interregional economy were the topic of investigation of Chapter 7. Unfortunately, in this conclusive section I cannot offer many conclusive answers. In Section 7.2 I wrote the unconstrained versions of the P.M. and the I.M. as systems of first-order difference equations. The purpose of this was to compare the system matrices of both unconstrained models, and to possibly derive meaningful conclusions as to how interregional trade affects the stability properties of the P.M. system. It turned out, however, that the P.M. system matrix is too complex to determine its stability properties, and of course the same holds for the even more complex interregional system matrix. Knowing the properties of the trade matrices as such (Section 7.3) does not help us to determine their impact on the stability of the interregional economy.

When the complexity of economic systems restrains us from deriving analytical solutions, the only road open is that of simulation. Section 7.2 offers the best justification for our reliance on this technique throughout this study. Simulation, however, is not without its drawbacks. As Orcutt [1960, p. 893] states: 'To determine how the behavior of the endogenous variables is more generally dependent on initial conditions, parameters and exogenous variables may require a very large number of simulation runs; and even then induction from specific results to general solutions will be required.'

Therefore, the following statement is only a supposition. Based upon simulations in this and previous chapters I conclude that the behavior of the economic agents as expressed in consumption and investment functions is responsible for the general character of a cycle. I believe that trade matrices do not alter the stability properties of an economic system as it would have been without the existence of buffers. Trade matrices do, however, determine the amplitude of the regional cycles' economies in terms of the composition of consumption goods and capital goods production. They also affect—due to the existence of ceilings—the length of the cycles since the trade matrices determine how close to the capacity ceilings the regional economies operate. I found this gap between actual and capacity output to be an active determinant of the cycle length.

Airov [1963], in what was the first comprehensive article on inter-regional business cycle models, makes a similar, although less far-reaching statement concerning the influence of trade on the cyclical behaviour of an interregional economy. He writes:

Given the diversity of regions, each will have a cycle that differs in amplitude depending (1) on its economic structure, that is, the internal composition of stable consumption and un-stable investment output, and (2) its ties through trade with other regions and their stability and instability. But the cycle in each region will be of the same general type—and in the nation as well.[18]

What Airov is saying is that given the trade matrices, or in general, the trade relationships between regions, these will affect the eigenvectors of each characteristic root and therefore the amplitude of the regional cycles. The question I attempted to answer in this chapter is: Do trade relation-ships affect the roots of the characteristic equation? Our supposition is that economic behaviour, and economic behaviour only, determines the character of the interregional model cycle as expressed in the roots of the characteristic equation.

If our hypothesis is correct it implies that an otherwise stable economy cannot become unstable because of the way in which interregional trade takes place. In that case the desirability of a particular trade pattern can be stated entirely in terms of our two goals of economic policy, namely interregional equity and regional stability. The 'well-behaved' matrices of Section 7.4.1 will give perfect interregional equity, when matched by identical levels of government expenditure in all regions. The cyclical fluctuations generated by these matrices are identical for each region and equal to those that would be generated by economic models without interregional trade. On the other hand, perfect stability (i.e. steady-state growth) on the regional level requires the concentration of production in a few regions such that the level of production in these regions is pushed up to the capacity ceilings. By doing this cycles that would be generated in an unconstrained economy are prevented from running their normal course. This causes 'upper' steady-state growth in the regions of concentration, and 'lower' steady-state growth in the other regions.

Allowing more flexible trade patterns by changing the 'actual production' section of the I.M., as I did in Section 7.5, certainly adds realism to the model. Even though in reality trade patterns may be stable, import coefficients are not fixed as in our certainty model, for importers will not stop their attempts to obtain the products they desire just because one region is unable to deliver them. Instead they will turn to other regions that also produce the desired product. Actual trade patterns may be stable enough to make the change of 7.5 an over-compensation, but at any rate the simulations of this section suggest the direction of the changes that take place when flexible trade patterns are allowed. Intuitively these changes appeal to us: a longer expansionary stage, higher peaks and lower troughs. And significantly enough, the familiar trade-off between stability and interregional equity is again present. Flexible trade means more equity because the productive capacity of the low-income regions is called upon during an expansion, but it also means heavier fluctuations for all regions. It is important to realize that flexible trade as I devised it can only take place under the assumption that the regions with excess capacity are able to provide the goods that are ordered by the excess demand regions. If stable trade matrices strictly are a sign of specialization, no additional output could take place in the excess capacity regions and I would have to accept fixed trade patterns as the only possibility.

Notes

[1] S. Engerman [1965, p. 299].
[2] See G. Borts [1960]; also R. A. Siegel [1966].
[3] As far as assumption (e) is concerned: it does not matter whether $w=0$ or $w=1$.
[4] See K. Lancaster [1968, p. 310] and M. Morishima [1964, Appendix].
[5] See A. C. Chiang [1967, pp. 551–2].
[6] See, for instance, A. M. Martirena-Mantel [1968, Appendix] who, facing a similar problem, developed such algorithms.
[7] The author would like to express his thanks to Professor K. G. Witz of the Mathematics Department of the University of Illinois for his assistance in searching for theorems that could be used in this part of my study. Professor Witz suggested the application of perturbation theory as a possible way to develop theorems on interregional systems. Perturbation theory, however, can only be applied if the perturbations are very small. For instance, taking three isolated regions as a starting point, interregional trade would have to be introduced as a perturbation of the 3×3 identity matrix; but this perturbation would necessarily have to be by a small matrix in order to derive any theorems, which means that the use-

fulness of perturbation theory for interregional economics is very limited. The interested reader is referred to P. Lancaster [1969] for a survey of perturbation theory.

[8] See A. Brauer [1946].

[9] See K. Lancaster [1968, p. 310].

[10] Actually, the dominant root will always be one when all entries are non-negative and the column entries add up to one.

[11] J. Airov [1963, p. 3].

[12] It does not really matter whether or not the regional marginal propensities to consume are equal to each other, as long as the marginal propensity of each region is non-negative and less than one. See L. McKenzie [1960, p. 56].

[13] The original multiplier-accelerator model by Samuelson gave investment as a function of $\{C(t) - C(t-1)\}$. See P. A. Samuelson [1939].

[14] As in other tables, the extreme u.r.s are extremes for the time interval that runs from the 24th to the 60th period. Because of the convergence of the time series in runs 1768 to 1772, and because of the two-period cycle these extreme rates must necessarily be recorded in periods 24 and 25.

[15] The trade matrices will give the actual production shares only if $F_i(t) = 1$ holds for all i. This is true for fixed trade as well as for flexible trade. Under the fixed-trade assumption, however, the variations of the actual production shares around the coefficients c_{ij} and k_{ij} will be much smaller than when I allow trade 'overflow'.

[16] Note that excess demand and supply here mean excess demand for and excess supply of productive capacity. They refer to the productive plans of a region. For instance, excess demand for productive capacity includes orders for region i from region j, and should not be confused with excess demand for goods by the inhabitants of region i.

[17] The first task, correcting the 'actual sales' part, would be easiest to carry out, were it not for the existence of inventories in each region. Inventories are a buffer between planned production and demand, and several arbitrary decisions would have to be made to determine what fraction of inventories is used to satisfy which region's demand.

[18] J. Airov [1963, p. 11].

8 Migration

8.1 Introduction

I now come to the last of our experiments with the I.M., the one in which I shall allow migration of labour to take place between regions. Thus far the I.M. has been a model in which productive resources were perfectly immobile, each region having its own labour market and its own capital stock. With the assumption of fixed trade patterns this means that certain trade matrices would give rise to large differences in structural unemployment between regions, that would persist because the immobility of the labour force prevented migration from operating as an equalizing mechanism.

In Chapter 4, I pointed out that the P.M. and the I.M. are two extremes. The former portrays a national economy in which resources are perfectly mobile, the latter represents the standpoint of regional economics, or the 'economics of resource immobility', as J. R. Meyer [1963] describes it, in which the national economy consists of separately operating regional economies, connected only through trade relationships. The P.M. overrates mobility, the I.M. under-rates it. In this chapter I shall take a position somewhere in between the two extremes: as before, I keep the already installed regional capital stock immobile, but I now allow migration of labour to take place.

What will affect the decision of an individual to migrate? According to neo-classical general equilibrium theory labour will migrate from low-wage to high-wage regions until wages are equalized. But the conditions under which this conclusion holds are virtually never met.[1] More recent theories view the decision to migrate as an investment decision. The investment in migration will only be undertaken if the expected present value of the investment exceeds the costs.[2] This evaluation of costs and benefits is also present in this quotation from A. Rogers: 'Current theories of internal migration view mobility as the resultant of the expulsive forces of adverse circumstances at a point of origin and the attractive powers of opportunities at a place of destination.'[3]

Because of the emphasis I have placed on employment throughout this study, and since prices and wages are not explicitly included in the I.M., it is only natural for us to take unemployment differentials as the best single indicator of the economic opportunities at the place of destination as well as the adverse circumstances at the place of origin. Statistical studies have suggested that a relationship between unemployment and migration can indeed be established.[4]

In the next section I shall introduce the changes in the I.M. that will make it an interregional model with migration. In Section 8.3, simulations with the migration version will be discussed. Simulations with migration and flexible trade patterns are the topic of 8.4, followed by some conclusions (8.5).

8.2   Migration as a Function of Unemployment

The simplest way to express the relation between migration and unemployment differentials is by the following equation:[5]

$$M_i(t) = -y_i[U_i(t) - U(t)].$$ (8.1)

Here, M_i is the rate of immigration in region i,
U_i is region i's unemployment rate, and
U is the national unemployment rate.[6]

The coefficient y expresses the intensity of the relation between migration and unemployment as it affects region i. Under the assumption that $y_{ij} = y_i$, equation (8.1) is the equivalent of the following equations:

$$M_{ij}(t) = -y_{ij}[U_i(t) - U_j(t)],$$ (8.2)

and

$$M_i(t) = \sum_j \frac{L_j^{eu}(t)}{\sum_j L_j^{eu}(t)} \cdot M_{ij}(t).$$ (8.3)

$$(i \neq j)$$

The variable $M_i(t)$ in (8.3) is the same as $M_i(t)$ in (8.1), that is, the rate of immigration will be the same regardless whether I compute it directly from (8.1) or indirectly from (8.2) and (8.3).

Equation (3.1) of the I.M. no longer measures the labour force in efficiency units correctly once I assume that migration takes place. In its place come

$$L_i^{eu}(t) = l_i N_{oi}(1 + p_i + m_i)^t,$$ (8.4)

for $t = 0, 1$

and

$$L_i^{eu}(t+1) = L_i^{eu}(t)[1 + M_i(t)](1 + p_i + m_i),$$ (8.5)

for $t \geq 1$

148

According to (8.5), the same population growth rate and rate of technical progress apply to the original population as to the immigrants (if $M_i(t) > 0$). I also implicitly assume that the immigrant population adopts the labour participation rate that prevails in the region of destination.

Finally, before I can simulate the migration version of the I.M. I have to decide on an appropriate value of the parameter y. Sensitivity experiments by Hamilton *et al.*, who for their Susquehanna River Basin study employed a similar migration function, 'seemed to show that the magnitude of the coefficient relating migration to unemployment was not of great importance.'[7] A low coefficient would, with a somewhat different time path, in the long run accomplish the same task as a high coefficient, the only difference being the speed of adjustment to unemployment differentials. I employed a coefficient $y = .5$ for most simulations, which means that a 1% unemployment differential will evoke $\frac{1}{2}$% migration; experiments with $y = .33$ and $y = .25$ gave only minor differences compared to runs with $y = .5$.

8.3 Simulations of the Migration Version of the Interregional Model

A summary of the simulations with the migration version of the I.M. can be found in Tables 8.1, 8.2 and 8.3. The first table brings together the non-optimal runs, the second the runs with (adjusted) optimal

Table 8.1

Interregional Model Simulations with Migration

Run	I.M. Run	Variation	Migration Model Run				I.M. Run			
			U low-high	Q low	F low	CL	U low-high	Q low	F low	CL
			2.4–4.5	.99	.99		1.1– 3.0	1.00	.97	
2503	1716	base run	2.6–4.5	1.00	.99	?	1.3– 2.1	1.00	.97	9
			1.6–6.7	.95	.91		5.5– 8.9	.95	1.00	
			3.2–4.9	1.00	.97		2.4– 3.0	1.00	.97	10
2501	1704	$b = .5$	3.2–4.9	1.00	.98	13	2.6	1.00	.93	—
			2.5–6.4	.96	.92		6.9– 9.2	.96	1.00	10
			1.9–4.2	.96	1.00		0.0– 3.4	.96	.98	
2515	1720	$b = 1.0$	2.1–4.0	.97	1.00	15	0.0– 3.1	.97	.99	12
			0.0–7.3	.92	.90		0.0–12.9	.88	.86	
			3.0–6.7	.97	.95		2.1– 5.5	1.00	.94	
2506	1717	$A_o = 0$	3.4–6.3	.98	.96	12	2.5– 5.1	1.00	.93	15
			2.5–7.1	.96	.85		1.0– 9.3	.94	.90	

Table 8.1 (continued)

Run	I.M. Run	Variation	Migration Model Run U low-high	Q low	F low	CL	I.M. Run U low-high	Q low	F low	CL
			2.8– 3.0	.99	1.00		0.6– 1.2	.99	1.00	10
2525	1719	$A_o=6$	2.8– 3.0	.99	1.00	D	0.4	1.00	.98	—
			2.4– 3.2	.95	1.00		7.2– 9.0	.94	1.00	10^{+2}
			2.9–17.5	.95	.85		2.6–10.0	.98	.86	
2524	1709	$w=0$	2.7–18.2	.97	.88	?	2.4–10.2	.97	.88	17
			2.7–18.5	.87	.64		2.6–22.4	.91	.70	
			4.9–13.4	1.00	.88		4.7–10.8	1.00	.87	
2523	1718	$A_o=0$ $w=0$	5.0–14.4	1.00	.89	?	4.8–12.6	1.00	.88	28
			5.0–13.8	.98	.77		4.7–19.0	.97	.73	
			2.5– 4.3	.99	.99		13.5–14.3	.88	1.00	
2516	1710	$G_o = \begin{bmatrix}18\\18\\18\end{bmatrix}$	2.6– 4.4	1.00	.99	13	1.7– 2.0	1.00	.89	11
			1.7– 6.3	.96	.93		1.0– 6.3	.96	.95	
			2.5– 4.3	.99	.99		8.4– 8.5	.97	1.00	
2529	1714	$G_o = \begin{bmatrix}27\\0\\27\end{bmatrix}$	2.5– 4.4	.99	.99	15	7.5– 7.6	.98	1.00	—
			1.8– 6.2	.96	.93		2.1	1.00	.90	
			2.1	1.00	.91		2.0	1.00	.90	
2507	1721	$G_o = \begin{bmatrix}42\\12\\9\end{bmatrix}$	2.0	1.00	.98	—	1.8	1.00	.92	—
			2.0	1.00	.92		5.5	.99	1.00	
			1.5– 2.8	1.00	.97		11.8	.94	1.00	
2517	1712	$G_o = \begin{bmatrix}21\\21\\21\end{bmatrix}$	2.0– 2.2	1.00	.91	10	2.1	1.00	.86	—
			2.0– 2.2	1.00	.92		1.9	1.00	.95	
			8.2– 8.3	.97	1.00		7.1	.98	1.00	
2528	1713	$G_o = \begin{bmatrix}30\\8\\7\end{bmatrix}$	8.2– 8.3	.97	1.00	—	4.1	1.00	1.00	—
			8.2– 8.3	.96	1.00		13.2	.92	.90	
			0.4	.99	1.00					
2520		$G_o=19.71$ $A_o= 6.93$	0.4	1.00	.99	—				
			0.3	1.00	.98					
			1.1	.96	1.00					
2521		$G_{o1,2}= 0$ $G_{o3} =59.13$ $A_o = 6.93$	1.1	.99	1.00	—				
			1.1	1.00	.97					

All simulations are with $y=.5$.
See also *Explanation* following Table 3.1.

Table 8.2

Interregional Model Simulations with Migration and (Adjusted) Optimal Distributions of Government Consumption

Run	I.M. Run	Variations			Migration Model Run				I.M. Run	
		G_o^*	A_o	z	U low-high	Q low	F low	CL	U low-high	CL
		34.39			3.1–6.7	.97	.95		2.6–6.2	
2512	1725	7.64	0	1	3.3–6.3	.98	.96	12	2.2–6.2	12
		11.97			2.4–7.1	.96	.85		1.6–9.3	
		33.49			3.1–6.6	.97	.95		3.0–6.4	
2511	1744	5.95	0	.8	3.1–6.3	.98	.96	12	3.5–6.4	12
		14.56			2.4–7.1	.96	.85		1.9–7.4	
		33.06			2.9–6.8	.97	.95		3.0–6.7	
2522	1743	5.13	0	.7	3.1–6.3	.98	.96	12	3.0–6.5	10/11
		15.81			2.4–7.1	.97	.85		2.1–6.4	
		33.31			3.0–4.2	.99	.99		2.0–4.4	
2509	1754	5.82	3	.95	2.6–4.2	.99	.99	15	2.1–4.4	16
		14.87			1.7–5.9	.96	.93		1.0–6.2	
		32.41			2.8–4.3	.99	.99		3.6–4.3	
2508	1747	4.17	3	.7	2.5–4.3	.99	.99	14/15	4.0–4.6	16
		17.42			1.7–6.2	.96	.93		1.1–3.9	
		33.34			2.6–4.0	.99	.99		1.8–4.2	
2513	1727	5.90	3.51	1	2.6–4.0	1.00	.99	15/16	2.2–4.4	16
		14.76			1.5–6.0	.96	.94		0.7–6.6	

All simulations are with $y = .5$.
For other key figures of the comparable I.M. runs see Table 6.1.
See also *Explanation* following Table 3.1.

distributions of government consumption and the third gives the national averages of some of the non-optimal and (adjusted) optimal runs.

Our over-all impression from these tables is that migration would provide the economy with a very powerful equalizing mechanism, if our migration function and the other behavioural equations of the I.M. held in reality. The simulations with the base-run distribution of government consumption (the first seven runs of Table 8.1) invariably show that migration pulls the average level of unemployment of our problem area, region 3, into line with the other regions' unemployment level. For regions 1 and 2 this means a higher average u.r., for region 3 this means a much

Table 8.3

National Averages of Interregional Model Simulations with Migration

Run	P.M. Run	National Averages				P.M. Run			
		U low-high	Q low	F low	CL	U low-high	Q low	F low	CL
2503	1604	2.4– 5.0	.98	.96	?	1.0– 5.5	.97	.94	14
2506	1601	3.1– 6.5	.98	.92	11	1.9– 6.8	.98	.90	13
2525	1605	2.8– 3.0	.99	1.00	D	1.7– 4.8	.97	1.00	D
2524	1608	2.8–17.9	.94	.78	?	2.0–19.2	.93	.74	17
2523	1603	5.1–13.5	.99	.84	?	4.0–23.5	.94	.70	16
2529	1604	2.3– 4.9	.98	.96	15	1.0– 5.5	.97	.94	14
2507	1622	2.0– 2.1	1.00	.94	—	2.1	1.00	.93	—
2528	1621	8.2– 8.3	.97	1.00	—	8.2	.97	1.00	—
2512	1601	3.0– 6.5	.99	.92	11/12	1.9– 6.8	.98	.90	13
2522	1601	2.9– 6.6	.98	.92	12	1.9– 6.8	.98	.90	13
2509	1604	2.5– 4.6	.99	.97	15	1.0– 5.5	.97	.94	14
2513	1646	2.3– 4.5	.98	.98	15	0.9– 5.4	.97	.95	14/15

See *Explanation* following Table 3.1.

lower average u.r. The benefits of migration for the economy as a whole are more interregional equity.

As far as the amplitudes of the fluctuations are concerned: both region 1 and 2 see the amplitudes of their cycles increase somewhat compared to a situation with no migration. Region 3, on the other hand, becomes more stable although it still remains the region with the largest fluctuations. Migration, while adjusting the regional labour forces to the needs of the regional economies, allows private investment to display its volatile character more than a fixed resources interregional economy will. This means that the ranges of national u.r.'s will be larger in the migration version of the I.M. (compare Tables 8.3 and 4.1), yet they are smaller than those in the P.M. (Table 8.3). From the standpoint of mobility the migration version is somewhere between the immobility of the I.M. and the full mobility of the P.M., and this position is reflected in the degree of fluctuations.

In terms of cycle lengths the migration runs show irregularities that have not appeared before. In the base run (2503) for instance, no clear cyclical pattern is discernible (see Figure 8.1) during the 40 periods of observation. In two other runs (2524 and 2523), the output paths are very stable for some 20 periods when suddenly the economy enters a depression that lasts for about 8 periods. In some instances the damped character of the runs can be held responsible for erratic output patterns.

u.r.

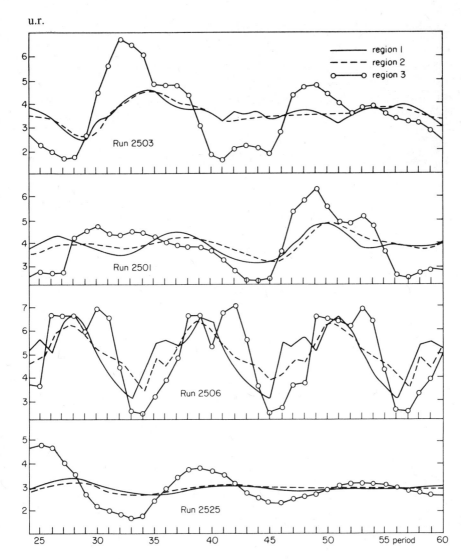

Figure 8.1   Migration Model Runs

For instance, additional simulations for periods 100 to 140 showed that the oscillations of runs 2516, 2517, 2508 and 2513 are clearly damped.

Runs 2516, 2529, 2507 and 2517, all with suboptimal G_o-distributions, are interesting because they show how well migration performs its equalizing function. The government consumption distributions 18/18/18 and 27/0/27 (runs 2516 and 2529) lead to virtually identical time paths. Labour adjusts itself perfectly to the demand for it in each region. Obviously, the regional labour forces have different sizes in the two runs. For the two runs 2507 and 2517 the situation is a little different, because the total initial amount of government consumption is higher than the amount required for a Golden Age economy. This does not prevent the economy of run 2507 from reaching the same position as in the comparable P.M. run (see Table 8.3), but in the case of run 2517 the capital shortage in all regions prevents a quick adjustment.

The last two experiments with non-optimal distributions were made with the Golden Age levels of government consumption and autonomous investment, but with the former distributed very unevenly. As runs 2520 and 2521 show, the migration mechanism alone is not sufficient to give steady-state growth with full employment in all regions. As soon as unemployment differentials are eliminated no migration takes place any more. Immobility of the capital stocks prevents the economies reaching full employment. The two examples show that even when labour is mobile it is still important to search for an optimal distribution of government expenditure. As it is in 2520 and 2521, during every period a fraction of planned government consumption cannot be realized because not all $\bar{F}_i$ are equal to one, while in the Golden Age all production plans are realized and output is at a higher over-all level.

Interesting for another reason are the runs of Table 8.2. Here I deal with two competing policy measures (supposing migration can be promoted by government authorities and therefore be seen as a policy instrument) that aim at the same goal: interregional equity. Remember from Chapter 6 that the optimal distributions of government consumption led to larger fluctuations in region 3 than in the other regions because of region 3's larger share in the production of capital goods. To compensate region 3 for these large fluctuations, I devised the z-method. Runs 2512, 2511 and 2522 show us that the migration model simulations produce the same time series regardless of the value of z for which we compute the optimal distribution of $\sum G_{oi}$. When migration can complement an optimal distribution policy, the z-method loses its importance. The same conclusion can be drawn for runs 2509 and 2508. With migration the fluctiations of all three economies are symmetrical around the same average rate.

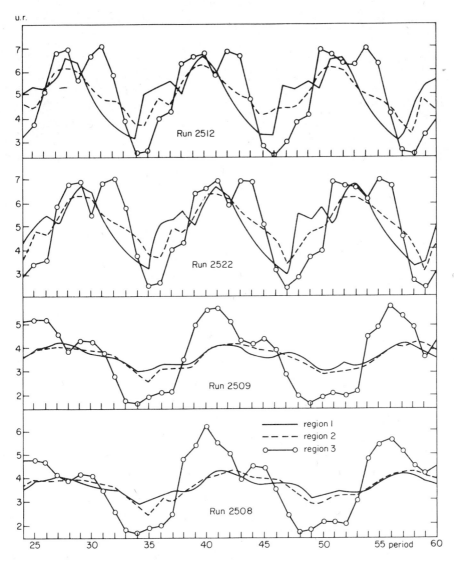

Figure 8.2 Migration Model Runs with (Adjusted) Optimal
Distributions of Government Consumption

8.4 Simulations with Migration and Flexible Trade Patterns

Remember from Section 7.5 that flexible trade alone gave a fair degree of equity, but also that it tended to make the economy less stable. When the migration version of the I.M. is run with flexible trade patterns, the difference with migration alone is the larger fluctuations in the first case. From Table 8.4 it is apparent that in general the amplitudes increase slightly because of the flexible-trade assumption, but a comparison with Table 7.4 shows that the fluctuations are milder here than for the runs with flexible trade and no migration. Migration not only equalizes, but also dampens the effects of flexible trade. In two of the six runs of Table 8.4 the time paths for migration plus flexible trade are the same as those for migration alone (runs 2605 and 2609). In these cases the regional economies over a period of time are so much alike in terms of the coefficient F, that the flexible-trade assumption does not lead to additional trade.

8.5 Conclusion

The addition to the I.M. of a migration function, in which migration is a function of unemployment differentials gives the model a powerful built-in equalizer. Migration corrects the regional labour forces such that each region will end up with a labour force proportional to its general level of production. The size of the coefficient that relates migration to unemployment is only important in that it determines the speed of adjustment to the unemployment differentials; given time, a high as well as a low coefficient will accomplish the same task.[8]

As an instrument of economic policy, subsidized migration is aimed at the same goal as reallocating government expenditure: both are used to increase interregional equity. In the first case, and in so far as migration takes place unsubsidized according to (8.1), the problems of congestion may trouble national and regional planners; on the other hand, shifting government services may meet considerable resistance from those involved. In this study I shall not ponder the difficulties that policy makers face in implementing their equity measures. Regional texts are available that deal with the problems and strategies of regional economic policy in much more detail than I would be able to do here.[9] They will tell us that general solutions do not exist because the problems of each region are unique. In some situations planned out-migration will be the optimal solution for a depressed region, in others, attracting government services or industries in general may be more justifiable.

In this study, however, I deal with an abstract model. When I make any comparison between reallocating government consumption and planned

156

Table 8.4
Interregional Model Simulations with Migration and Flexible Trade

Run	Migration Model Run	Variation	Migration and Flexible Trade				Migration Model Run			
			U low-high	Q low	F low	CL	U low-high	Q low	F low	CL
2601	2503	base run	2.1–4.4	.98	.98	16	2.4–4.5	.99	.99	?
			2.5–4.2	.99	.98		2.6–4.5	1.00	.99	
			1.6–5.8	.95	.92		1.6–6.7	.95	.91	
2604	2506	$A_o=0$	2.4–7.1	.96	.95	12	3.0–6.7	.97	.95	12
			2.6–6.6	.98	.95		3.4–6.3	.98	.96	
			2.6–9.5	.96	.83		2.5–7.1	.96	.85	
2605	2507	$G_o=\begin{bmatrix}42\\12\\9\end{bmatrix}$	2.1	1.00	.91	—	2.1	1.00	.91	—
			2.0	1.00	.98		2.0	1.00	.98	
			2.0	1.00	.92		2.0	1.00	.92	
2608	2511	$G_o=G_o^*$ $A_o=0$ $z=.8$	2.6–7.6	.95	.96	12	3.1–6.6	.97	.95	12
			2.7–7.0	.97	.96		3.1–6.3	.98	.96	
			2.6–8.6	.96	.83		2.4–7.1	.97	.85	
2606	2508	$G_o=G_o^*$ $A_o=3$ $z=.7$	2.2–4.4	.98	.98	14/15	2.8–4.3	.99	.99	14/15
			2.4–4.3	.99	.99		2.5–4.3	.99	.99	
			1.7–6.1	.95	.92		1.7–6.2	.96	.93	
2609	2513	$G_o=G_o^*$ $A_o=3.51$ $z=1$	2.6–4.0	.99	.99	15/16	2.6–4.0	.99	.99	15/16
			2.6–4.0	1.00	.99		2.6–4.0	1.00	.99	
			1.5–6.0	.96	.94		1.5–6.0	.96	.94	

All simulations are with $y=.5$.
See also *Explanation* following Table 3.1.

157

migration as tools for economic policy, I have to realize that every conclusion I draw only holds under the assumptions I used with respect to the optimality of distributions of government consumption, and only for the type of function I used as our migration function. If I do this, then it seems that:

(a) Migration is somewhat more effective as an equalizing mechanism than optimal distributions of government consumption are. Regardless of the initial distribution of $\sum G_{oi}$, regional unemployment will in time be largely the same when the migration function is included in the model, because the regional labour force adjusts itself to the regional demand for labor.[10] Examples are runs 2503, 2516, 2529, 2509 and 2508 (with the base-run parameters), and runs 2506, 2512, 2511 and 2522 (with $A_o = 0$). On the other hand, when I try to achieve interregional equity through the reallocation of a given amount of government consumption in an economy in which no migration takes place, it is difficult to find distributions that produce regional cycles around a common average unemployment level. The trend method and its offspring, the z-method, both have their shortcomings. None of them is as equitable as migration.

(b) While migration alone is more equalizing than a reallocation of government consumption alone, a combination of the two instruments is more desirable since it will require smaller adjustments of both labour and government expenditure. In some cases it will also increase the over-all level of output.

(c) Migration alone will not reduce the fluctuations inherent in the investment behaviour of the economic agents. Reallocating government consumption can increase stability, but at the expense of interregional equity. Migration, however, will nullify the greater stability accomplished by a particular distribution of government consumption, by restoring the long-term equality of the unemployment rates.

Notes

[1] They include: zero migration costs, wage differentials as the only determinant of migration, constant returns to scale, homogeneity of labour markets, perfect competition in the labour markets and perfect information.

[2] The main exponent of this view is L. A. Sjaastad [1962].

[3] A. Rogers [1968, p. 4].

[4] See, for instance, H. R. Hamilton et al. [1969, pp. 147–52].

[5] Realize that this equation holds under similar conditions as the neoclassical migration function I mentioned above: zero migration costs (unless migration is to a large extent subsidized by the government), unemploy-

ment differentials as the only determinant of migration, perfect competition and perfect information in homogeneous labour markets.

[6] $U(t) = \sum_i \dfrac{L_i^{eu}(t)}{\sum_i L_i^{eu}(t)} \cdot U_i(t)$. Since by assumption technical progress is

identical for all regions, it does not matter whether I use labour efficiency units or men to weight the regional u.r.s.

[7] See Hamilton *et al.* [1969, pp. 150–1].

[8] Needless to say, the value of y has to be plausible. Empirical studies will have to give us the range within which I can expect the value of y to be.

[9] See, for instance, H. W. Richardson [1969] and E. M. Hoover [1971].

[10] The only situation in which the initial distribution is of importance to the end result is when $\sum G_{oi}$ exceeds the Golden Age level (which is 59.13 for our base-run parameter values). In that case the capital stock is always the scarcer of the two resources, labour and capital stock, and this slows down the labour force adjustment through migration. An example is run 2517.

9 The Timing of Changes in Government Expenditure in a Cyclical Economy

9.1 Introduction

All forms of government intervention in regional economic affairs in Chapters 6, 7, and 8, were concerned with structural or long-term changes in the regional economies. The reallocation of government expenditure, changes in the location of industry (implied by changes in the trade pattern) and migration, whether or not subsidized by the central government, were all intended to bring the long-term output levels of the regions in line with each other and to make the regional economies more stable in the long run. The emphasis in the previous chapters has been a little more on inter-regional equity than on regional stability. Stability was pursued as a long-term goal, but in most cases priority was given to regional output equalization. On the other hand, short-term adjustments in the I.M. have been exclusively aimed at stabilizing the economy. Measures such as contra-cyclical investment and unemployment benefits both reduce the fluctuations of output with time, while applying equally to all regions.

In this chapter I shall add one short-term policy measure to the ones I have already discussed. That is the single or once-and-for-all government expenditure, which may be implemented for all kinds of purposes. Specifically, I want to look at the aspect of the timing of the expenditure. Clearly, it makes a difference in a cyclical economy whether I inject our single out-lay during the expansionary or contractionary phase of a cycle. In Section 9.3 I shall report on the results of simulations with single expenditures injected at different phases of the cycle.

Since it is the cyclical aspect I am interested in, it does not matter whether I use the P.M. or the I.M. for these experiments. For convenience I chose the base run of the P.M. for our simulations.

Timing is as important for long-term policy as it is for short-term adjustments. While in a short-term adjustment it is only the short-term effect that counts, when implementing structural policy I am also interested in the short-term effects of the structural change. The timing of the measures discussed in Chapters 7 and 8 admittedly is difficult to control, as the adjustments there take place in the private sector, and *a priori* the government will not know how effective measures such as subsidies to migrants or investment allowances to industries will be. Government expenditures, on the other hand, are to a large extent controllable, and it is important for the policy maker to know during which cyclical phase a structural change such as a reallocation of government consumption can be best implemented. Therefore, in Section 9.4 I shall look at the effects of a permanent increase in government expenditure during different phases of the cycle, again by using the base run of the P.M. for the experiments.

Both experiments are examples of dynamic multiplier analysis. Therefore, Sections 9.3 and 9.4 are preceded by a short section on multipliers in a dynamic model.

9.2 Dynamic Multiplier Analysis

In macro-economic dynamics a distinction is usually made between two kinds of multipliers: the impact multiplier and the dynamic multiplier. The impact multiplier gives the initial effect of an exogenous change in expenditure on an endogenous variable in the macro-economic model. Dynamic multipliers incorporate the effects which the lag structure of the model has on the change in the endogenous variable, after one or more periods have elapsed. Dynamic multipliers can be computed for every period following the one in which the initial expenditure was made.

In comparative static analysis only one multiplier is computed from the reduced-form solution of the economic model. This multiplier gives the over-all or total effect of an exogenous disturbance on an endogenous variable. It is the multiplier to which the dynamic multiplier converges in the long term, provided, of course, that our model is stable in the equilibrium dynamics sense of the term.

This all holds for linear models. When inequalities are introduced several complications arise. A reduced-form solution of the model can no longer be obtained (just as it was impossible in Chapter 7 to reduce the P.M. and the I.M. to a difference equation), and the long-term multiplier can only be estimated by simulating the model. This, of course, is what I shall do below. Simulation of the P.M. with exogenous shocks injected at different stages of the cycle will provide us with all dynamic multipliers.

When the multiplier is defined as the multiple by which output will change because of a change in autonomous spending, the latter change is usually thought to be a permanent change in expenditure, as opposed to a single, once-and-for-all injection (after which autonomous spending drops to its previous level). If the economy is stable the once-and-for-all injection will have no permanently lasting effect on output. In other words, the long-term multiplier is zero. In an unstable economy, however, output will not converge back to its equilibrium path. Understandably, the distinction between a stable and an unstable economy is just as important when the autonomous change is permanent. In our models instability is kept in check by the ceilings, and even though a long-term value of the multiplier cannot be computed in such a case, the simulations will give us the range within which unemployment moves after the change.

The experiments in the following two sections are examples of dynamic multiplier analysis, conducted with the P.M. Because of the large number of possible interregional reactions involved I preferred the P.M. to the I.M. for these experiments. I did, however, compute comparative static multipliers for the I.M. under the special assumption of steady-state growth with $\bar{Q}_i = 1$ and $\bar{F}_i = 1$. These multipliers are presented and discussed in the Appendix to this chapter.

9.3 The Timing of a Single Government Expenditure

By injecting the P.M. with a single increase in government consumption—and later with single increases in government investment—during each of the 14 periods of the base-run cycle (which therefore amounts to 14 simulations for each type of exogenous shock), I am able to get an impression of how dynamic multipliers differ, depending on the timing of the shock. Tables 9.1 and 9.2 give dynamic multipliers up to ten periods following the shock, and for each of the 14 periods in which the shock, a 1% increase in government expenditure, takes place.[1] The multipliers measure the percentage increase in employment with respect to the base run at each point in time. The final four columns of both tables give cumulative percentage changes over three, five, and ten periods, and over the whole cycle, with adjustments made for changes in length caused by the exogenous shock.[2]

I can draw the following conclusions from our experiments. In general:
(a) To raise employment with a single government expenditure, government consumption is generally more effective than government investment. The explanation is that the former adds to total demand, while the latter is partly a substitute for private investment.
(b) Single increases in government consumption and government investment are most effective when made during the downswing phase.
(c) Single increases in government consumption and government investment may disturb the cyclical pattern by lengthening or shortening the cycle depending on the phase of the cycle in which the shock occurs. Increases in government consumption made during the trough and early upswing periods will shorten the cycle; increases made during the late up-

Table 9.1

Dynamic Multipliers of a Single Increase in Government Consumption on Employment

Period of Expenditure	Dynamic Multiplier Per Period										Cumulative Dynamic Multiplier			
	1	2	3	4	5	6	7	8	9	10	3	5	10	cycle
29 (P)	0	1.1	1.0	0.7	0.4	0	-0.3	-0.5	0.1	0	2.1	3.2	2.5	4.1
30	1.0	0	1.0	0	0.6	-0.3	0.2	0.3	0	-0.2	2.0	2.6	2.6	4.1
31	1.0	0.1	1.0	0	0.7	-0.3	0.2	0.2	0	-0.1	2.1	2.8	2.8	3.0
32	1.0	0	1.0	0	0.2	0.4	0.3	0.2	0.1	-0.2	2.0	2.2	3.0	2.9
33	1.0	0	0.6	0.3	0.3	0.4	0.4	0.4	0.2	0	1.6	2.2	3.6	2.2
34 (T)	1.0	0.1	0	0.2	0.4	0.6	0.9	0.7	0.1	-1.0	1.1	1.7	3.0	2.2
35	0.8	0.1	0	0.3	0.5	0.9	0.7	0.1	-0.9	-0.3	0.9	1.7	2.2	2.2
36	0.1	0	0.1	0.5	1.0	0.9	0.2	-1.2	-0.5	-1.0	0.2	1.7	0.1	1.5
37	0	-0.1	0.1	0.6	0.6	0.2	-0.4	-0.1	-0.4	0.1	0	1.2	0.6	0.8
38	0	-0.1	0.1	0.3	0.2	-0.1	-0.1	-0.1	0.1	0	0	0.5	0.3	0.8
39	0	0	-0.1	0	0	0.5	0.4	0.4	0.2	0.1	-0.1	-0.1	1.5	1.2
40	0	-0.1	-0.1	-0.1	0.7	0.5	0.5	0.2	0.1	-0.2	-0.2	0.4	1.5	2.5
41	0	-0.1	-0.1	0.7	0.5	0.5	0.2	0.1	-0.2	-0.2	-0.2	1.0	1.4	3.0
42	0	-0.1	0.8	0.6	0.5	0.3	0	-0.2	-0.3	0.1	0.7	1.8	1.7	3.5

(Rows 30–34 are bracketed as *downswing*; rows 38–41 are bracketed as *upswing*.)

Explanation

1. *Period of expenditure*: period in which government expenditure takes place (if increase is permanent: period in which expenditure level is increased).

2. *Multipliers* are measured as changes in employment, following a 1% increase in government expenditure.

Table 9.2

Dynamic Multipliers of a Single Increase in Government Investment on Employment

Period of Expenditure		Dynamic Multiplier Per Period										Cumulative Dynamic Multiplier			
		1	2	3	4	5	6	7	8	9	10	3	5	10	cycle
29 (P)		0	0.9	0.5	0.2	−0.1	−0.4	−0.5	−0.5	−0.1	−0.2	1.4	1.5	−0.2	3.0
30	downswing	1.0	−0.2	0.5	−0.5	0.1	−0.6	0	0	−0.2	−0.3	1.3	0.9	−0.2	2.6
31		1.0	−0.2	0.5	−0.5	0.1	−0.6	0	0	−0.2	−0.2	1.3	0.9	−0.1	2.3
32		1.0	−0.2	0.5	−0.5	0.1	0.2	0	−0.2	−0.4	−0.7	1.3	0.9	−0.2	1.5
33		1.0	−0.2	0.5	−0.5	0.1	0.2	−0.1	−0.1	−0.5	−0.4	1.3	0.9	0.1	0.6
34 (T)		1.0	−0.2	0.3	0.4	0.2	0	−0.1	−0.5	−0.6	−0.2	1.1	1.7	0.3	0.8
35		0.8	0.1	0.3	0.4	0.3	0.2	0	−0.2	−0.1	0.1	1.2	1.9	1.8	1.4
36		0.1	0.4	0.4	0.5	0.6	0.4	−0.5	−0.5	−0.3	−0.7	0.9	2.0	0.9	0.3
37		0	0.3	0.4	0.6	0.4	0.1	−0.2	−0.3	−0.6	−0.2	0.7	1.7	0.2	0
38	upswing	0	0.3	0.5	0.4	0.1	−0.4	−0.2	−0.5	−0.1	−0.3	0.8	1.3	−0.2	0.1
39		0	0.3	0.2	0	−0.1	−0.1	0	−0.1	−0.1	0.1	0.5	0.4	0	0.1
40		0	0.3	0.2	−0.3	−0.2	−0.4	−0.1	−0.1	0.2	0.1	0.5	0	−0.2	0.1
41		0	0.3	−0.3	−0.3	−0.3	−0.1	−0.1	0.2	0.1	0.2	0	−0.6	−0.3	0.1
42		0	0.3	−0.4	0	−0.3	0	−0.2	0.1	0	−0.1	−0.1	−0.4	−0.6	−0.1

See *Explanation* following Table 9.1.

swing and early downswing periods will prolong the cycle. Increases in government investment will prolong the cycle when made during the downswing phase.[3]

(d) It depends on the time horizon of the policy maker when a single expenditure should be made. The immediate effects (measured by the impact multiplier) are greatest when the economy operates far enough below the capacity ceilings to permit a 1% employment increase. The cumulative impact over three periods is greatest for an expenditure made during the downswing phase. Five-period effects are best for downturn injections of government consumption and for early upswing injections of government investment. Longer-term impacts become more difficult to interpret as the cumulative effects depend on whether or not one adjusts the comparison for a change in cycle length.

What is not apparent from the tables is that a single expenditure still affects the cycle around 60–70 periods later. This shows the inherently unstable character of the base-run economy. Cumulative changes in employment over a cycle length, however, run from $+0.3\%$ to -0.4%, in other words, are very moderate. There is no clear pattern in these changes. The long-term range of u.r.s remains 1.0–5.5%, as in the P.M. base run. Specifically:

(e) A single increase in government consumption is most effective when made in the early periods of the dowswing phase, when the c-u.r. is at its lowest level; it is least effective when made during the upswing phase, when the production realization rate is less than one.

(f) A single increase in government investment is most effective during the downswing phase, if the time horizon of the policy maker is not longer than three periods, or during and immediately after the trough period, if the time horizon is five periods. It is least effective when made during the late periods of the upswing when the demand for capital goods is already falling.

9.4 The Timing of a Permanent Increase in Government Expenditure

The impact of permanent 1% increases in government consumption and government investment on employment in the base-run economy is tabulated in Tables 9.3 and 9.4. The organization of these tables is the same as those of Tables 9.1 and 9.2. Only the column giving the cumulative impact over a cycle is omitted, because of changes in cycle lengths and shifts in the timing of turning points.

Obviously, the long-term effect which a permanent 1% increase in government expenditure has on employment over a period of time greatly depends on the state of the economy prior to the change. Using the base-

Table 9.3

Dynamic Multipliers of a Permanent Increase in Government Consumption on Employment

Period of Expenditure	Dynamic Multiplier Per Period										Cumulative Dynamic Multiplier		
	1	2	3	4	5	6	7	8	9	10	3	5	10
29 (P)	0	1.5	1.9	3.0	2.9	3.0	2.1	1.5	1.6	1.6	3.4	9.3	19.1
30 downswing	1.0	1.0	2.1	2.0	2.1	1.3	0.9	1.3	2.0	2.5	4.1	8.2	16.2
31	1.0	1.1	1.9	2.0	1.0	0.6	1.1	2.0	2.6	2.2	4.0	7.0	15.5
32	1.0	1.0	1.8	0.9	0.3	0.9	1.7	2.5	2.2	0.8	3.8	5.0	13.1
33	1.0	1.0	0	0.2	0.5	1.4	2.2	2.2	0.9	−0.6	2.6	3.3	9.4
34 (T)	1.0	0.8	−0.1	0.1	0.7	1.6	2.1	1.0	−0.3	−0.9	1.8	2.6	6.1
35	0.8	0.1	0	0.3	1.1	1.8	1.2	−0.1	−0.9	0.7	0.8	2.2	4.9
36	0.1	0	0	0.5	1.2	1.0	0	−0.6	0.7	1.7	0.1	1.8	4.6
37	0	−0.1	0.1	0.6	0.8	0.2	−0.4	0.8	1.6	3.1	−0.1	1.3	6.6
38 upswing	0	0	−0.2	0.2	0	−0.3	1.0	1.6	3.0	3.4	0	0.2	8.9
39	0	−0.1	−0.1	−0.2	−0.2	1.1	1.6	2.9	3.3	3.9	−0.2	−0.6	12.2
40	0	−0.1	−0.2	−0.2	1.1	1.7	3.0	3.4	3.9	3.3	−0.2	0.7	16.0
41	0	−0.1	−0.2	1.1	1.7	3.0	3.4	3.9	3.4	3.0	−0.2	2.5	19.2
42	0	−0.1	1.2	1.8	2.9	3.4	3.9	3.4	3.0	2.8	1.1	5.8	22.3

See *Explanation* following Table 9.1.

Table 9.4

Dynamic Multipliers of a Permanent Increase in Government Investment on Employment

Period of Expenditure	Dynamic Multiplier Per Period										Cumulative Dynamic Multiplier		
	1	2	3	4	5	6	7	8	9	10	3	5	10
29 (P)	0	1.9	1.3	1.5	0.7	0.5	−0.2	−0.3	0.3	0.7	3.2	5.4	6.4
30 downswing	1.0	0.8	1.4	0.8	0.9	0.3	0.2	0.7	0.9	0.6	3.2	4.9	7.6
31	1.0	0.8	1.3	0.8	0.9	0.3	1.1	1.1	0.7	0.2	3.1	4.8	8.2
32	1.0	0.8	1.3	0.8	0.9	1.2	1.1	0.9	0.4	−0.4	3.1	4.8	8.0
33	1.0	0.8	1.3	0.9	1.0	1.1	1.1	0.9	0.4	0	3.1	5.0	8.5
34 (T)	1.0	0.8	0.7	0.9	1.1	1.4	1.5	1.2	0.2	−1.8	2.5	4.5	7.0
35	0.8	0.5	0.6	1.0	1.4	1.8	1.5	−0.3	−1.7	−1.2	1.9	4.3	4.4
36	0.1	0.4	0.7	1.2	1.8	1.5	0	−1.6	−0.9	−0.9	1.2	4.2	2.3
37 upswing	0	0.3	0.7	1.3	1.4	0.7	−1.3	−0.1	−0.7	0.5	1.0	3.7	2.8
38	0	0.3	0.8	0.9	0.7	−0.5	0.2	−0.1	0.6	0.2	1.1	2.7	3.1
39	0	0.3	0.5	0.5	0.2	0.2	0.4	0.5	0.5	0.5	0.8	1.5	3.6
40	0	0.3	0.5	0.4	0.2	0.6	0.5	0.7	0.5	0.4	0.8	1.4	4.1
41	0	0.3	0.5	0.7	1.0	0.7	0.7	0.3	0.2	−0.1	0.8	2.5	4.3
42	0	0.3	1.1	1.2	1.0	0.7	0.5	0	−0.2	0.5	1.4	3.6	5.1

See *Explanation* following Table 9.1.

168

run parameter values, an increase on government consumption means that the economy will operate closer to the productive capacity ceiling. This shows itself in the ex-post range of u.r.s: 1.3–3.5%, over what is then a 20-period cycle (consisting of 8- and 12-period subcycles), compared with a 1.0–5.5% range before the increase, along with a 14-period cycle. An increase in government investment on the other hand does not change the cycle length, nor does it improve the long-term range of u.r.s, which becomes 0.7–5.4% over a 14-period cycle. The reason is again that government investment in the P.M. is a substitute for private investment, and as such it competes with private investment.[4]

In addition to the possibility of a permanent change in cycle length, a permanent increase in government expenditure may, and—more likely than a single increase—will very often change the length of the cycle in which the permanent increase takes place. One-percent increases in government consumption will shorten the cycle by as much as three periods when made during the downswing periods. These increases will leave the cycle length unaltered when made during the late upswing periods. Permanent 1% increases in government investment prolong the cycle by as much as two periods when made during the downswing. One can imagine that a combination of single and permanent changes, or just single shocks alone—added to a model as Adelman and Adelman did, in the Klein-Goldberger model[5]—will generate patterns in which regular business cycles are no longer discernible.

It should be clear that no such thing as the long-term value of the dynamic multiplier exists for the kind of cyclical model which the P.M. is. I can only express long-term impacts in terms of ranges of u.r.s as we just did. This is also the way in which I evaluated reallocations of government expenditure in Chapter 6. With the amount of instability inherent in the model, no convergence to the steady-state growth rate takes place, except when the levels of activity are very high or very low.

With respect to the effectiveness of the 1% increases in government expenditure at the different phases of the cycle I can draw the following conclusions. In general:

(a) The over-all short-term effectiveness of government consumption is not greater than that of government investment when the increase in expenditure is a permanent one. Only during the peak period, immediately before, and up to three periods after is the cumulative impact of government consumption greater than that of government investment.

(b) Again, changes are more effective when made during the downswing than during the upswing phase.

(c) The ranking of cumulative gains over three periods does not differ much from that over five periods and, as we are dealing with a structural change the long-term gains are obviously the same regardless of the time of implementation. In the short run it is only the ranking itself that is important. Specifically:

(d)   The short-term impact of an increase in government consumption is greatest when the change is made just before, during and just after the upper turning point. It is smallest for changes made during the upswing phase.

(e)   The short-term impact of an increase in government investment is greatest when the change is made during the downswing phase; it is smallest for changes made during the late part of the upswing phase.

The conclusions in this and the previous section pertain to increases in government expenditure in an economy characterized by the base-run parameter values. In general, of course, the effects of changes in expenditure depend on the level of economic activities relative to the ceiling and the floor of the economy. One should keep this in mind when considering what the effect of similar 1% decreases in government expenditure will be.

Appendix: Comparative Static Multipliers for the Base Run of the Interregional Model

In his excellent article on regional stabilization policy, S. Engerman [1965] uses comparative static multiplier analysis to evaluate a number of alternative stabilization targets. I shall apply the same analysis with the same targets to the I.M., under the simplifying assumptions of steady-state growth at $\bar{Q}_i = 1$ and $\bar{F}_i = 1$. The multipliers I compute this way obviously only hold under these special conditions of full capacity utilization and full realization of production plans. Table 9.5 gives the comparative static multipliers of regional government consumption [6] on regional output for the parameter values of the I.M. base run, and for three different cases: (I) $w = 1$, $h = .3$;   (II) $w = 0$, $h = .3$;   (III) $w = 0$, $h = 0$.

The extremely low values of the multipliers in Case I are explained by the presence of two built-in stabilizers: contracyclical investment and unemployment benefits. As soon as we drop the first (Case II), or both the first and the second stabilizer (Case III), the multiplier rises.

I can now apply Engerman's stabilization targets to these multipliers, [7] and compare his conclusions regarding the efficiency of a certain policy with ours. His first target is a maximum increase in national employment. Engerman concludes that the increase in national income will be the same regardless of where the initial expenditure is made, so long as the marginal propensities to consume are the same in all regions. This is true for our multipliers too, although I have to make the additional condition

Table 9.5

Comparative Static Multipliers of Regional Government Consumption on Regional Output, Assuming Steady-State Growth with $\bar{Q}_i = 1$ and $\bar{F}_i = 1$

	G_{o1}	G_{o2}	
Case I: $w=1$, $h=.3$			
$\bar{X}_{o1}$	.5608	.0284	.0257
$\bar{X}_{o2}$	.0459	.5641	.0459
$\bar{X}_{o3}$	.0403	.0545	.5754
$\bar{X}_o$	.6470	.6470	.6470
Case II: $w=0$, $h=.3$			
$\bar{X}_{o1}$	1.2436	.1523	.1411
$\bar{X}_{o2}$	.2421	1.2749	.2421
$\bar{X}_{o3}$	.2263	.2848	1.3288
$\bar{X}_o$	1.7120	1.7120	1.7120
Case III: $w=0$, $h=0$			
$\bar{X}_{o1}$	1.8071	.6339	.6215
$\bar{X}_{o2}$	1.0580	2.1259	1.0580
$\bar{X}_{o3}$	.8883	.9936	2.0739
$\bar{X}_o$	3.7534	3.7534	3.7534

Explanation
The column totals give the national multipliers.

that the investment parameters are also the same, which is the case in the examples above.

The second target is a maximum increase in employment in one region. Engerman argues that an expenditure made in the region itself is more efficient than an equal expenditure anywhere else, provided that the other regions' propensities to consume and propensities to import are less than one. Although a direct comparison with our model cannot be made because of different import functions, it can be seen from the multipliers of Table 9.5, that to increase employment in a region most efficiently I should allocate government consumption in that region. This is so because one unit of government consumption in a particular region generates less than one unit of imports from any other region (see the trade matrices $[c]$ and $[k]$), which is in effect what Engerman is stating.

The third target deals with different regional distributions of employment changes, resulting from a one-unit increase in government expenditure. In this case, the policy maker is interested in the spill over of employment increases in the regions other than the one in which the expenditure is made. The spill-over ratio will be higher (that is more spill over will take place): (a) the higher the marginal propensities to consume, (b) the higher the marginal propensities to import of the region in which the expenditure is made, (c) the lower the marginal propensities to import of the other regions. All these conclusions make sense intuitively. In our model, for example, a one-unit increase in government consumption in region 2 gives more spill over in region 3 than in region 1, because region 2 imports more from region 3 than from region 1.

Notes

[1] Note that in an economy with buffers an increase in government expenditure will not necessarily affect employment over a time period in the same way that a decrease will.

[2] In the long run the cycle does not change in length. The shock, however, may affect the length of the cycle in which the shock takes place. It makes a great difference whether the total cycle effect of a shock is measured over a stretch of just 14 periods, or by matching the comparable periods for each phase of the cycle while adjusting for a change in length of the new cycle.

The dynamic multipliers for each period compare periods that carry the same period number: they are not necessarily the result of matching comparable periods in terms of cyclical behaviour. One should realize this in interpreting the many negative dynamic multipliers in the tables. An adjusted comparison will give less negative multipliers.

[3] This change in cycle length by an exogenous shock is one reason why empiricists encounter so many difficulties in measuring cycles.

[4] It is indeed a weakness of our model that it does not include government investment projects which do not compete with fixed business investment. Improvements of the regional infrastructure are often dependent on government initiative. Even though carried out by private enterprise, these investment projects are of an entirely different nature than fixed business investment.

[5] I. and F. L. Adelman [1959].

[6] The assumption $\bar{Q}_i = 1$ makes government investment no longer an independent parameter, but rather a variable whose relation to $\bar{X}_{oi}$ is fixed by the requirement $\bar{Q}_i = 1$. The equation which expresses this relation is the one I referred to in Chapter 5 as the second reduced-form equation.

[7] See S. Engerman [1965, pp. 300–11].

10 Summary

In this study I construct and experiment with an interregional model of economic fluctuations, with the purpose of answering two questions: (a) How are regional and national fluctuations of output and unemployment affected by the economic characteristics of regions and by the trade relationships that exist among them? (b) Through what forms of regional intervention can the central government attain its goals of interregional equality of unemployment and economic stability at the lowest possible level of unemployment?

In the first part of this study (Chapters 2, 3 and 4) I attempt to answer the first question for the type of economy described by the interregional model. The second part (Chapters 5 to 9) is concerned with regional economic policy in a fluctuating economy.

The interregional model (I.M.) of this study is an analytic, dynamic model of economic fluctuations, in which the interrelationships among regions are established through two trade matrices: one for private consumption and one for private investment. Fluctuations in the model are primarily generated by the private-investment function, which is a flexible-accelerator type function. An essential feature of the model is the presence of buffers (ceilings and floors) in the economy, which keep the movement of output in check over a period of time. In the author's opinion, capacity constraints are a necessary feature of interregional models of economic fluctuations. Capacity bottle-necks may limit the expansion of a particular region, even if the country as a whole is characterized by excess supply of productive capacity. Because of its non-linearities, no analytical solution of the I.M. can be obtained. I use the simulation technique instead to gain insight into the behaviour of the model over an interval of time.

In Chapter 1, besides reviewing the business cycle and regional economics literature relevant for this study, I state the assumptions that underlie the interregional model. Rather crucial assumptions are:

(a)   Immobility of resources. Labour and capital stock are mobile within the region, but not between regions. Capital goods are traded, but once installed can be shifted no longer. Migration of labour (introduced in Chapter 8) reduces immobility of all resources to immobility of capital stock alone.

(b)   Only final products are traded and the trade coefficients are stable (this assumption is relaxed in Chapter 7). Resource endowments have led to a certain production pattern among regions such that no inter-regional trade of raw materials and semi-finished goods has to take place. (c)   The monetary sector does not affect the course of the real variables with time. For instance, the rate of interest is not included in the invest-ment function; monetary policy on the regional level is ruled out, and so are regional tax policies.

(d)   Prices do not affect the course of the real variables with time. For instance, movements of prices and wages have no influence on fluctuations of real variables during a cycle. Prices are not used as an allocative mechanism, nor do wage differentials affect migration.

When I assume that no interregional trade takes place, the I.M. col-lapses to a national model of economic fluctuations. This model is called the prototype model (P.M.). It is a 28-equation model, and its presenta-tion in Chapter 2 is meant to make the reader familiar with the cyclical properties of the I.M. Just like the I.M., the P.M. is capable of generating cycles as well as steady-state growth. For a large range of acceptable parameter values it will generate cyclical output paths. Whether or not the actual time paths of a simulation will be cyclical depends on the relative position of output with respect to floor and ceiling of the system.

In two cases steady-state growth will be the outcome: (a) When the de-mand structure is such that an excess demand of stable demand com-ponents (e.g. private and public consumption) causes planned production continually to exceed maximum possible production. This I call 'upper' steady-state growth: output moves along the ceiling. (b) When govern-ment autonomous investment and contracyclical investment (which responds to the unemployment level) cause an excess supply of capital goods, relative to the total demand level, such that the accelerator mechanism of private investment demand ceases to operate. This I call 'lower' steady-state growth: output moves along the floor.

If cycles are generated, the length and amplitude of these cycles depend on the instability of investment behaviour, and on the extent to which the central government will attempt to mitigate instability through the use of built-in stabilizers. Fluctuations will be heaviest and cycles will be longest when all fiscal policy is eliminated.

The I.M. is presented in Chapter 3. The simulations in this and the following chapters are made for a hypothetical three-region economy. They show that it is possible for some regions to experience steady-state growth, while others grow cyclically. If cycles are generated, the cycle length with respect to that of comparable P.M. simulations will depend

174

on the interregional distribution of economic activities. Usually, the I.M. cycles will be shorter. The composition of regional output in terms of stable consumption and unstable investment output determines the amplitude of the regional cycles and also the timing of turning points. The regions that predominantly produce consumption goods lag behind the other regions. The length of the cycle, however, will be the same in all regions.

In Chapter 4 I compare national averages of I.M. simulations with P.M. simulations that were made for the same parameter values. That is, I confront 'the economics of resource immobility' with the perfect-mobility assumption that underlies the P.M. In general, the P.M. economy will generate longer fluctuations than the I.M. economy, but because of its mobile production factors the P.M. economy will have less unemployment than the I.M. economy. The actual differences between the two will depend on the interregional distribution of economic activities in the latter.

In Chapter 5 I develop a method to compute trends in analytical models of economic fluctuations. Trend rates of unemployment, capital utilization, and planned production realization are computed by writing the trend version of the P.M. model, that is, by forcing steady-state growth conditions upon the model. Seven trend types and subtypes can be distinguished for the P.M. The parameter values determine by what type of trend a particular simulation of the model is characterized. If a simulation generates steady-state growth, the trend rates are the steady-state rates. Although developed for the P.M., the trend determining method can also be applied to the I.M. For the purposes of the following chapters, however, I need only to know the national trend rates provided by the P.M.

The promotion of national and regional growth, and interregional equality in conditions of unemployment are often mentioned in the regional economic literature as goals of regional economic policy. Interregional inequalities in the I.M. cannot result from differences in the structural growth rate among regions. This growth rate, the sum of population growth and technical progress, is assumed constant and identical for all regions in our model. Interregional inequalities only result from differences in the levels of activities and from the different susceptibility of regions to fluctuations. Therefore, I define as our first goal of regional economic policy the equality of trend rates of unemployment among regions at the lowest possible level. This goal I label: interregional equity. Our second goal is regional, and therefore also national, stability. As a goal of economic policy, stability is measured as the range of fluctuations of the unemployment rate with time, perfect stability being steady-state growth.

Throughout the second part of this study some priority is given to interregional equity as a goal. Stabilization policies are pursued, but I recognize that the instability of investment behaviour is inherent in the economy, and that a certain amount of fluctuations will have to be accepted, unless the level of activities is so high that the regional economies operate close to their productive capacity ceilings all the time. When the level of activities in the national economy is not high enough to eliminate fluctuations altogether, it is impossible to attain both goals of economic policy completely at the same time.

Either one of the two can be fully accomplished: I can have perfect stability in all regions, with interregional differences in unemployment, or I can have equal trend rates of unemployment in all regions, but with cycles. The only way to escape this dilemma is by raising the over-all level of expenditure such that the gap between the trend levels of output and the productive capacity ceilings is too small to allow cycles, the ultimate being a level and distribution of expenditure which gives full employment, full capacity growth in all regions. This 'optimum optimorum' is Golden Age growth.

The trade-off between interregional equity and stability is apparent in all chapters dealing with structural regional economic policy. In Chapter 6 the distribution of a given amount of government expenditure is the instrumental variable to attain the two goals. I define an optimal distribution of government expenditure as one which gives equal trend rates of unemployment among regions. In the mathematical specification of optimality I include the interregional equality of capital utilization and planned-production realization in the objective function. This allows us to use the trend determining method of Chapter 5 most effectively.

When the trend rates of unemployment are required to be identical among regions, the problem of finding an optimal distribution of government expenditure is reduced to that of finding an optimal distribution of government consumption alone, since all regions can claim the same amount of government investment under this requirement. An optimal distribution of government consumption will give all regions the same trend rate of unemployment, but will not eliminate those interregional differences in economic fluctuations caused by the interregional distribution of the production of capital goods. To compensate the capital goods producing regions for the heavier fluctuations they experience, I can rewrite the trend version of the I.M. by under-representing the trend level of private investment.

The result of this correction will be an adjusted optimal distribution of government consumption which allocates more government consumption in the capital goods producing regions than the optimal distribution does. This reduces the fluctuations in these regions; it also increases over-all stability. Reducing the weight of private investment in the trend

176

version of the I.M. more and more, and computing the accompanying adjusted optimal distribution of government consumption will finally result in steady-state growth in all regions, however with considerable interregional inequity.

In Chapter 7 our main concern is stability in the equilibrium dynamics sence of the word. The question is: How does interregional trade affect the stability of the interregional economy? It is not possible to obtain a direct answer to this question. I can write the unconstrained version of the I.M. as a system of first-order difference equations, but the resulting system matrix is of too high an order, and does not possess any desirable properties that would allow us to find a relatively easy answer to the stability problem. The same holds for the P.M. system matrix.

Knowing the properties of the trade matrices, therefore, does not help us to determine their impact on the stability of the interregional economy. Our indirect answer to the question of the impact of interregional trade can be no more than a supposition. From the simulations of Chapter 7 and previous chapters, I conclude that only the behaviour of the economic agents as expressed in consumption and investment functions, is responsible for the general character of a cycle. I believe that trade matrices do not alter the stability properties of an economic system as it would have been without the existence of buffers. Trade matrices do, however, determine the amplitude of the regional cycles since they determine the structure of the regional economies in terms of the composition of consumption goods and capital goods production. They also affect—due to the existence of ceilings— the length of the cycles since the trade matrices determine how close to the capacity ceilings the regional economies operate.

If our hypothesis is correct it implies that an otherwise stable economy cannot become unstable because of the way in which interregional trade takes place. In that case the desirability of a particular trade pattern can be stated exclusively in terms of our two goals of economic policy. Well-behaved', symmetrical trade matrices, matched with the same amounts of government expenditure in all regions, will produce perfect interregional equity with regional cycles identical to the national cycle. On the other hand, trade matrices that concentrate production in a few regions will give a perfectly stable economy, with 'upper' steady-state growth in the regions of concentration, and 'lower' steady-state growth in the remaining regions.

Allowing regions to import from regions that have excess productive capacity, when the usual trading partners cannot meet all demand, changes the I.M. from a fixed-trade to a flexible-trade model. In this change the trade-off between equity and stability is present again. Flexible trade means more equity because the excess productive capacity of high-unemployment regions is called upon during an expansion, but it also means heavier fluctuations in all regions.

Adding a migration function to the I.M., as in Chapter 8, in which the migration of labour is a function of regional unemployment differentials, provides the economy with a powerful equalizing mechanism. Migration corrects the regional labour forces such that each region will end up with a labour force proportional to its general level of production. Comparing planned migration with reallocations of government consumption as tools of regional economic policy, and realizing that any conclusion only holds for the type of migration function I used, it seems that:

(a) Migration performs its equalizing function somewhat better than optimal distributions of government consumption will.

(b) While migration alone brings more interregional equity than a reallocation of government consumption alone, a combination of the two instruments is more desirable since it will require smaller adjustments of both labour and government expenditure.

(c) Migration alone will not reduce the fluctuations caused by investment behaviour. Reallocating government expenditure can increase stability, but at the expense of interregional equity. Migration, however, will, by restoring interregional equity, nullify the greater stability accomplished by a particular distribution of government consumption.

In Chapter 9 I examine a particular aspect of fiscal policy: the timing of single or permanent changes in government expenditure in a cyclical economy. It is important for the policy maker to know during which cyclical phase a single change in government spending can be best implemented, or when a structural reallocation of government expenditure can be made most effectively. In general, the impact of changes in expenditure depends on the level of economic activities relative to the ceiling and the floor of the economy. Changes are most effective when made during the downswing phase of the cycle; they are least effective when made during the upswing phase. Very often, changes in expenditure will disturb the cyclical pattern by lengthening or shortening the cycle in which they occur.

List of References

Adelman, I., and Adelman, F. L. [1959], 'The dynamic properties of the Klein-Goldberger model', *Econometrica*, vol. 27, October 1959, pp. 596–625.

Airov, J. [1963], 'The construction of interregional business cycle models', *Journal of Regional Science*, vol. 5, Summer 1963, pp. 1–20.

Allen, R. G. D. [1967], *Macro-economic theory*, London: Macmillan.

Barten, A. P. [1970], 'Some reflections on the relation between private consumption and collective expenditure in an expanding mature economy', in Paelinck, J. H. P. (ed.), *Programming for Europe's collective needs*, Amsterdam: North-Holland, pp. 82–98.

Baumol, W. J. [1961], 'Pitfalls in contracyclical policies: some tools and results', *Review of Economics and Statistics*, vol. 43, February 1961, pp. 21–6.

Beckmann, M. J., and Sato, R. [1969], 'Aggregate production functions and types of technical progress: a statistical analysis', *American Economic Review*, vol. 59, March 1969, pp. 88–101.

Belsley, D. A. [1969], *Industry production behavior: the order-stock distinction*, Amsterdam: North-Holland.

Blyth, C. A. [1969], *American business cycles 1945–50*, London: Allen and Unwin.

Borts, G. H. [1960], *Regional cycles of manufacturing employment in the United States, 1914–1953*, National Bureau of Economic Research Occasional paper, no. 73, Princeton University Press.

Bowen, W. G., and Finegan, T. A. [1965], 'Labor force participation and unemployment', in Ross, A. M. (ed.), *Employment policy and the labor market*, Berkeley: University of California Press.

Brauer, A. [1946], 'Limits for the characteristic roots of a matrix', *Duke Mathematical Journal*, vol. 13, pp. 387–95.

Bronfenbrenner, M. (ed.) [1969], *Is the business cycle obsolete?* New York: Wiley Interscience.

Chenery, H. B. [1952], 'Overcapacity and the acceleration principle', *Econometrica*, vol. 20, January 1952, pp. 1–28.

Chiang, A. C. [1967], *Fundamental methods of mathematical economics*, New York: McGraw-Hill.

Childs, G. L. [1967], *Unfilled orders and inventories*, Amsterdam: North-Holland.

Chipman, J. S. [1950/1], 'The multi-sector multiplier', *Econometrica*, vol. 18, October 1950, pp. 355–74.

Chipman, J. S. [1950/2], *The theory of inter-sectoral money flows and income formation*, Baltimore: Johns Hopkins Press.

Duesenberry, J. S. [1958], *Business cycles and economic growth*, New York: McGraw-Hill.

Engerman, S. [1965], 'Regional aspects of stabilization policy', in Musgrave, R. A. (ed.), *Essays in fiscal federalism*, Washington D.C.: Brookings Institution, pp. 7–62; reprinted in Needleman, L. (ed.) [1968], pp. 277–334 (references in text refer to reprint).

Evans, M. K. [1967], 'The importance of wealth in the consumption function', *Journal of Political Economy*, vol. 75, August 1967, pp. 335–51.

Evans, M. K. [1969], *Macroeconomic activity: theory, forecasting and control*, New York: Harper and Row.

Goodwin, R. M. [1948], 'Secular and cyclical aspects of the multiplier and accelerator', in *Income, employment and public policy: essays in honour of Alvin H. Hansen*, New York: W. W. Norton.

Goodwin, R. M. [1951], 'The non-linear accelerator and the persistence of business cycles', *Econometrica*, vol. 19, January 1951, pp. 1–17.

179

Goodwin, R. M. [1953], 'Static and dynamic linear equilibrium models', in *Input-output relations*, Leiden: Stenfert Kroese.

Gordon, R. A. [1961], *Business fluctuations*, 2nd ed., New York: Harper and Row.

Hahn, F. H., and Matthews, R. C. O. [1964], 'The theory of economic growth: a survey', *Economic Journal*, vol. 74, December 1964, pp. 779–902.

Hamberg, D. [1971], *Models of economic growth*, New York: Harper and Row.

Hamilton, H. R., Goldstone, S. E., Milliman, J. W., Pugh, A. L. III, Roberts, E. B., and Zellner, A. [1969], *Systems simulation for regional analysis: an application to river-basin planning*, Cambridge, Mass.: M.I.T. Press.

Harrod, R. F. [1939], 'An essay in dynamic theory', *Economic Journal*, vol. 49, March 1939, pp. 14–33.

Hickman, B. G. [1965], *Investment demand and U.S. economic growth*, Washington D.C.: Brookings Institution.

Hickman, B. G. [1969], 'Dynamic properties of macroeconomic models: an international comparison', in Bronfenbrenner, M. (ed.) [1969], pp. 393–435.

Hicks, J. R. [1950], *A contribution to the theory of the trade cycle*, London: Clarendon Press.

Hoover, E. M. [1971], *Introduction to regional economics*, New York: Knopf.

Isard, W. [1960], *Methods of regional analysis*, Cambridge, Mass.: M.I.T. Press.

Jorgenson, D. W., and Stephenson, J. A. [1967], 'The time structure of investment behavior in U.S. manufacturing, 1947–60', *Review of Economics and Statistics*, vol. 49, February 1967, pp. 16–27.

Kaldor, N. [1940], 'A model of the trade cycle', *Economic Journal*, vol. 50, March 1940, pp. 78–92; reprinted in Kaldor, N. [1960], pp. 177–92.

Kaldor, N. [1951], 'Hicks on the trade cycle', *Economic Journal*, vol. 61, December 1951, pp. 833–47; reprinted in Kaldor, N. [1960], pp. 193–209.

Kaldor, N. [1960], *Essays on economic stability and growth*, London: Duckworth.

Kalecki, M. [1939], *Essays in the theory of economic fluctuations*, London: Allen and Unwin.

Klein, L. R. [1950], *Economic fluctuations in the United States, 1921–1941*, Cowles Commission monograph no. 11, New York: Wiley.

Klein, L. R., Ball, R. J., Hazelwood, A., and Vandome, P. [1961], *An econometric model of the United Kingdom*, Oxford: Basil Blackwell.

Kuh, E. [1966], 'Measurement of potential output', *American Economic Review*, vol. 56, September 1966, pp. 758–76.

Kuznets, S. [1961], *Capital in the American economy*, Princeton University Press.

Lancaster, K. [1968], *Mathematical economics*, New York: Macmillan.

Lancaster, P. [1969], *Theory of matrices*, New York: Academic Press.

Levy, M. E. [1963], *Fiscal policy, cycles and growth*, New York: National Industrial Conference Board.

Martirena-Mantel, A. M. [1968], 'A model of economic fluctuations', *Yale Economic Essays*, vol. 8, Spring 1968, pp. 83–151.

Matthews, R. C. O. [1954], 'Capital stock adjustment theories of the trade cycle and the problem of policy', in Kurihara, K. K. (ed.), *Post Keynesian economics*, New Brunswick, N.J.: Rutgers University Press, pp. 170–91.

Matthews, R. C. O. [1959], *The trade cycle*, Cambridge: University Press.

McKenzie, L. [1960], 'Matrices and economic theory', in Arrow, K. J., Karlin, S., and Suppes, P. (eds.), *Mathematical methods in the social sciences*, Stanford: Stanford University Press.

Metzler, L. A. [1941], 'The nature and stability of inventory cycles', *Review of Economics and Statistics*, vol. 23, August 1941, pp. 113–29.

Metzler, L. A. [1942], 'Underemployment equilibrium in international trade', *Econometrica*, vol. 10, April 1942, pp. 97–112.

Metzler, L. A. [1950], 'A multiple-region theory of income and trade', *Econometrica*, vol. 18, October 1950, pp. 329–54.

Meyer, J. R. [1963], 'Regional economics: a survey', *American Economic Review*, vol. 53, March 1963, pp. 19–54.

Modigliani, F., and Weingartner, H. M. [1958], 'Forecasting uses of anticipatory data on investment and sales', *Quarterly Journal of Economics*, vol. 72, February 1958, pp. 23–54.

Morishima, M. [1964], *Equilibrium, stability and growth*, Oxford: Clarendon Press.

Needleman, L. (ed.) [1968], *Regional analysis*, Harmondsworth, Middlesex: Penguin Books.

OECD Economic Studies [1966], *Economic growth 1960–1970*, Paris: OECD.

Okun, A. M. [1962], 'Potential GNP: its measurement and significance', *Proceedings of the American Statistical Association*, 1962, pp. 98–104.

Orcutt, G. H. [1960], 'Simulation of economic systems', *American Economic Review*, vol. 50, December 1960, pp. 893–907.

Phillips, A. W. [1954], 'Stabilization policy in a closed economy', *Economic Journal*, vol. 64, June 1954, pp. 290–323.

Richardson, H. W. [1969], *Regional economics*, New York: Praeger.

Robinson, J. [1966], *The accumulation of capital*, London: Macmillan.

Rogers, A. [1968], *Matrix analysis of interregional population growth and distribution*, Berkeley: University of California Press.

Samuelson, P. A. [1939], 'Interactions between the multiplier analysis and the principle of acceleration', *Review of Economics and Statistics*, vol. 21, May 1939, pp. 75–8.

Siegel, R. A. [1966], 'Do regional business cycles exist?' *Western Economic Journal*, vol. 5, pp. 44–57.

Sjaastad, L. A. [1962], 'The costs and returns of human migration', *Journal of Political Economy*, vol. 70, special supplement, October 1962, pp. 80–93.

Solow, R. M., and Samuelson, P. A. [1953], 'Balanced growth under constant returns to scale', *Econometrica*, vol. 21, July 1953, pp. 412–24.

Strand, K., and Dernberg, T. [1964], 'Cyclical variation in civilian labor force participation', *Review of Economics and Statistics*, vol. 46, November 1964, pp. 378–91.

Suzuki, K. [1971], 'Observations on the stability of the structure of the interregional flow of goods', *Journal of Regional Science*, vol. 11, August 1971, pp. 187–209.

Tinbergen, J. [1952], *On the theory of economic policy*, Amsterdam: North-Holland.

Tinbergen, J. [1954], *Centralisation and decentralisation in economic policy*, Amsterdam: North-Holland.

Vining, R. [1946/1], 'Location of industry and regional patterns of business-cycle behavior', *Econometrica*, vol. 14, January 1946, pp. 37–68.

Vining, R. [1946/2], 'The region as a concept in business cycle analysis', *Econometrica*, vol. 14, July 1946, pp. 201–18.

Vining, R. [1949], 'The region as an economic entity and certain variations to be observed in the study of systems of regions', *Papers and Proceedings of the American Economic Association*, vol. 39, May 1949, pp. 89–104.

Index

acceleration coefficient 6

accelerator: in business cycle models 5–10; flexible 9, 11, 15, 17, 19, 28, 31, 50n., 173; interacted with multiplier 5–7, 14–16; inventory 16, 17, 19; naive 9, 10, 19; in P.M. and I.M. 30, 46, 60, 70, 174

adjustment coefficient: in fixed-investment function 9, 16, 32, 38, 46; in inventory-investment function 28, 37

Abramowitz, M. 82n.
Adelman, F. L. 169, 172n., 179
Adelman, I. 169, 172n., 179
Airov, J. 10, 11, 15–19, 22n., 23n., 130, 144, 146n., 179
Allen, R. G. D. 12, 22n., 23n., 99n., 179
Arrow, K. J. 180

balance of trade 57, 59
base run: comparison between P.M. and I.M. 73; of the I.M. simulations 35, 40–4; of the P.M. simulations 60, 63, 67
Belgium 37
Brookings model 80
buffers: see ceilings and floors
built-in stabilizers 83, 104, 174
business cycle: models: see fluctuations, models of economic; phases 20–1

Ball, R. J. 180
Barten, A. P. 37, 179
Baumol, W. J. 72n., 179
Beckmann, M. J. 26, 50n., 179
Belsley, D. A. 50n., 179
Blyth, C. A. 51n., 179
Borts, G. H. 145n., 179
Bowen, W. G. 27, 179
Brauer, A. 146n., 179
Bronfenbrenner, M. 179, 180
Burns, A. 82n.

capacity 21, see also ceilings; constraints 1, 9, 173
capital-output ratio 16, 25–6, 36–7; optimal 9
capital stock 8–10, 26, 31, 34–5, 40, 57, 59, 78;

desired or optimal 9, 31–2, 34–5, 47–8, 50, 50n., 56, 78
capital stock adjustment principle 6, 8–10, 15, 19, 22n., 28
capital utilization rate (Q) 21, 29, 40, 51n., 81, 82n.
ceilings 1, 6–9, 21, 44, 47, 68–9, 71, 75, 79–81, 82n., 83, 85, 87, 109, 111, 144, 163, 170, 173–4, 176–7
Central Planning Bureau, Dutch 82n.
characteristic equation 128, 131, 144; roots 129–30
characteristic matrices, of P.M. and I.M. 127–8
congestion 158
consumption: autonomous 92; public: see government consumption
consumption function 30–1
contracyclical expenditures: see government contracyclical investment
cycles: amplitudes 40, 43–4, 46, 67, 70, 76, 104, 107, 109–10, 138, 144, 152, 174, 177; asymmetry around the trend 109, 111–13; in the base run 40, 43, 67; building 78–9, 82n.; explained by the interregional distribution of economic activity 67–70; inventory 78–9; Juglar 78–9, 82n.; Kondratieff 78; Kuznets 78–9, 82n.; leads and lags 70–1; length 41, 47, 67, 69, 70, 73, 78–81, 144, 152, 163–4, 166, 169, 172n., 174, 177, 178; major 78, 79, 82n.; NBER 78, 79; turning points 79–81, 175; two-period 70–1, 72n., 138–9, 146n.

Chenery, H. B. 9, 10, 179
Chiang, A. C. 145n., 179
Childs, G. L. 27, 179
Chipman, J. S. 10, 12, 14–5, 129–30, 179

demand: anticipated 28; in the I.M. 54–6, 58, 59; in the P.M. 30–3, 35, 38; realized 57, 59
depreciation, rate of 8, 15–19, 23, 32, 38–9
difference equation solution: of the I.M. 128–9; of the P.M. 127–8
disbursements 14
distance 4

183

unemployment rate (U) 27, 29, 40–1, 63, 75, 81, 82n., 91, 122–3n., 175

United Kingdom 81
United States 26–7, 37–8, 43, 50n., 51n.; Council of Economic Advisers 51n.

Vandome, P. 180
Vining, R. 10–12, 22n., 180

Weingartner, H. M. 33, 181
Witz, K. G. 145n.

Z-method 112–3, 119–20, 136

Zellner, A. 180